I would like to dedicate this book to my parents,
Richard Arthur Lewty and Marjorie Lewty.
Simon Lewty, 2010

THE SELF AS A STRANGER

SIMON LEWTY

black dog publishing
london uk

9 FOREWORD IAN HUNT
15 CHOSEN SUBJECTS SIMON LEWTY
45 THE SADNESS OF DREAMS STUART MORGAN
49 NOTES TOWARDS A BIOGRAPHY PAUL HILLS
53 MATERIALS MATTER PAUL HILLS
56 VISIBLE WORDS PAUL HILLS
62 A WALK IN SUTTON PARK PAUL HILLS
71 SIMON LEWTY PAUL HILLS
79 VOICES FROM LOST FIELDS PETER LARKIN
84 EPISODES PAUL HILLS
96 ECLIPSES: A RESPONSE JESSICA DUBOW
107 CAPTURING A CONSCIOUSNESS CATHY COURTNEY
127 PITT RIVERS MUSEUM CATHY COURTNEY/SIMON LEWTY
133 THE SELF AS A STRANGER SIMON LEWTY
150 REVERIES AND TRANSFORMATIONS SUSAN MICHIE/SIMON LEWTY
178 ARCHIVE PHOTOGRAPHS
184 LIST OF PLATES
187 BIOGRAPHY/LIST OF EXHIBITIONS
189 CREDITS
190 ACKNOWLEDGMENTS

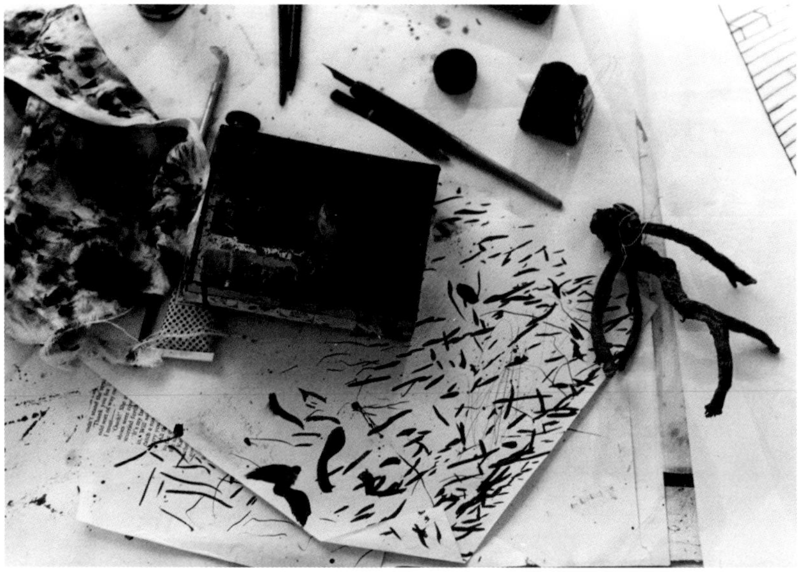

FOREWORD

IAN HUNT
2010

I

Imagine an encounter with one of Simon Lewty's more recent works, from which image as such has been banished, and that you approached it with little knowledge of the context of its production other than as a contemporary artwork. I have in mind a work such as *Gift*, from 2007 (plate 64). How would you seek to understand what it was that you saw or characterise the qualities of your encounter with it?

What you see from a distance is clearly writing, forming a rectangle of pinkish colour, and you quickly see that it is in English. The familiar shape of repeated words such as pronouns and connectives is part of what helps you to recognise this, before you are close enough to follow what it is the text relates, or have even decided to begin reading. The writing is placed squarely on the paper, with regular margins top and bottom, right and left. The words and letters, in soft coloured pencil, are formed in what appears to be a careful performance of a habitual handwriting. This handwriting has nevertheless been organised with some reference to printed pages, as the right-hand margin is justified not ragged. In printing, spaces and letters are squeezed closer together or spaced out to achieve this regularity within a notional frame (for most of printing history, this was the result of a laborious manual process, inside an actual frame; now, it is performed by an automated computer calculation). The hand moving the pencil to make *Gift* has been able to calculate with impressive but not perfect control: there is a slight unevenness down the right-hand edge. The many dashes, which function as the principal mark of punctuation in the text, are particularly visible here, and draw your attention to the significance of the dash in your experience of the work itself—when you settle down to reading it. For there appears to be no alternative to reading, and also to calculating how long this will take, as you shift your weight to and fro on your feet. The lines are extraordinarily long—to 'follow' the text, if that is what you are meant to do, involves a conscious effort to begin again at the next line down. You may have to scan from right to left, against the usual direction of reading, to do this successfully—it is a bit like ploughing up and down a visual field. The demand to read is also an unexpected one. We tend to expect artworks to give themselves to us more easily than this. There is one way in which *Gift* could give itself easily—by analogy with abstract painting, perhaps the kind offered especially for contemplation. Paintings by Agnes Martin, for example, offer themselves to the gaze instantaneously, while also rewarding long looking. But whatever the visual pleasures caused by the variation of pressure of the red pencil in *Gift*—which have resulted in subtle variations of tonality and colour seen in relation to channels and flurries of white space that open out between the words—it would clearly be an evasion of the demand to read simply to concentrate on these formal features.

A lot more should be said at this point about the text itself: how it consolidates around the notional 'I' that is the speaking subject, and seeks to convey something to the reader with a varying pressure of urgency. This urgency is traversed by less clearly directed thoughts, and then by renewed attempts to communicate. To read this text is sometimes to feel like an eavesdropper on a mind talking to itself, and sometimes to feel that the speaking self becomes aware of your impatience for meaning. This process takes two: both the text and the reader are involved in a repeated process of beginning again, at each dash. The top left position, strongly coded as the place to start reading a text, begins with a dash—a sign for an interruption, a change of direction. What chain of thought or narrative was already underway here, before being interrupted? A life, a chain of thought, was already continuing before you got here, and may continue after you leave. The dashes allow you to enter the text at almost any point, to return to an earlier thread of thought, and also to leave—to follow a personal association, or to subside into momentary inattention. Becoming aware of one's inattention or failures of attention towards the work can start to feel like an emotional subject in itself.

Ultimately, to make any sense of the value of the work, it should be possible to give an account of the text and an interpretation of its meaning, along with the title, *Gift*. This word is eventually encountered in the text itself. Titles are part of the public space surrounding and situating artworks. Lewty clearly sets out to say something about what it means to give or to be given something. But interpretation is not straightforward, because all but the most determined viewers will question the possibility or the validity of reading the work consecutively. However, you do become aware of a development in the text—there is enough forward-driven sense here, and enough urgency in what is being said, to make you feel that you might at any point miss something supremely important. In this way, *Gift* tackles the question of meaning. The proportion of meaning spectators bring to works of art, and the proportion that should or can derive from their physical facts and assumed cultural and historical context, is much debated, especially since Dada. But can it be a matter of complete arbitrariness what we think any work is about? Artists themselves are often rather casual about defending the area of meaning their works seek to delimit—feeling, perhaps, that it is wrong to preach, or to disabuse viewers of their own interpretation. The experience of trying to read *Gift* can be seen within this debate, and also as a powerful dramatisation of it. Meaning does seem to matter here. The act of reading involves some frustration, some effort, and a feeling that you are in some way bound to fail to grasp what is being said. At the same time the effort is productive, exciting and stimulating to your own thought processes. The meaning that you encounter is hard to encapsulate, but it does not feel arbitrary. It emerges through your patient engagement with the physical facts and demands of the work, and also with a process that is more free-floating: more like becoming a radio receptor and tuning in to what is being said. The encounter is charged with a physical drama, too: the drama of the unique work of art, that exists in only one place and time. At any point you could walk away, perhaps to return, perhaps not.

I have spent some time demonstrating how complex an encounter with Simon Lewty's work can feel in order to inaugurate a general discussion about what type of art it really is. When reviewing the ways it has been characterised, and looking at its development, it is important to keep in mind the actual experiences his works produce. They are what matter.

II

Lewty's work has too often been seen as a kind of special case, even by those who have praised it. In a book such as this, which includes commentary, context, interpretations from different perspectives and the artist's own words, both spoken and written, a sense of chronological development becomes clearer. Some mysteries and misconceptions are cleared up. Lewty's own interests and preoccupations, from Medieval graffiti to psychoanalysis, are set out, and his education and working methods are explored. It becomes possible to see his work in a longer art-historical context, which can be briefly sketched by considering some of the significant names and art movements that are mentioned by the artist: Paul Klee, Giorgio De Chirico, Jean Dubuffet, Surrealism, Abstract Expressionism, Conceptual Art. His responses to significant exhibitions such as *Art of a Decade* at the Tate Gallery in 1964 (an influential show of American Abstract Expressionism) and When Attitudes Become Form at the ICA in 1968 are explored. In discussion with Susan Michie, he sets his excitement at seeing the first works of conceptual art within its moment, which included Land Art and Arte Povera. Lewty clearly understands this point in art history not as a supposed triumph of language over material but as a deepening and opening out of the complexities of their relationship. That kind of understanding provides a valuable way into thinking about the relationship his work makes between language and material—specifically, for Lewty, a surface. His recognition of the significance of abstraction is also worth noting, because he came to prominence in the 1980s, a period that did not make the kinship his work has with some forms of abstraction easy to see. Lewty's interest in such developments, though he is neither an Abstract Expressionist nor a Conceptual artist, places him firmly within the generation of post-war British artists who were responding to the significant developments of their time.

However, artists are marked not just by the period of their education and apprenticeship—by what they are responding to, looking at and thinking through—but by the period when they first begin to exhibit, and the wider tendencies they then appear to be part of. Lewty's reception as an artist is not explored in detail in the essays that follow, and so some aspects of it need to be set out here. It was not until the 1980s that Lewty emerged to wider public view, with exhibitions at Ikon Gallery in Birmingham, followed by regular shows in London. Lewty rapidly gained an appreciative audience. He entered this period with quiet assurance, having worked through the 1960s and 1970s somewhat secretively (or at least, relatively unobserved), developing his own path while working full-time teaching art.

This was a heterogeneous period of art in Britain, with a confusing number of developments, including a backlash against weak versions of formalism and abstraction (often in the name of myth and imagination), alongside a continued critical exploration of language and media. Sculpture in Britain had taken a significant and interesting turn. When Lewty exhibited at the Serpentine Gallery in 1985, it was in the company of Richard Deacon. The weightlessness of Lewty's figures (brilliantly described in the essay by Stuart Morgan, included in this book) must have compared intriguingly with the elusive sense of 'figure' that clings to Deacon's forms. British art, however, was quite considerably caught in a figurative revival that was more closely allied to realism, alongside some local versions of neo-expressionism or what was then called New Image—the tendencies emerging in painting from Italy, Germany and the US. Lewty had seen the Royal Academy Exhibition A New Spirit in Painting in 1981, and found this period exciting, but little imagined that it would be the trend for New Image which would in some way inform the reception of his work—quite apart from anything else, he did not identify himself as a painter. But it was the context of figuration, nationally and internationally, that was decisive in defining his position and reception.

Lewty clearly shared an interest in myth and the imagination with many artists of the 1980s: more specifically, he devised a procedure of working from dream diaries. His work was open, in its own way, to the current mode of unlikely combinations and strange conjunctions, and it conveys a sense of temporal and spatial discontinuity, though he developed this differently from the New Image painters, with their casual manipulation of symbols. Despite the extent to which he overlapped with them, he seems to have been regarded with suspicion by some in the figurative camp. It is striking that he remembers a studio visit from Jon Thompson and Marjorie Allthorpe-Guyton, as they were working on the selection of artists for *The British Art Show: Old Allegiances and New Directions* 1979–1984, but not from Alexander Moffat, the selector for the show who put himself forward as the defender of the figurative tradition. It was the more experimental and open-minded selectors who were curious to visit Lewty. To look at the catalogue today (Lewty was not included, but easily could have been) is to see a moment in British art where the figurative and imaginative revival was given credit, but not seen as the only or even the main possibility. It was precisely the openness of this situation at the beginning of the 1980s which Lewty himself found exciting, and which provided some support and confirmation of the particular path he had been following.

However, the figurative revival and New Image which in some ways provided a context for Lewty's work also limited how it was understood. He was included in books such as *The New British Painting*, 1988, which documented and celebrated the figurative revival. Did he really fit within that company? There are some points of contact—the feeling for childhood in riotous early works by Paula Rego, perhaps. But a much closer visual connection for his work at the time would have been outside painting altogether. The spatial strangeness of the sculptor Edward Allington's drawings—their mood of removal from the world, their use of an alternative but coherent form of perspective, and their frequent use of a pre-existing surface, such as ledger paper—make for a suggestive comparison with Lewty's practice. The first comparison that seems to have formed in many people's minds, however, was with so-called outsider art. It is easy to see why the connections were made—and which artist would not like their work to be connected, at some level, with the fertility and inventiveness of artists such as Adolf Wölfli, Arthur Bispo do Rosario or Henry Darger? At the same time, there could be no pretence here. As David Maclagan noted in his essay "Outsiders or Insiders", "Simon Lewty's work comes from a context that seems to be largely 'artistic' in that he has the stylistic self-consciousness that professional training implants; yet the striking coincidence between his style, and especially its linguistic inventions, and the neologisms of certain psychotic works is the result of mysterious convergence rather than conscious imitation" (*The Myth of Primitivism*, ed., Susan Hiller, 1991, p. 46). Such careful discriminations were not always made. When discussing Lewty's work it is still possible to encounter lazy reactions that simply assimilate it to outsider art. In discussion with Susan Michie, Lewty makes reference to Klee's rebuke to those who could see only childishness in his style of drawing, and seems to identify strongly with Klee's feeling that his work was misunderstood.

As Lewty's work developed, the whole question of depiction clearly became a difficult one. His eventual abandonment of figuration as such in the 1990s shows his distance from those artists committed to it as a faith, and also perhaps served to distance him from the reactions to his work that assimilated it to outsider status. His position is complicated, however. There were aspects of Lewty's work that were strongly interested in human life, in showing its strangeness and complexity. And there is one area of his work that suggests a human emphasis very strongly. Lewty's longstanding commitment as an artist is to making a worked surface, analogous to a palimpsest and to skin—hence his interest in Didier Anzieu's theories of the "skin ego" as a stage of infant development, deriving from the young child's earliest experiences of its own and its mother's body. The whole surface of a Lewty is what matters, and works from different periods show signs of being carefully prepared, delicately touched, worked, flooded, preserved and restored from the attack or alteration of it which drawing and writing at some level represent. In discussion with Susan Michie, Lewty becomes animated at the comparison between inscribing the surface with deliberate calligraphic forms, and ice-skating. At the same time his understanding of surface is of something capable of healing itself from wounds, as skin does: "To alter it while letting it remain the same", Lewty writes in his essay "The Self as a Stranger". This could count as a credo.

Lewty's work can be seen to rest on an implicit metaphor: seeing surface as skin, or, more obscurely and mysteriously, as person. This dimension of his work can be seen as answering, in a very different way, the sometimes shrill and anxious demands that could be heard in the art of the 1980s: that art become 'more human'. The 1984 exhibition *The Hard Won Image*, held at the Tate Gallery, was one example of this demand, which presented itself as a defense of traditional subject and technique: nude, landscape, still life. Royal Academicians were shown among the more dramatic works of Leon Kossoff, Frank Auerbach and Lucian Freud. There were interesting misfits included, such as the delicately constructed watercolours of Leonard McComb, and a painting by Richard Hamilton—as though to acknowledge that the whole exhibition's premise was open to question. Lewty hated this exhibition, its title and the melodramatic idea of struggle. He hated the fact that the artists did not, in his terms, respect the surfaces they worked on. Against the idea of a hard-won image, his work proposes as a serious alternative an art of play, which activates what he thinks of as "a metaphysical surface, a plane of continuity which can take in ambiguities and opposites, and reconcile them on the surface and as a surface". In its current mode, the surface can incorporate new technical innovations: photocopies, for example, of anonymous drawings, which keep alive Lewty's interest in drawing and symbolisation in a new way, opening out the collective dimension that has always been present in his work.

I began by considering *Gift*, from the period of Lewty's production that is probably less familiar than the earlier work. This was a deliberate choice, because although Lewty has had consistent support, his recent work especially is less well known than it should be. The early work, and the confusing aspects of its reception, still define too much what we might think Lewty's concerns are. The self-consciousness he has shown around the issue of the surface—as distinct from the picture plane, the favoured term in art discussions for much of the last century—is as present in the later work as in the earlier, and it emerges frequently as an issue in the essays and interviews that follow. I think it is crucial, and would argue that the surface acts as an extremely subtle formal basis for thinking about how his work both is, and is not, to be understood as writing. The surface is changed by the process of inscription, but is never reducible to the meaning of the words written on it: it seems to come before and after the words, and makes a complex and mostly unconscious or unverbalised impression on the viewer's reception of what the work gives.

The photograph in the foreword shows Lewty's work table with a mandrake root, 1995.

CHOSEN SUBJECTS

MEAD GALLERY
UNIVERSITY OF WARWICK
1992

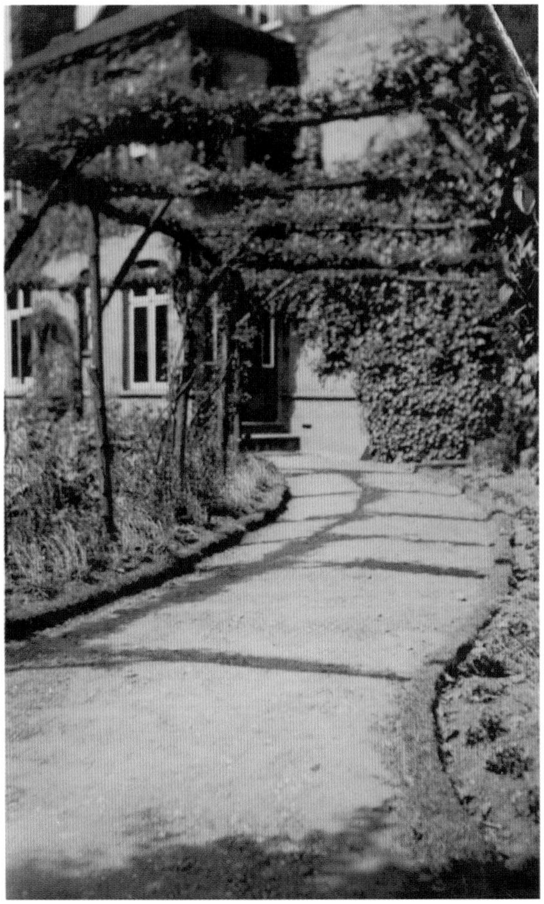

Childhood home in Sutton Coldfield,
photographed c 1941.

These fragments from childhood and later seem to me to have some bearing on my work. Although they might appear at times to have little to do with art, they have much to do with the life of an artist. I hope that through them, and the thoughts to which they give rise, I may be able to come at things obliquely which I am unable to tackle head-on.

LONG AGO

c 1947 One day when I was aged about six, I took a large bottle of bluish glass, and into it put a mixture of leaves and flower petals, some earth, a bone button, tobacco ash, fragments of cloth and leather, a few iron nails and some ink. There may have been other ingredients which I have forgotten. I topped the bottle up with rain water, corked it, and hid it in a dark part of the cellar, where it remained for several months. Occasionally I went to look at it, but would not disturb it until the appointed time. I have no idea what I was expecting, but I was quite unprepared for the abominable stench loosed upon the air at the moment of uncorking. Peering into the depths, I could dimly make out a few shapes floating in the fetid juice or lying at the bottom in a black silt : the moon-like button, still pale; rusted nails like wrecked spars gleaming dully. It was a let-down; but my disappointment was soon followed by the most intense curiosity. I had not created life—quite the reverse; yet the contents of the bottle had become a new reality. All was changed. The 'experiment' had failed; but the ritual had worked. Out of the commonplace had come something utterly alien. A wonder.

Many years later I read of the stage in alchemy called *nigredo*: a strange incubation where matter undergoes a transformation akin to death, evidenced by blackening and decay prior to the rebirth and exaltation of its sublimated body. But of course the child knew nothing of this. In the weak 'alchemy' of my ignorance, I had done everything back to front, taking fair matter and making of it a foul chaos. 'Perhaps if I had left it for a year... for two years... ?'

At about the same time the mistress of my kindergarten brought in a rare treat for us. It was a box of stones, which she had polished on a lapidary machine. To each child she gave a stone. My turn came late, but I was not disappointed. My stone was finely speckled with black and white, like the markings on a bird's egg. Of irregular shape, and cooler than glass to the touch, it lay vibrant in my hand.

Two years or so later, during a walk in the park, I found a cigarette lighter. It was broken and of no intrinsic value, but for me it had both meaning and worth. It nourished and fulfilled a need. To discover a tiny silver box, lying in the long, wet grass! I picked it up and took it home—mine now!

To have a strange thing come from nothing. To receive an unexpected gift of beauty. To find a disquieting key to an unknown door. Later I knew that these were stages on a journey, whose beginning is lowly, whose end unknown. But this was not yet art. Childhood knew nothing of the 'hard-won'. Appropriation and transformation had to do their own day-labour, while the young creator rested; whereas in art I am with the journey (a journey through myself) at every stage. I plod on. Yet there is always the other way, the child's way, who gives a push to the things of his world out of curiosity to see what happens. Art may be a willed thing; but it is also an adventure. Who does the willing, and why?

ALONE, YET WATCHED BY INNUMERABLE EYES

1959 The barn, made entirely of brick, stood isolated in the middle of the field where I, an art student, had come to sketch. Sheep were grazing there, and made a loud commotion at my approach. It was a very hot day in summer. I opened the barn door and entered the cool, damp interior. There were no windows, and the only light came in through the door, which I left slightly ajar. As I stood there, my eyes growing accustomed to the dimness, I saw something hanging in deep shadow on a wall to one side of the door; something I knew had once lived, but was now too still for life. I came closer and saw that it was the dead body of a large lamb, dangling stiffly from a nail, its head sunken, its legs trailing stick-like from a stained huddle of greyish-brown wool, caked with dried mud.

I knew that I had to make a drawing of it. I knew also that in order to see it properly I would have to turn it towards the light. But there was something else prompting me, less rational. I felt that unless I touched the carcass, not only could I not see it, but I could not know it, and so would not be entitled to draw it. The idea revolted me, yet conscience kept saying; this is the price you must pay for your drawing. At length I put down my drawing-board, and coming closer in the half-darkness, I embraced the shrunken thing and turned it to the light. I cannot adequately describe the feelings of that moment. I knew that it was just a creature, not alien to me; and yet the reality which had been an animal was utterly changed. It hardly seemed like a once-living thing, now in decay, but rather a kind of nothing, become stubborn, clotted substance.

There will be some who find this probing of chaos merely morbid. Yet I am convinced that curiosity—whether 'pure' or 'impure'—

lies behind much of what the artist does. From it springs the need to scrutinize surfaces and to peer beneath them, to touch the unclean, to transgress in order to know. Entering that barn out of a clear, bright day, I was confronted with a presence very near and yet unapproachable. My business with the lamb was to possess something dark and fearful, that in coming close to it I might come closer to myself. So what happened was a necessity, and the recalling of it serves a better end than that of simply stirring up mental mud.

The lamb has long since returned to its elements. The drawing, and the painting I did from it later, likewise. A housing estate now covers the fields where the barn was. So nothing is left now, of substance. Yet the essence of the experience remains: to question.

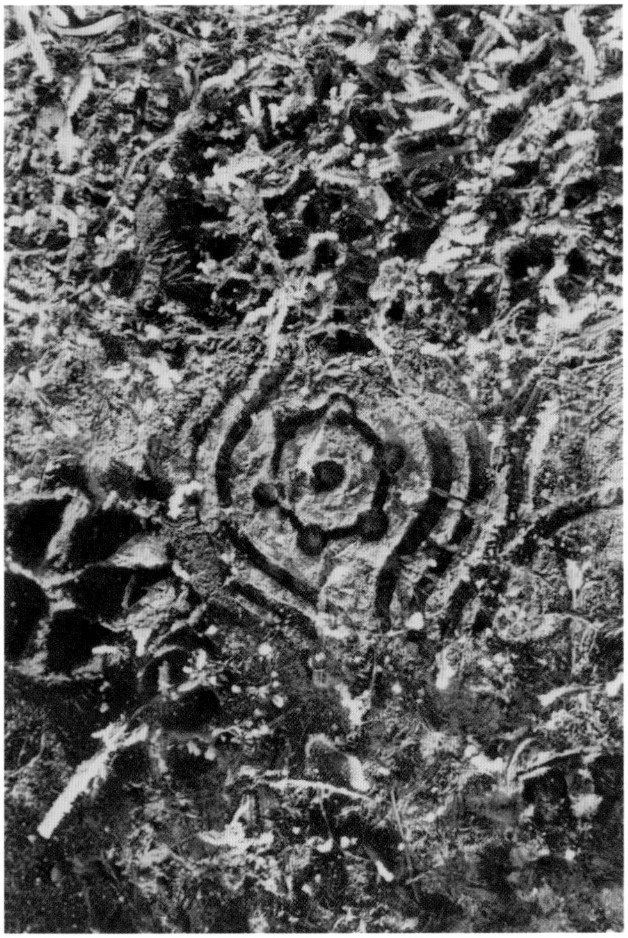

Human and dog footprint in frozen ground.

WAYFARING

'No dog?' enquires the lady I meet on the path through the field one hot summer's morning.
'No...' I reply, glancing at the small brownish creature that snuffles now at my feet, 'I don't have one.'

Conversations are rare with us field-walkers. One doesn't stop. 'Morning' and 'Afternoon' are nodded over the shoulder in passing, if at all. But this morning is fine, and, for some reason, I am moved to prolong the exchange. 'Sometimes I wonder if I am the only person who comes this way without a dog,' I say.
She turns and looks back. 'Yes... ' she murmurs, 'There aren't many now....'

And so we go our ways.

Perhaps she is right. It would seem that fewer people go for walks on their own just for the sake of walking. Not to get anywhere in particular; not in pursuit of health; not as a work of art; and dog-less. Again I fail to conform—even in open country. I think of my pictures of tracks and walking men, and as I continue along the dry field-path, I begin to remember the emotions associated with other walks, at other times.

1962 North London sleeps late on Sunday mornings, but I am out of the house today by soon after eight o'clock, and walking through streets of brick-built villas, red in the early, slanting sun. Not a sound comes from any of the houses. I turn into a long main road, equally deserted and equally silent. A single car drives past, the trail of its exhaust slow to disperse in the still air; then silence again, but not quite as profound. The envelope of quietude has been picked open at the corner.... there are other people on the earth. And a short time later I see some of them, out to buy Sunday papers. In the distance a church bell starts up, in a tentative monotone, but without eliciting any obvious response. Others, more hectoring and insistent, join in, and a jangling carillon rings out over the rooftops from unseen belfries.

Of the few people abroad at this time, the vast majority seem to be over sixty, and once in this road I saw an old man who looked nearer to ninety. He was walking so slowly that he seemed hardly to move, yet gradually he made progress. I began to think. 'If he is ninety or thereabouts, he would have been born in, say, 1872, which would have made him about my age at the time of Queen Victoria's Diamond Jubilee. He would have seen horses on these London streets; been middle-aged at the outbreak of the first World War....'

The character of the road is changing now. The houses are less prosperous-looking, and interspersed with shops—delicatessen, second-hand clothes and furniture, tobacco and sweets, newspapers; and yet more endless terraces. One house there looks derelict; no, it isn't; it is just withdrawn: dark windows hung with grey net curtains, peeling green paint, blackened pebbledash walls. It stands like one in mourning among a merry crowd. A house decayed. And London has many such, each with its own story.

I come to a large park. By now I must have walked several miles. Just a little further, to see what happens round that corner.... And on I go, until the sun stands high in the sky, people appear, and cooking smells and gathering road traffic proclaim the day in earnest. That's enough. I must turn back now, or find another route. The heat closes in. I turn and take a last look at my road, as it loses itself in the mazed tentacles of the East End, moving ever closer to the city's ancient heart.

1981 I climb a steep, rubble-strewn path leading up the side of a great chalk cliff in Dorset. Some time in the last century a thoughtful soul placed a massive rectangular block of stone at the top of this path, for the benefit of the weary walker, and had it inscribed with the words, 'REST AND BE THANKFULL'. This I do; and am.

Sheep have for centuries cropped the grass up here, leaving a wide track of short, springy turf, strewn at the edge with lumps of chalk. The light breeze makes walking comfortable; and I step out, moving into a high, bright emptiness. Below me, sea, heath, and again sea. The light gives a sharp clarity to all it touches. A large chunk of gritty aggregate, relic of some wartime emplacement, stands abandoned in the path, casting a shadow like a black hole cut into the ground at its base. All around me, the bubbling songs of larks arise on currents of warm air. I feel as though I am walking on the roof of the world.

Then, some two hundred yards in front of me, a ragged white cloud of sea-mist blows across the sunlit path. Others follow, and soon they are funnelling up the side of the cliff, like steam escaping from an invisible chimney. I look down, and already the sea is blotted out. Above me, the sun fades to a glowing white disk, then it, too, is gone. Thicker with every moment, the surging vapour rolls across the hill, smothering everything in a dripping blanket of whiteness. Abruptly the temperature drops. The path becomes an ethereal track, marked only by the forward motion of my feet. Within minutes, my face and hair are beaded with water, and the thin shirt clings damply to my back. All sound is stifled. The larks' songs dissolve into nothing; the wash of the sea dies

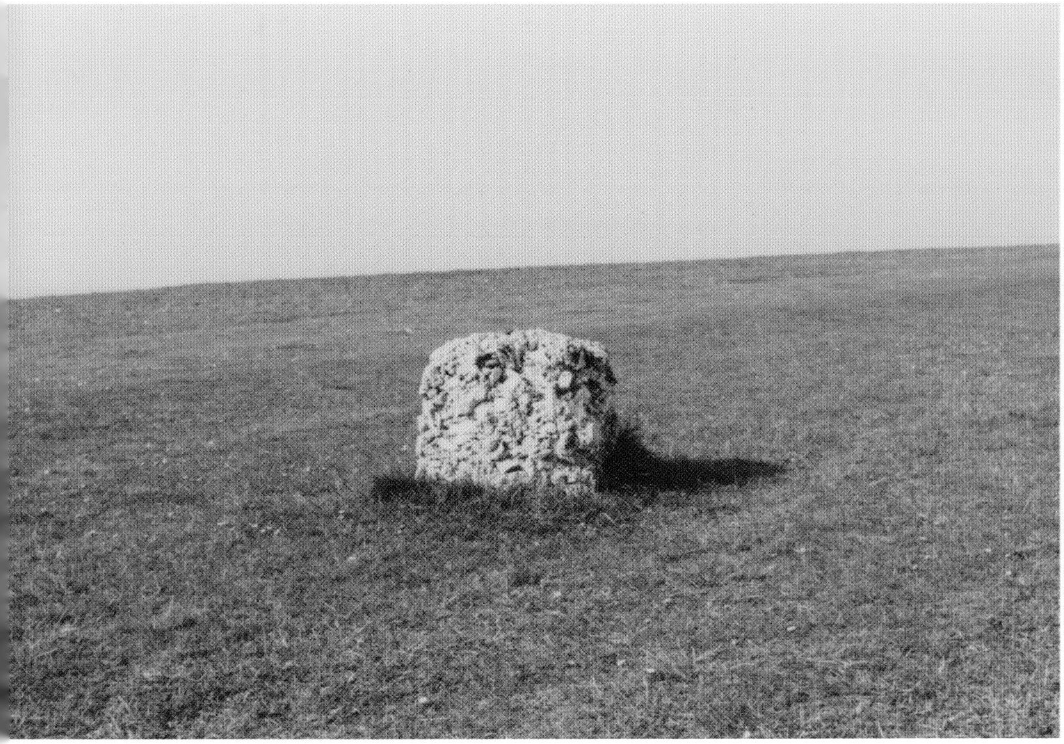

Ballard Down, Swanage, Dorset.

away far below me. I can hear only my own breathing, and muffled footfall, as I penetrate the glaring blankness.

I come eventually to a large mound, an ancient barrow, and scrambling up the soaked grass, I stand, cocooned in mist, upon the bones of some beaker-using hill-dweller long gone. I might be the last man on earth. I had woken up that morning in the twentieth century, and there I hope to lie down to sleep, but at this moment I feel as though time itself has fallen from me, or I from time. Unseeing and unseen, I stand on the blurred tumulus. Then slowly I pick my way down, and press on into the void.

And only a minute later I am out of it, and blinking in bright sunlight. The 'hedge of mist' could only have extended for a quarter of a mile, and must have been shifting constantly. Yet for the time I was in it, I was in a world cut off; a white, silent territory where all was changed. I look back to where it lies behind me, already retreating like a fading dream as I walk on into the burning day.

Recalling these past walks I am by now nearly at the end of the 'dog-path', where the green road crosses a bridge, before arriving at the tarred one. At this spot, a few summers ago, I picked up the sole of an old leather shoe. It was lying in the dust at the edge of the field. Brownish-black, and fissured like the ground itself, to guess its age was impossible, but it had stubbornly resisted dissolution for many years. Probably it had been brought to the surface by the plough. To me it was a relic of someone I would never know. A dessicated token of the man who once wore it and walked in it. How many miles?

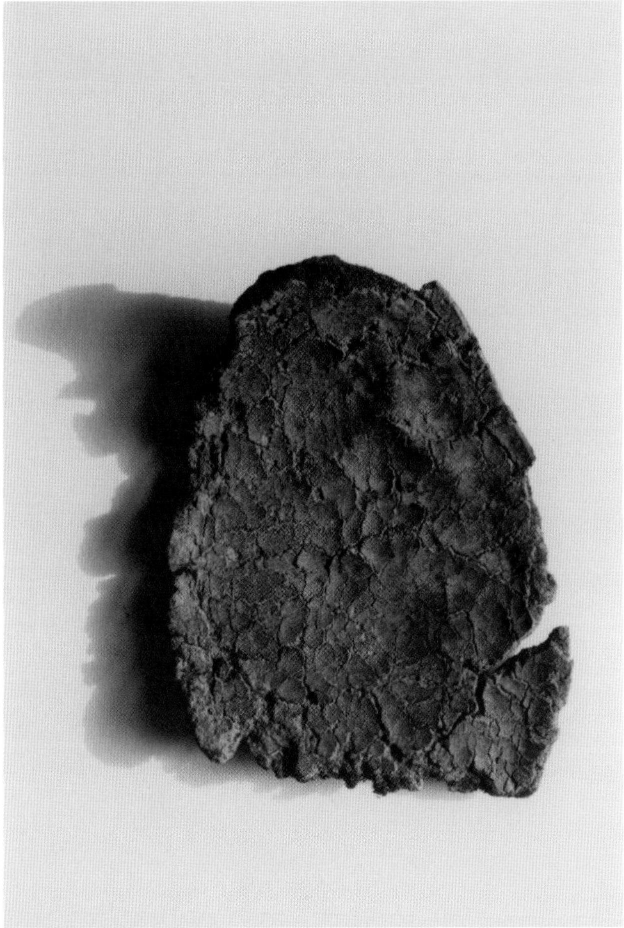

Fragment of leather shoe sole, South Warwickshire.

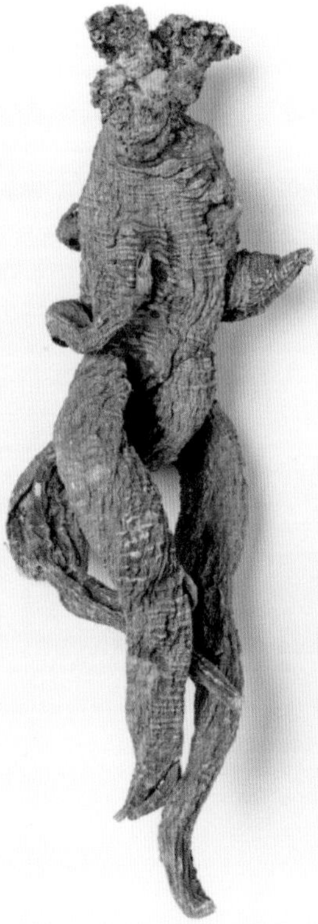

Mandrake root from the Pitt Rivers Museum, Oxford, labelled:
England, Headington, Oxfordshire. Root of Black Briony brought in by a labourer as a 'mandrake', believed to have magical potency, 1916.

A WILD SHOUT

About half way through the orchestral work 'Eventyr', by Frederick Delius, there is a climactic moment when a concealed chorus of men's voices is instructed to give 'a wild shout'. I understand that this office is usually performed now by members of the orchestra. Such a shock tactic is unique in the music of Delius, and is, of course, the sort of thing which, once done, should not be repeated by anyone else, unblushingly. The effect is of a primitive release of tension. It is like an electric flash, lighting up for an instant a deep chasm under the surface texture of the music. Occasionally life throws at us something equally untamed, and the earlier this happens, the stronger the impression it makes.

1948 Aged about seven, I was on a visit to the zoo. As we watched the leaping monkeys at play, a large chimpanzee sprang suddenly towards me. In a moment I glimpsed his wrinkled hand dart through the wire and snatch my tie (a new, bright red one, and fortunately loosely knotted) from my neck. Almost before I realised what had happened, he was off, with a shout of triumph, to the stunted, leafless trees, gleefully waving his newly acquired finery. It was all over in seconds.

This was life; but there are times when art, too, must call upon the ape within. But what does this mean in practice? Chimpanzees, as we know, can, if supplied with paints and brushes, turn out a good imitation of a splashy abstract painting. They can also, with a wild shout, have the tie off your neck. What, then, might not the artist do?

But not too often! Shouting is not to be advocated as a way of life, or of art: there is too much of it today, in both. It should be the exception, not the rule. Once is enough: a wild shout! and then silence.

Another 'shout' echoes from the past: the shriek, bringing death or madness to the hearer, of the mandrake, as its roots are pulled from the earth. This job was soon delegated to the huntsman's luckless dog. Mandrakes are mentioned in the Old Testament, but it was Josephus, the first century Jewish chronicler, who first put about the story of their shrieking. As early as the Middle Ages this was known to be superstition, yet it continued to grip the imagination of later times, in outlying areas, and the body of folk-credulity waxed fat on every kind of belief connected with this forked, human-seeming vegetable. It was supposed to have both narcotic and aphrodisiac properties, if eaten, and also to induce pregnancy. There are accounts of country people dressing the roots as manikins, with grains of millet for eyes. They were called 'poppets' or 'mommets', kept in special cupboards and even consulted as oracles.

The mandrake is a recent-comer to my pictures. I show him as a mouthed root, proxy for a man; and have him play within the spaces of my world and along familiar paths. Both scapegoat and accuser, yet he is also an innocent, a laughing stranger, and wears his symbolism lightly: a vagrant of the imagination.

A real mandrake root lies in a glass case at the Pitt Rivers Museum, along with various other 'charms'. Dried and labelled and of course silent now—what is it supposed to mean to us today? What does it take as we peer at it on an Oxford afternoon, to breathe the air of a younger, wilder time, when the root lived, and shrieked in the minds of men?

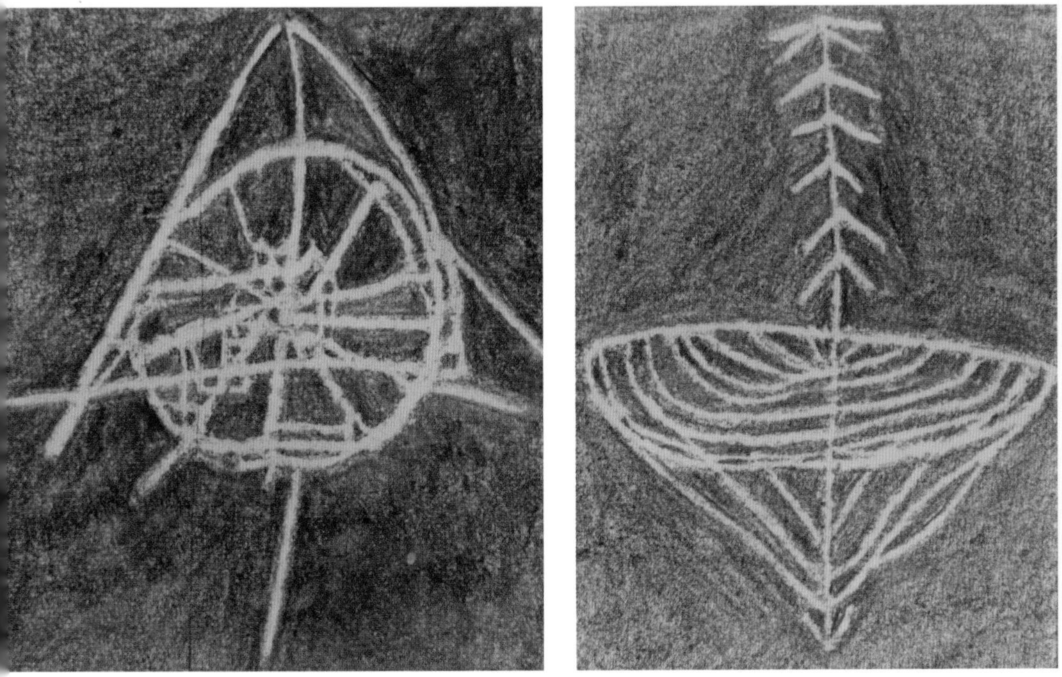

Rubbings taken by the author from a discussed school desk, c 1950?

THE MAN WHO POINTS

Graffiti—the ones I am concerned with—certainly date back to the ancient world, and probably far beyond. They are the cries of individuals throughout the ages, and there is great poignancy in such unofficial art. It is wonderful that these scratched mementoes of the forgotten people of past ages have survived into the present —for the most part unremarked, unprotected and unrecorded.

Modern aerosol ephemera are not true graffiti, strictly speaking, which have always been drawn or scratched into a surface rather than painted on it; which tend characteristically to be small and private, secretive even; and are born out of a desire for commemoration and permanence, unlike the gaudy superficial defacements of a throwaway age. Carved tokens of love long outlast the lovers who made them. 'X was here'—yes, and here will remain! until the score-marked wall comes down, until the notched school desk is broken up.

Older graffiti, many of them in churches, are often of great beauty, and obviously the work of skilled hands. Others are very crude. Those which include writing are ipso facto the work of the educated, in a largely illiterate society. Sometimes they are puzzles, to which we will always lack the key. Sometimes they are cries of pain and fear: the words 'God help me' speak for themselves, throughout the ages. Yet whenever and wherever made, and by whatever makers; whether scratched by sword-point, chisel, pocket knife, kitchen knife or scribing pencil lead, graffiti are the stuff of enigma. They speak of half-forgotten customs, secret rituals and galling obsessions. Deeply incised on the stone coping of a railway bridge is a strange image. It appears to be a stylized hand, with four fingers curled inwards and the thumb also bent and lying across the palm. As I place my own hand on it, fitting my fingers to the lichened stone ones, I wonder at the mark: how it came to be there, and who made it; and when, and why?

One day, many generations ago, someone probably very like us carved the following words on a church wall:

A yong rewler wytles
A pore man spendar haveles
A ryche man thif nedeles
A old man leche(r loue)les
A woman rebolde sameles

Who was he, the unknown man who, like the boy in *The Emperor's New Clothes*, blurted out these words, so like a finger pointed in derision, and went away? The verse is a variant on a text popular in the thirteenth and fourteenth centuries, *The Abuses of the Age, or Five Evil Things**.

Was he then a disillusioned being? A misanthrope? Soul-sick? Or simply mischievous? There is no way of knowing. Man and woman, rich and poor, young and old, not one of them is spared. The words are cut; the jabbing finger points; the brief, mocking laughter rings out—and he is gone.

* See V Pritchard, *English Medieval Graffiti,* (Cambridge 1967).

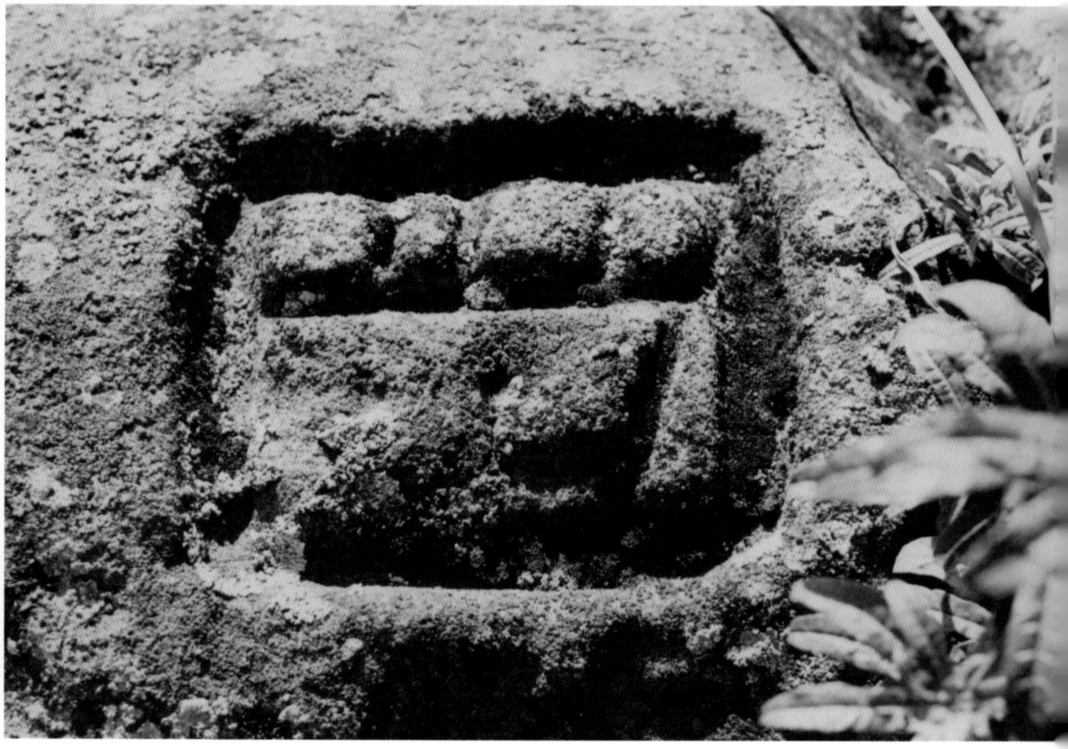

Stylized hand from a coping stone, railway bridge, South Warwickshire.

THE BEACH

Few people come this far along the beach, and those who do tend not to stay for long. Indeed, there is little reason why they should. The beach starts out as sand, but pebbles pile up into ever steeper ridges, until at its extreme northern end it becomes a true storm beach, with almost vertical terraces of shingle, some as much as eight or ten feet high. This part of the beach is quite different from what has gone before. It is the untamed region: rough, steep and narrow, and not without its dangers. The great chalk cliffs which rise up behind are unstable, and regularly feed the sea below with slumping falls of stone. The beach itself is a result of these falls: a desert of tumbled white rocks and silent cascades of scree. Here is no easy foothold, and in summer, no shelter from the sun. A fierce light pours down on blanched boulders and splinters on piles of smaller stones, some still jagged, others worked smooth by the sea. Some are porous, as though in decay, riddled with hundreds of tiny holes, like stone sponges, streaked with ferruginous orange and grey-green ochre: *terra cariosa*. Clouds of tiny flies hover round those places where perhaps some death lies beneath the shingle.

The whole detritus of stone is threaded with other leavings, washed by the sea to this end of the beach. Gorse roots, torn from the cliffs, lie here dried and bleached, their twisted lineaments a silent record of the force that once flowed in their lost pith. Weathered fragments of driftwood, one still bearing a rusty iron bolt; bedraggled sea-birds' feathers and the bones of fishes. Here also lie the residues of our own consumption: countless bits of plastic; bottles and cans; a broom head; a child's sandal. The colours of man's spilt debris are garish: acid chromatic flicks on a ground of pale cream and grey. Sometimes an abandoned object speaks with the pathos of the forsaken—a cerise hair ribbon; sometimes the absurd breaks through—a green polystyrene anchor. Some things invite closer scrutiny: a half-burnt chunk of sodden printed paper turns out to be the charred remains of an 'explicit sex' book.

There are larger offerings also: a whole tree, its roots waving dryly in the salt air; the rusted remains of a motor cycle; a great timber baulk from some destroyed jetty, resting across the rocks like a bench for a giant. All this is interwoven with dense tangles of seaweed and nylon fishing line, orange and green, crumpled sail-canvas and lengths of frayed rope, stained and clotted with oil.

Coarse shore-plants have gained a root-hold in places. Sucking what nourishment they can in a marginal life, their fibrous tendrils and fat leaves creep across the hot stones. They are the only vegetation in this desert, apart from the great rafts of seaweed which lie over the shingle. Sallow green hair, laced with thick straps of brown gristle, these stinking ferments are alive with hopping sandflies. Crossing them is like treading on an enormous sponge.

At the sea's edge the wind is fresher, the smells cleaner. Squinting into the dazzle of sunlight on breaking water, I look out to sea. The rocks here are smooth and rounded. The surf breaks over them and withdraws, leaving pools of thousands of tiny bubbles. The wind dusts my face with spray, which dries immediately in the sun. My lips taste of salt.

I stand at an edge where the precarious certainties of land-life give way to an immense unknown. Behind me, vertical and rigid, the embedded past sleeps in the sunlit chalk; before me, the rippling expanse of the sea points towards an indiscernible futurity—a vast and glittering vertigo of the horizontal. This is a place of thinking;

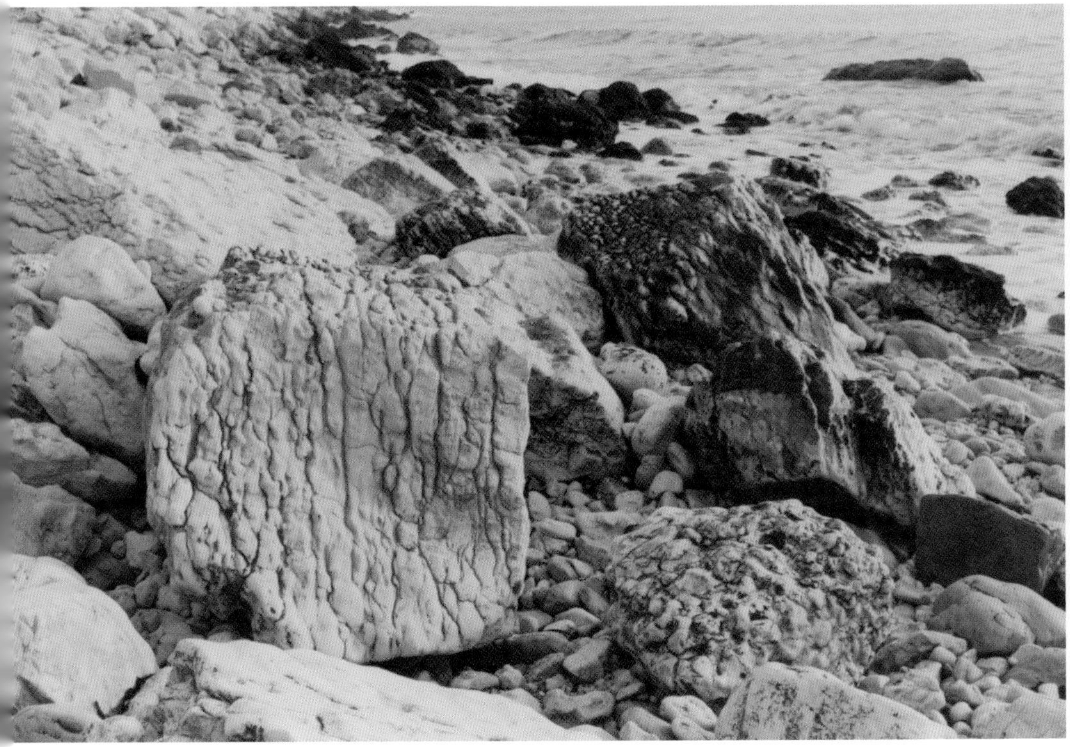

The beach, Swanage, Dorset.

it is also a place of the end of thinking. On this ancient yet ever-shifting margin the brain is overwhelmed in a burning solitude. Splintered fragments of words and images beat upon the overloaded consciousness until it can take no more, and is drained, as by the flux and reflux of waves breaking on a mental shore. Here I stand: and reach after some absolute which I do not find.

Yet beneath the glitter of the moving surface lie hidden depths of unhurried stillness. The beach, like the other places of which I tell, cannot be possessed, any more than the past can be re-lived. Yet it is by memories of such things as these that I am formed, and through imagination that I create. What I contemplate, I may become. I may discover something of myself in the found flotsam; I may come to know a mystery in the kept stone; I may recognize an unexpected joy on the lost beaches of a stirred dream.

November 1991

ISBN 0 902683 17 9
Chosen Subjects is published to mark the exhibition
Simon Lewty: *Terra incognita*
at Mead Gallery, University of Warwick
16 November – 19 December 1992
under the editorial direction of
Katharine Eustace, Curator, Mead Gallery
Victoria Pomery, Assistant to the Curator

Design: *pro*graphics, Coventry
Printed: M E Wilkinson, Nuneaton

Chosen Subjects
is printed in a limited edition
of 500 copies
of which this is

No ....

I cannot tell of all, for around the corner lies this place unspeaking of his arrivals and departures throughout the years – and it is rightly the place of a lifeless summer morning – or urgent in the cold following rains of spring. "So this is best left?" "Yes, you cannot enter, in any case, and you can have no recollection of him – the one who passed there over 20 years before – and even less of the great loads of stone as they were hauled along the dusty road!" Now I do not wish to insult you! That is a pleasant use to which the stone has been put. That tree grows there because of the custom of the place, once, and in high memory. BUCUORN. Idle on the green! Rightly told, this is too much here, not too little, as they think, who heedlessly pass through. BALUORN. Then of this sufficiency, which as he walks moves low at the edge of the road in waving bands: AND WILL GO WITH HIM, AT HIS SIDE. It is of those who left, and those who will not leave, and those who have returned. Then is it enough? Better, in fact, to reject the hopes turned bitter over four years ago, and in silence to watch there? But – STOP THIS! The waving band here falters, and now breaks; and there, where those careless beasts once trod, and lay under their gabled shelters, reared upon the dragged stones, now light voices are heard, and the stepping of those who will break them. This was not his intention – (Perhaps he was rash!) AND THIS – UNWANTED!

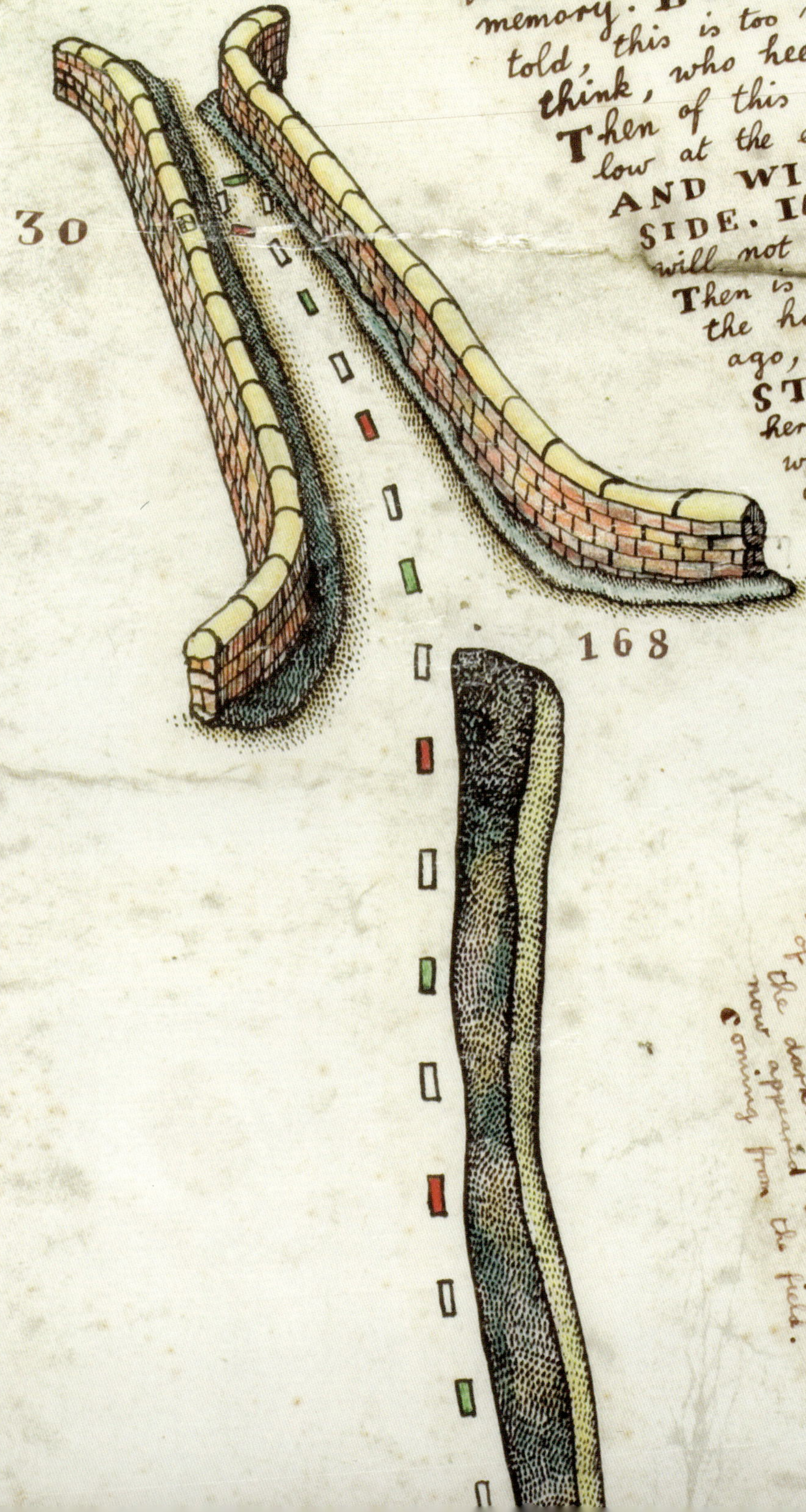

and could only find the way after
since any man had seen there. He ma
He awoke very early, and went out, int
where have you come from?" He woul
were to say to them: "I come from the
satisfy their curiosity. For in truth th
from that slatted shelter where he
of the field. Inside that dark pla
the darkness of evening had beg
now appeared at the door. A ng
coming from the field.

opposite and below 1. *Path*, 1991.

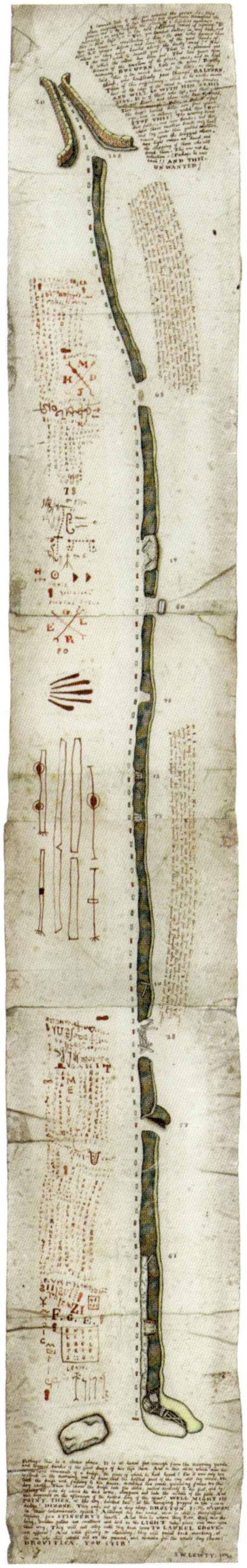

top 2. *Chalk Script Ballard Down*, 1994.

bottom 3. *Box Pew*, 1994.

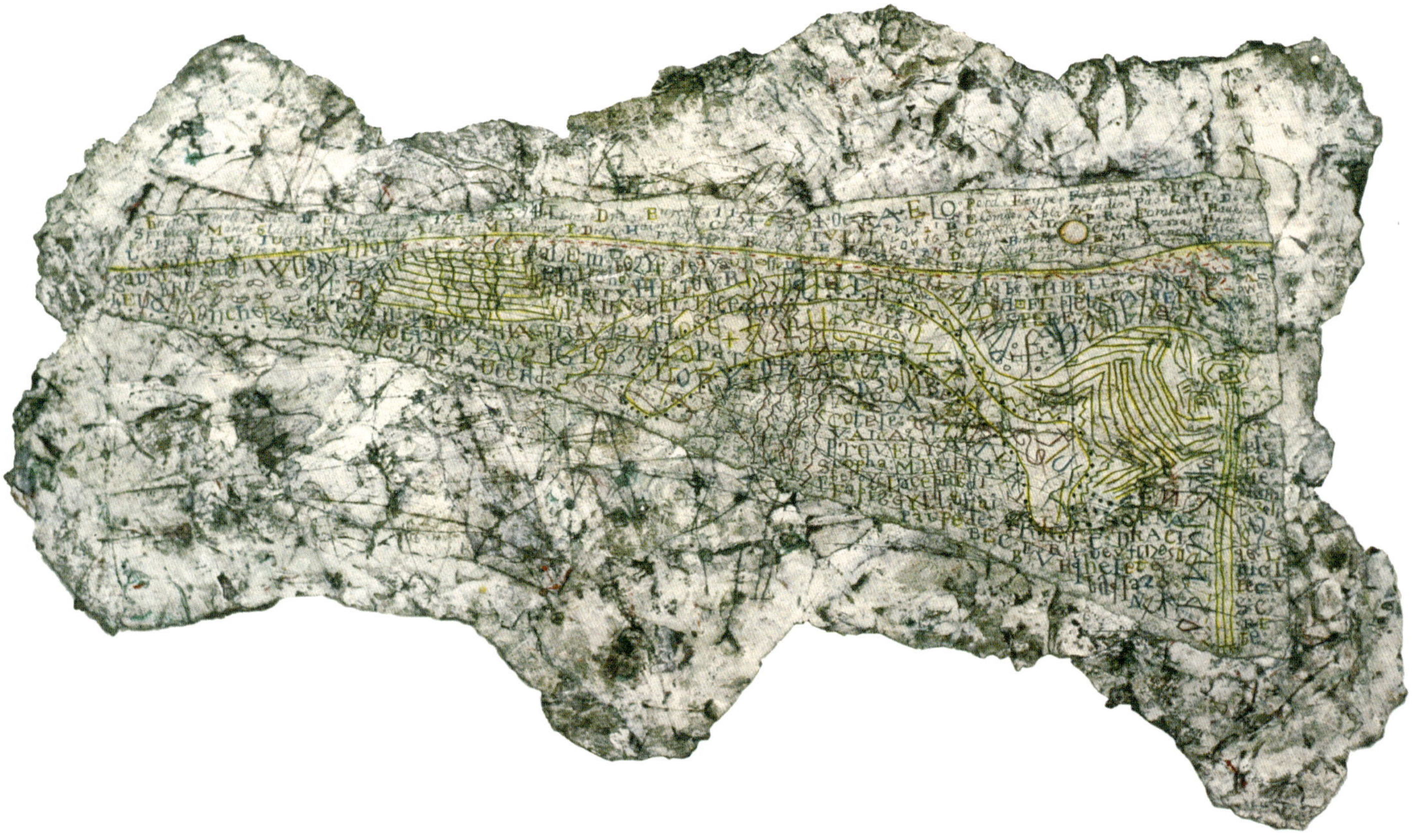

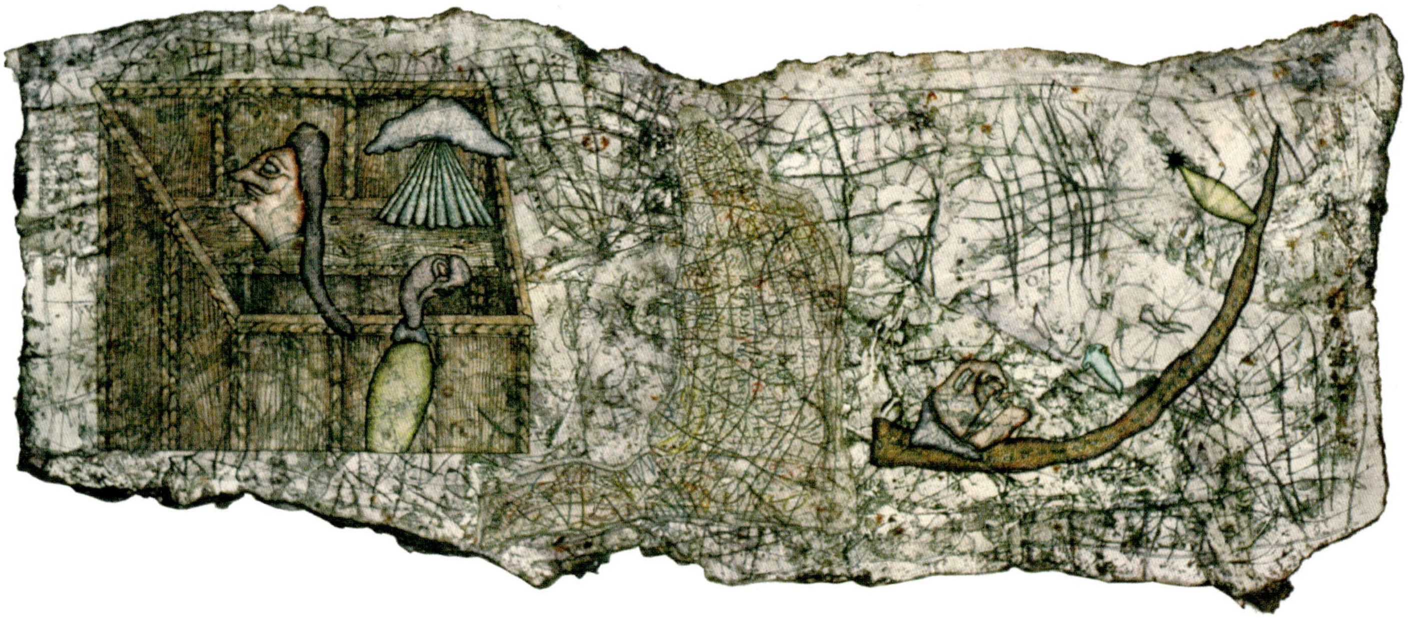

4. *Pointing Man*, 1990.

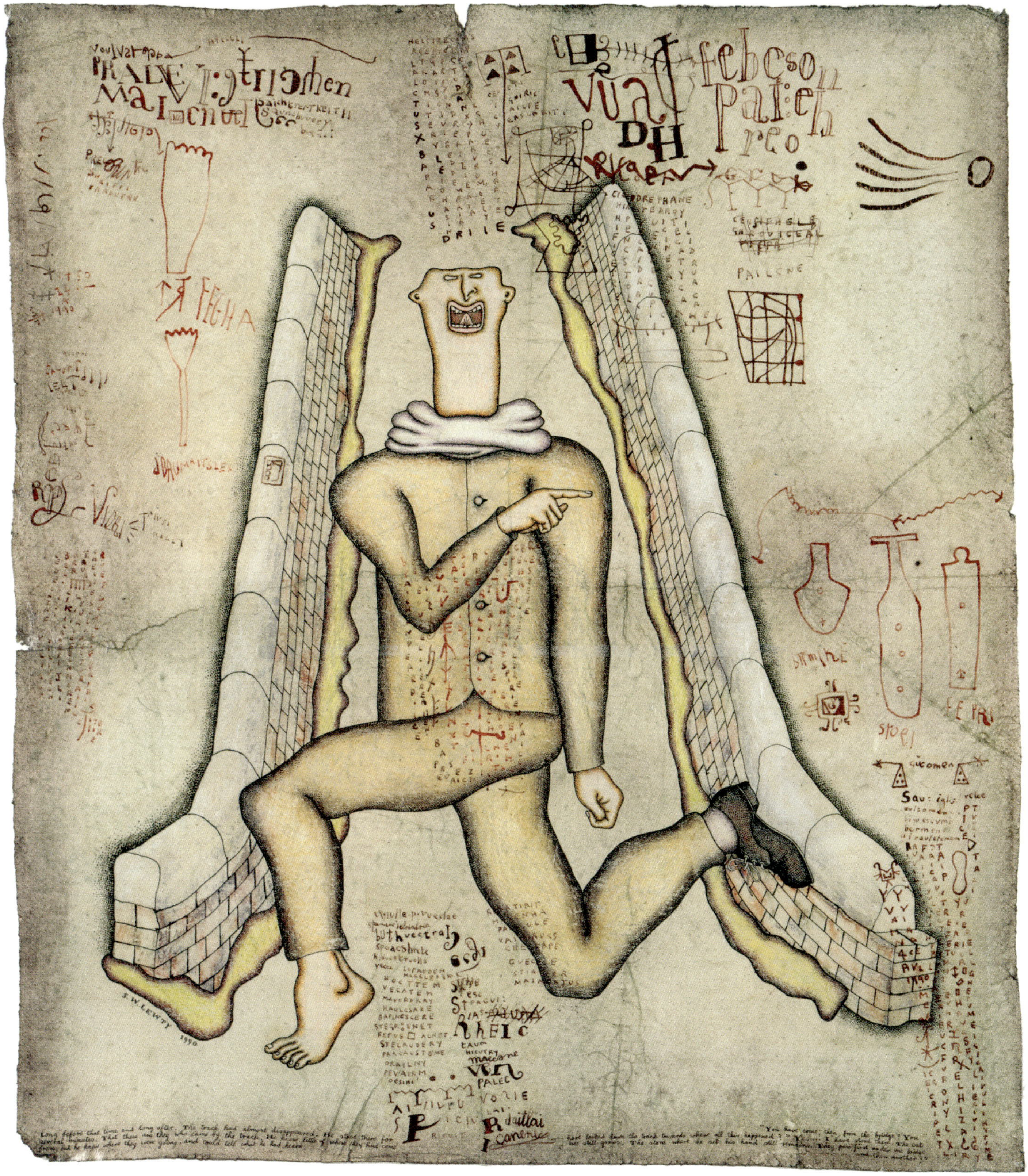

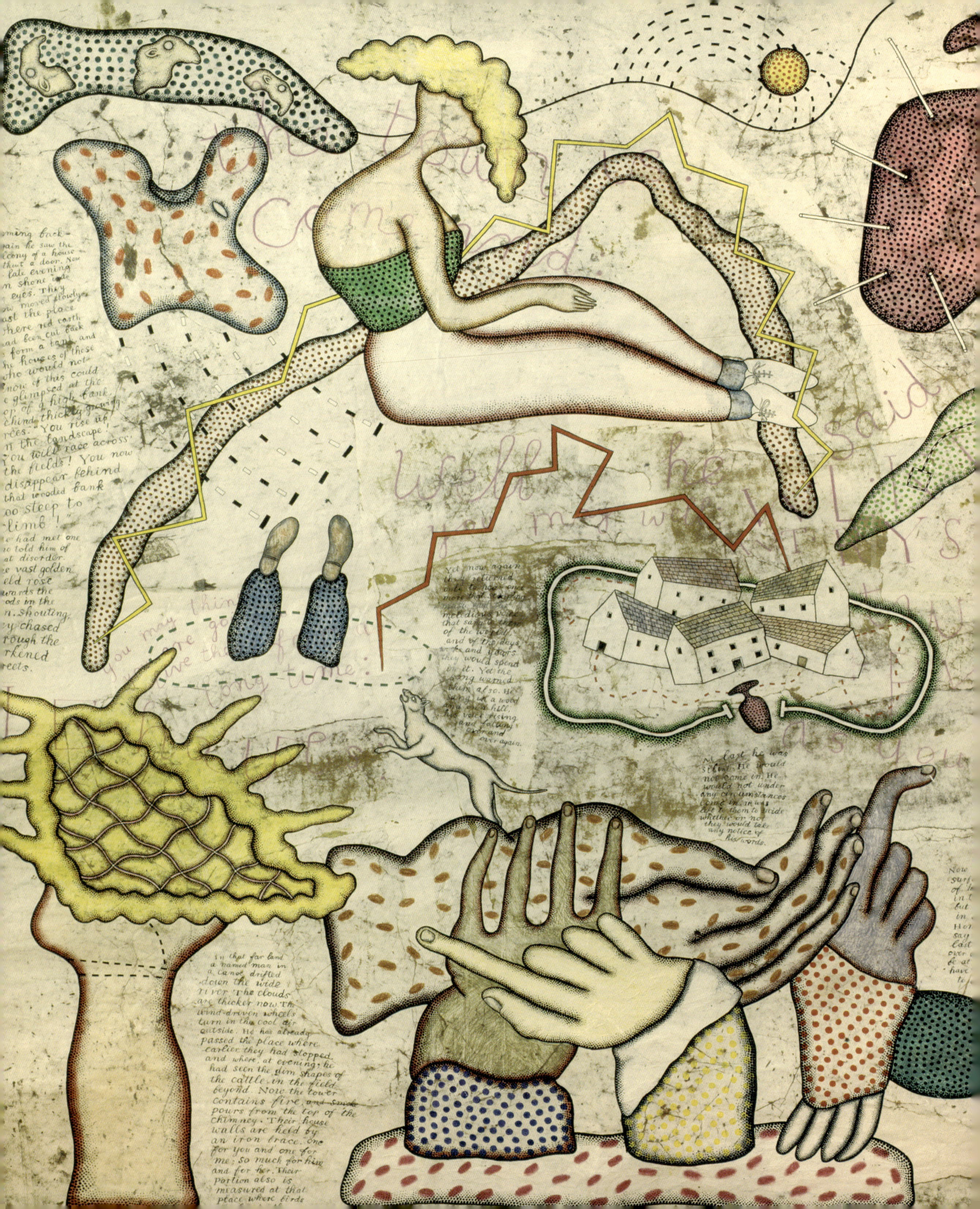

ming back-
gain he saw the
lcony of a house
thout a door. Now
late evening
n shone into
eyes. They
w moved slowly
ast the place
there red earth
ad been cut back
form a tank and
he houses of those
who would not
now of this could
e glimpsed at the
op of a high bank
ehind thickly growing
rees. "You rise up
n the landscape!
You will race across
the fields! You now
disappear behind
that wooded bank
oo steep to
limb!"
e had met one
o told him of
at disorder.
e vast golden
eld rose
wards the
ods in the
n. Shouting
ey chased
rough the
rkened
reets.
Yet now again
and of the days
and years
they would spend
in it. Yet the
song warned
them also.
over again.
At last he was
silent. He would
not come in. He
would not under
any circumstances
left to them to decide
whether or not
they would take
any notice of
his words.
In that far land
a named man in
a canoe drifted
down the wide
river. The clouds
are thicker now. The
wind-driven wheels
turn in the cool air
outside. He has already
passed the place where
earlier they had stopped
and where, at evening, he
had seen the dim shapes of
the cattle in the field
beyond. Now the tower
contains fire, and smoke
pours from the top of the
chimney. Their house
walls are held by
an iron brace. One
for you and one for
me; so much for him
and for her. Their
portion also is
measured at that
place where birds

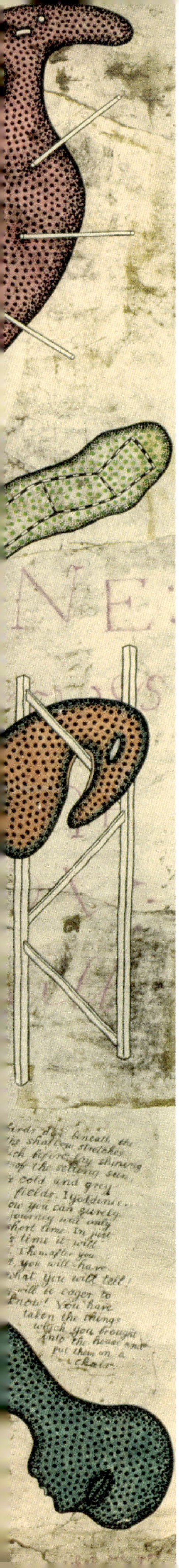

opposite 5. *Well He Said,* 1985.

THE SADNESS OF DREAMS

STUART MORGAN
SEPTEMBER 1985

It is hard to know what to think about the figures in a Simon Lewty drawing. Half child, half dirigible, they float untethered around the picture space, like single-celled animals which rotate around their own axes. Arms and legs are in short supply. And they have no identifiable expressions. Common politeness makes us regard them as victims of their own passivity. These infant zeppelins elicit a single response: deep sadness, as muffled and unspecific as their predicament itself.

Don't get me wrong. Every part of a Lewty drawing is logical enough in isolation. Workers are mending a fence. Sheep are munching grass. A man falls head downward into a swamp, with his legs waggling in the air. The drawing itself leaves no room for vagueness. A tangle of boundaries, it shows where things stop and other things begin, as in mapping. Doubts arise when we begin thinking of the entirety. Visually speaking, it is a model of clarity. In terms of logic—the terms a map should occupy—all hell has broken loose. To say that size, gravity, perspective, direction and surface have been rejected is not strictly true. The truth is that there are pieces of a lot of things here. And no single rationale connects them.

Even the elements of a Lewty drawing are quite different in kind. Paper has been marked and rubbed in the way Joan Miró did, as a means of unleashing inspiration. Unlike Miró, Lewty writes invented words as quickly as possible over the surface. They look and sound like words but never are. Nor do they fit together to make sense. In quite different calligraphy are the passages of prose. It would be going too far to call them 'narrative'; events never reach climaxes, nor do plots or characters emerge. There are only nameless figures in particular settings. In longer passages the confusion may be heightened by interruptions; other, different texts have been introduced.

Bringing together these apparently disparate areas of concern gives the entire drawing the effect of having been worked and overworked, like a wall covered with graffiti by various hands and from various periods. The new-coined words, in particular, sinking as they do into the depths of the 'background', suggest a step into the past, as if, by X-ray, rock strata could be viewed at the same time. (This play of levels also contributes to the making of the picture. Black outlines, like those of a stained-glass window, are painted on tissue. When this is stuck onto the treated cartridge paper the resulting effect is sometimes like that of a precious old document. The title and date and the name SW LEWTY are almost always present too.) There are direct historical allusions; the interpolation of capitals in the prose recalls eighteenth-century typography, while the rendition of animals in particular looks back to Medieval models. Yet the entire effect is of liberation from history. While half-human, buried forms resembling specimens from textbooks of marine biology are reminiscent of fossils, the same drawing may include the latest fashions or, in one case, a television set.

6. *The Passage Towards Stone*, 1983.

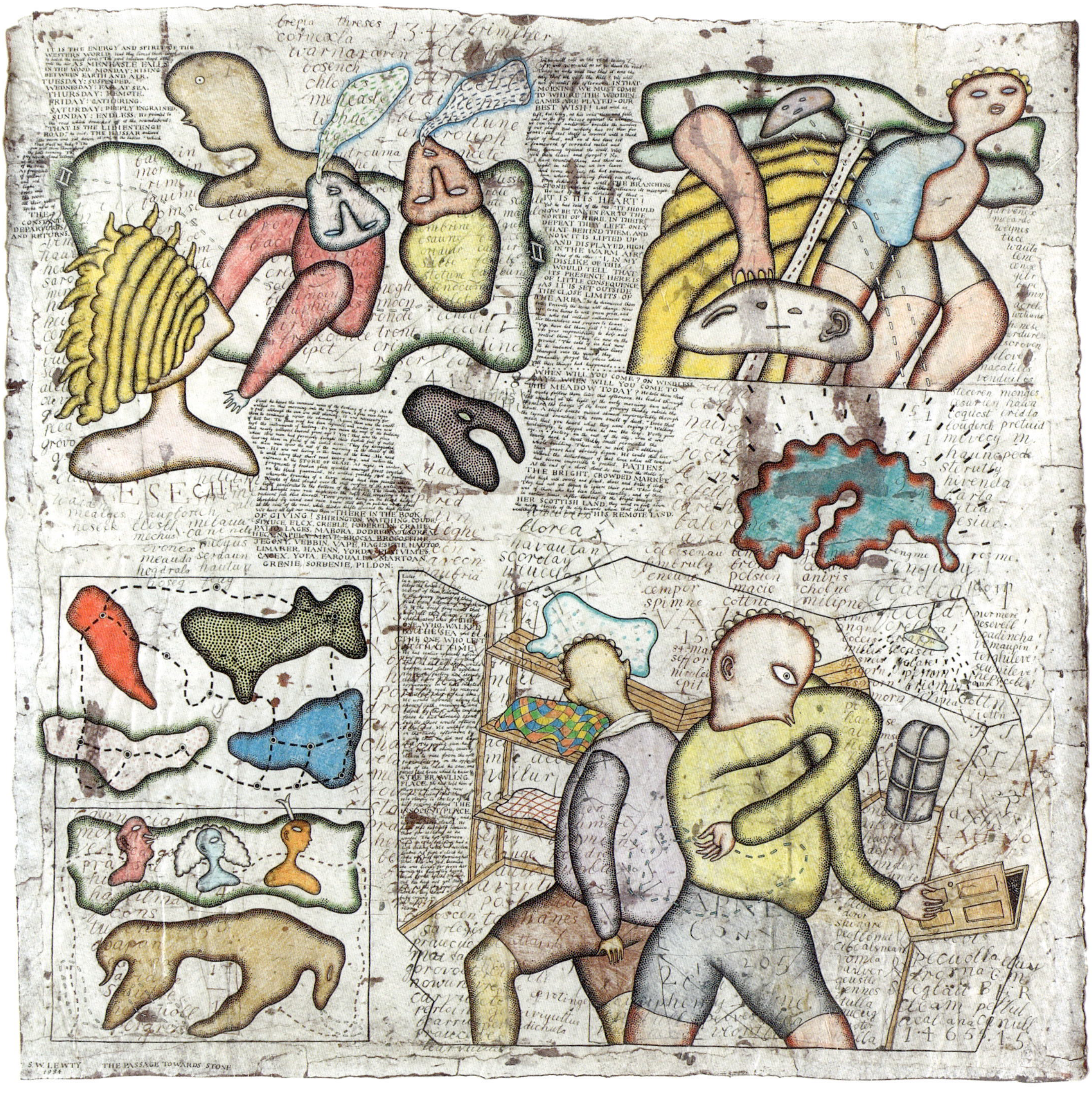

7. Study for *The Passage Towards Stone,* 1983.

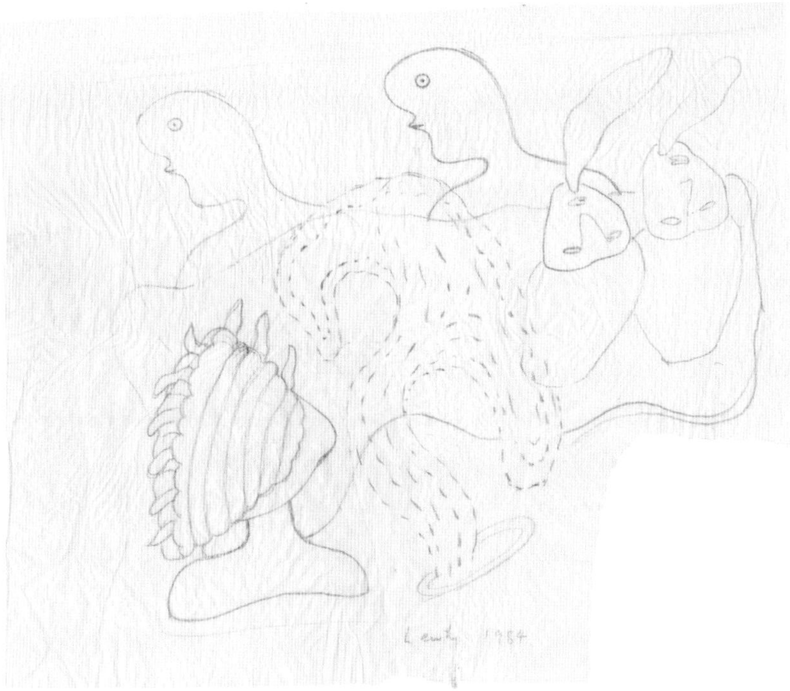

If Lewty cleverly sidesteps the issue of time, he operates differently with regard to place. It seems that a given number of settings are repeated over and over again. A field, a street, a barn, a yard.... They crop up throughout Lewty's work, less as realistic delineation than as psychological impressions of different spaces, ways of conveying different states of mind.

Though each of the drawings is a free improvisation, one source is used more than any other. Given the particular quality of abeyance in his art, it should come as no surprise that this is his Dream Book, in reality a whole series of blue exercise books containing reports of dreams. The state of suspension encountered in the drawings: the regular, unexcitable rhythms of the prose; the constant evidence of a creativity shown by the lists of words all find their parallel in the dream state, a permanent mystery to the waking world and one which has to be read 'between the lines'. Similarly, it is hard to tell where the meaning arises in a Lewty drawing. It seems to emerge from the cracks between the different parts and media.

Above all that obscure pain which first strikes the viewer about the blameless protagonists of this universe becomes more comprehensible when considered in the context of sleep. If the wounds inflicted on these figures are all staunched and healed within the limits of the dream experience, it should come as no surprise that they are inhuman, distanced, insufficiently pitiable. They are necessary sub-Lewties, participants in a charade of his own devising, which takes as its perennial subject the maintenance of his own identity.

8. The Writing on the Wall, 1957.

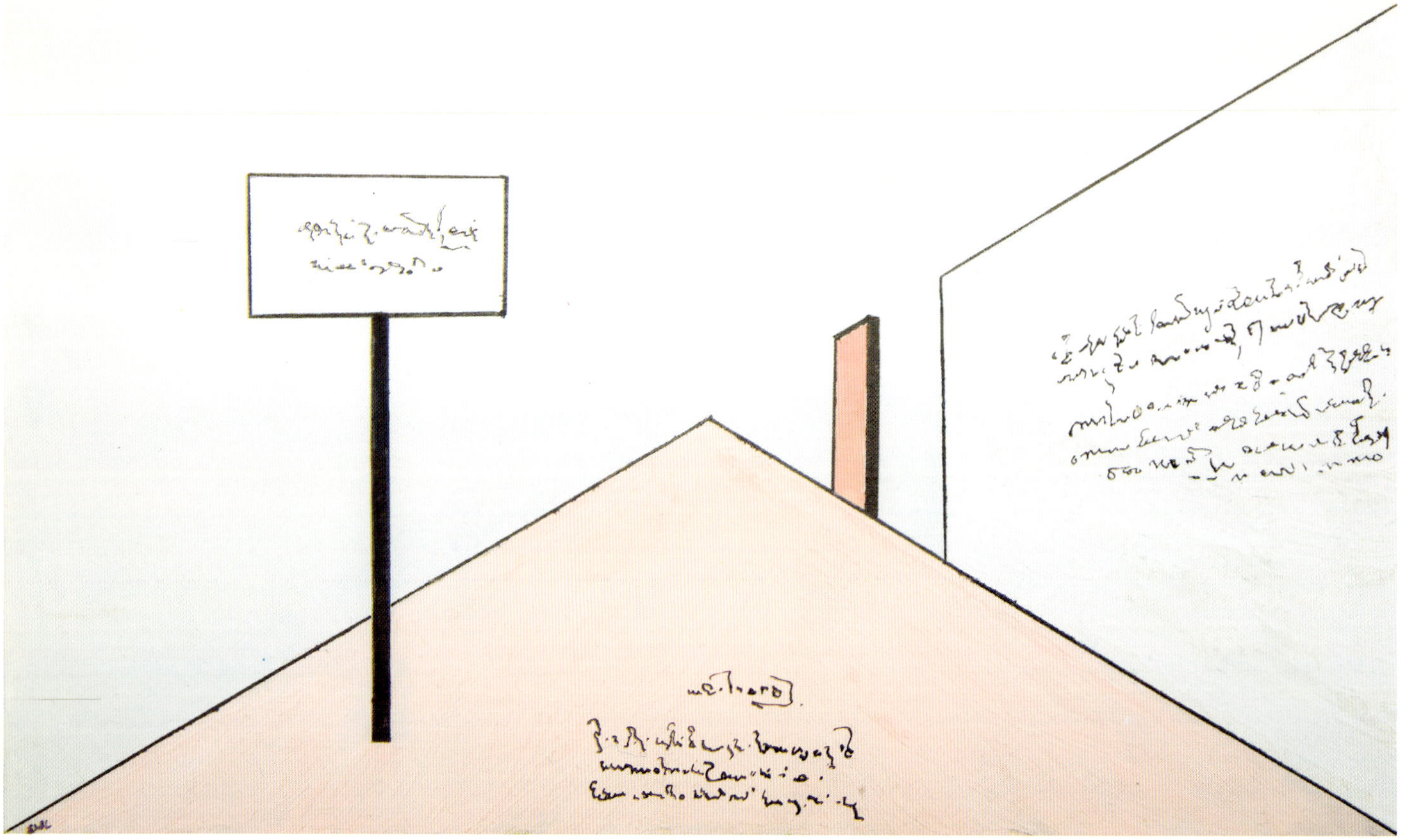

NOTES TOWARDS A BIOGRAPHY

PAUL HILLS
1991

Some events of Simon Lewty's journey may briefly be told. He was born in 1941 at Sutton Coldfield. His parents were not churchgoers and decided to leave the matter of baptism to their children to decide for themselves at a later stage. From an early age near the top of the class at school, Simon was just as likely to be found devouring the eight volumes of *The New Book of Knowledge*, bought for him by his mother from a travelling salesman, as reading Eagle. (Another artist for whom the alliance of text and picture was to be important, Eduardo Paolozzi, was familiar with the same illustrated encyclopaedia.) Untrammelled by any set of religious beliefs, the young Simon Lewty was left to himself to discover where we have come from. He did so with inquisitive energy, turning for enlightenment on evolution to the 1947 edition of B Webster Smith, *The World in the Past*. Its pictorial reconstructions of prehistoric sub-marine life, and its illustrations of amoeba and the skeletons of fishes were not to be forgotten.

At six or seven Lewty spent the best part of a year in bed with suspected rheumatism. In the end it turned out that there was nothing seriously wrong with him, but the experience had set the seal on his bookishness and by putting him out of step with his contemporaries gave him that sense of being an outsider that has never entirely left him. The experience of childhood illness may have been one root of that characteristic of his creativity which Simon Lewty ironically refers to as "negative capabilities", or, as one title (of 1987) has it, "gross deficiency masquerading as abundance".

It was in order to send their son as a day-boy to Warwick School, that the Lewty family moved, in 1950, 20 miles south to Leamington Spa. Apart from his time at Hornsey College of Art, and a year spent in Swanage in 1982–1983, Leamington has been Simon Lewty's home ever since.

In his teens at Warwick School he drew and painted still lives observed with hypnotic clarity, or empty landscapes haunted by a standing stone, a moon, or a slanting fence. Some are redolent of Paul Nash, others of Klee or de Chirico. What they have in common with the mature work is the singular election or choice of objects, which by their isolation take on the property of signs. He drew mainly at home, secretively, on a small scale, high in the attic of the tall house. (The place is recalled in a painting of 1990, *The Landing* (plate 10), which shows the top landing and the door to what became his studio.) At school he was put in the academic 'A' stream that wasn't allowed to do art. With access to the art room denied, his pictorial worlds were made in privacy.

What he excelled at publicly was music. He played the clarinet; he spent a lot of time on music theory. In the school's eyes he was either to go up to Oxford or to study music. "Music was useful to me at school, it gave me status as a non-games person", he recently explained. Music compensating

9. *Of Ancient Breathing,* 1991.

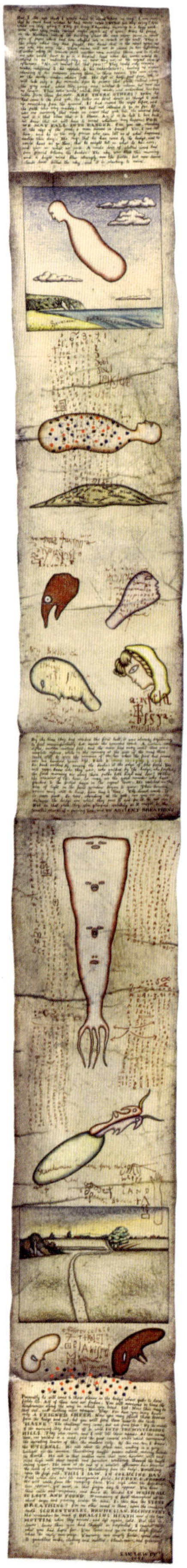

for ineptitude on the sports-field? The way he put it brought to mind the sense of perilous, even infernal sport—hurdles and trip-wires, warning voices on the touch-line—of his later paintings. Could it be that the playing-fields which he shunned re-emerge as the fields of his imagination, places where the notations of sounds and the incantations of words take the place of the trajectories of the cricket ball? Not literally perhaps; but if as a loner the young Lewty denied himself the socially acceptable outlet for physical aggression which sport provides, do not the older Lewty's paintings still bear the traces amidst their visual music of earlier anxieties and latent aggressions? It is at school that the less gregarious first suffer "taunts along the way" (a title of 1986) and the mockery of pointing fingers, the first of harrowings, foretaste of purgatorial journeys.

Reading music, particularly choral music, Lewty's eye became attuned to the visual relationship between words and the sign-language of musical notation. In an interview in 1986 he will observe that, "a map is diagrammatic but it also functions as a surrogate for experience, in the way a score relates to musical performance".

It was at Warwick School that Simon Lewty first went to a church service, and what seems to have struck him most was the declamatory and musical aspect. "I had to learn to chant the psalms", he told me. It called to mind the many published statements in which he has spoken of the importance of the sound as well as the look of his texts, for indeed if we look and listen there is something almost psalm-like about their strange litanies. Each sentence, or even phrase, stands entire, and between each there is a slight gap in the story—a pause for breathing, and a break in continuity. Such texts are more like houses built of bricks with clearly visible beds of mortar than a plastered wall without joint or division. Breathing measures our life in time, and breath-control is important in playing the clarinet: Lewty long ago gave up his clarinet, but recently entitled a painting *Of Ancient Breathing* (plate 9).

At 16 Simon Lewty disappointed his teachers by leaving Warwick School and going to the Mid-Warwickshire School of Art in Leamington. Exposed to the art school studio, privacy was lost, and fantasy grew dim. He learnt to paint in oil; Sickert, and even Rembrandt became models. He went on to London, to Hornsey College of Art, where his paintings were by his own account "very Euston Road". But visits to the Tate widened horizons: he was looking at Dubuffet, Pollock and de Kooning, as well as rediscovering earlier enthusiasms. Herbert Read's book on Surrealism opened doors. By 1962 he had discovered the abstractions of Antoni Tapies. Under their influence he gave up oil painting, turned towards abstraction, and set out on a fruitful period of experiment with materials.

10. *The Landing*, 1990.

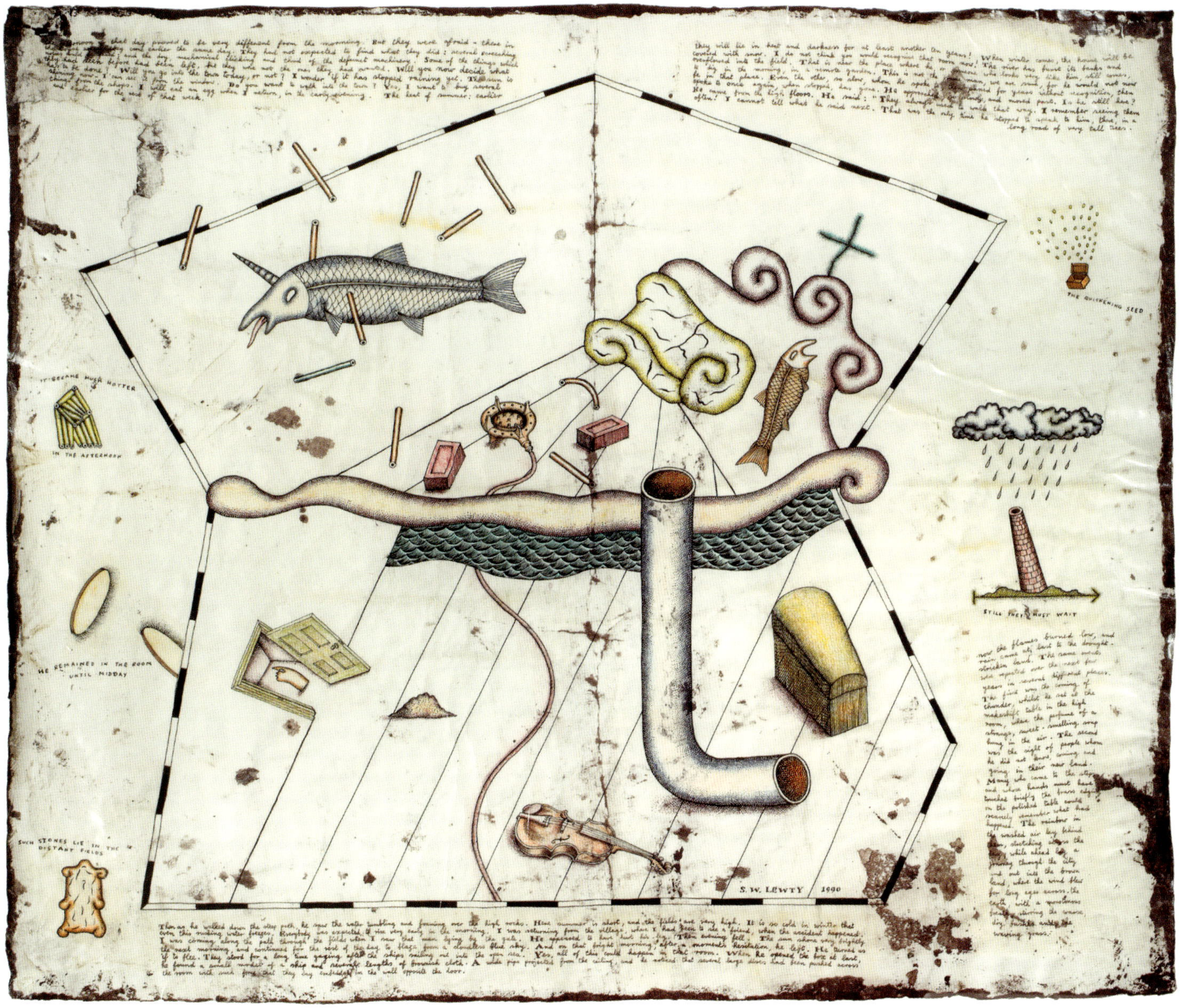

11. *Over Old Fields*, 1980.

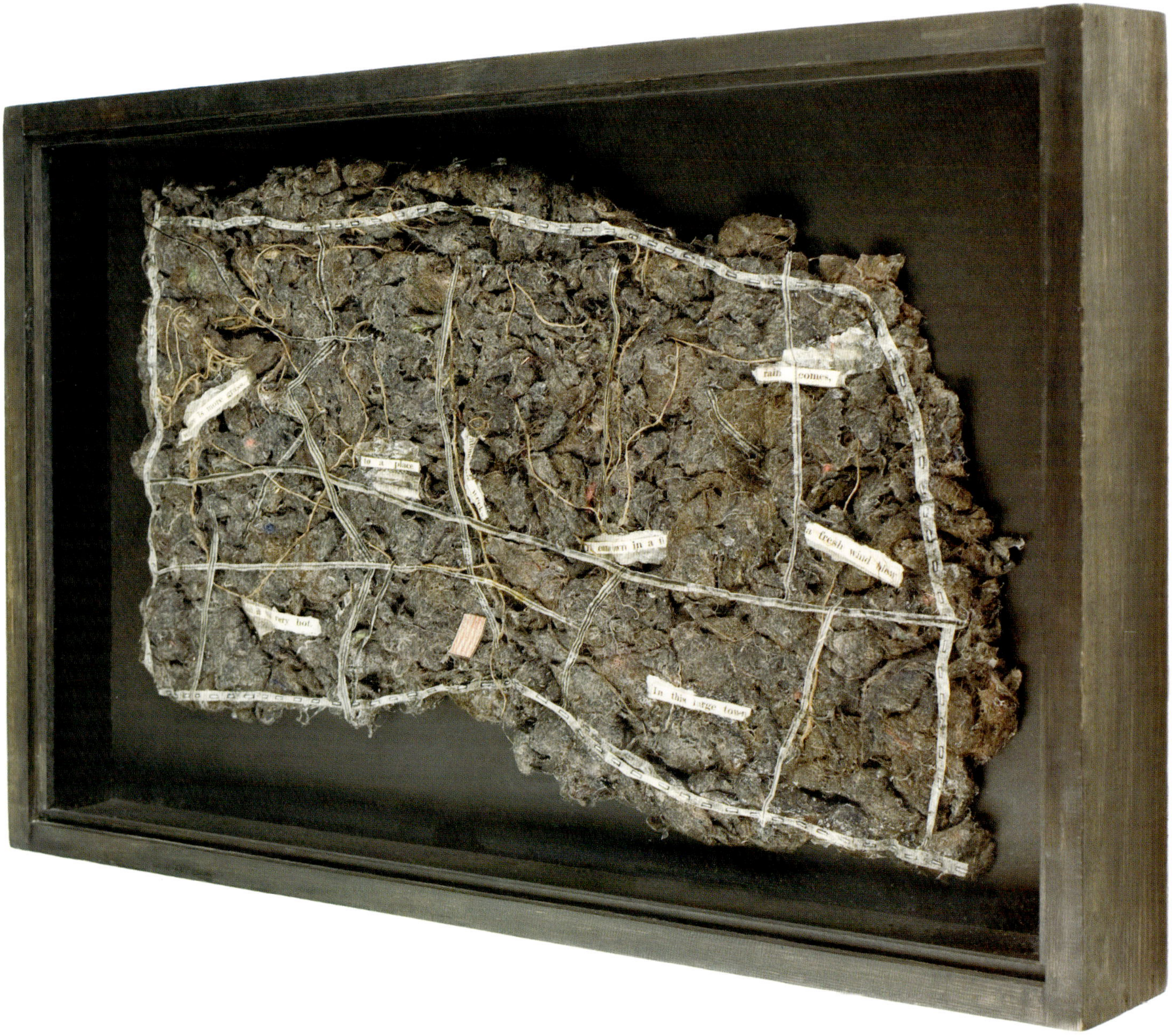

MATERIALS MATTER

PAUL HILLS
1991

Simon Lewty recently affirmed: "I need the material, the process, to knock up against. It's necessary to the imagination." In the artist's statement attached to the catalogue of his first solo show in 1965 he had written:

> The artist today is not restricted to using paint on canvas. In these pictures I worked with various materials which attracted me on account of their individual colour, texture or relief. As well as these distinctive formal qualities, they possessed in certain combinations the power to touch points of recollection and association.... The artist is working to release a significance latent in the material itself rather than attempting to match it to some external reality.

Allegiance to the truth-to-materials school is married here to something less 'pure', an appeal to recollection and association. 24 years later, in the catalogue of his exhibition Chosen Objects at Birmingham City Art Gallery, he will declare, "All art should tell us something beyond the limits of its physical volume, and in this sense, all the works in the exhibition have stories." In the 60s, the materials that he constructed into reliefs and collages, like those of the Cubists, often bore the signs of previous manufacture. A reviewer of his first show responded to signs of the temporal: "In collage No.10 hessian is replaced by a faded furnishing fabric. Here the wear and tear of an earlier existence reveals the occasional underlying pure yellow and black of original dyestuff." In the tradition of a British Romantic, Lewty had enlisted the weather as an accomplice by leaving out fabrics in the rain and the sun. If he kept one eye on the Continent, the other was on the clouds.

The introduction, since the mid-70s, of words into Lewty's paintings and drawings lures us into thinking about messages, codes and meanings. Lewty has described one of the functions of the writing as being "to draw you in closer". The cursive script, often little larger than handwriting, is small in relation to the totality of the picture, so that the viewer is pulled inwards to read, then steps back again to take in the whole. An oscillating viewing distance is space-shifting, for no frame demarcates the space in front of the surface from the space within; and the close reading-points bring us up against the 'smell' of the surfaces, their physical presence. Since the 60s, hessian and furnishing fabrics have been discarded, but the works are still collages, sometimes with as much relief as a crinkled parchment.

In the last 12 years or so, Simon Lewty has fashioned his own technique, and with it has invented a world. He starts with small notebooks, lined school notebooks, in which he records his dreams, and jots down, often just before falling asleep, great chains of impossible words. Little scribbles and diagrams also accompany the dream notations. Then he will draw with pencil on pieces of tissue paper, pushing them around on a table to choreograph the bouncy shapes. He may turn them over to reverse an image, or twist and tilt them, for the torn papers have no mandatory top or bottom. Bodies may sail through the air with the greatest of ease. As William Blake knew, when the body is freed from the forces of gravity the spirit is liberated.

12. *As Soon as the Skies Darken*, 1979.

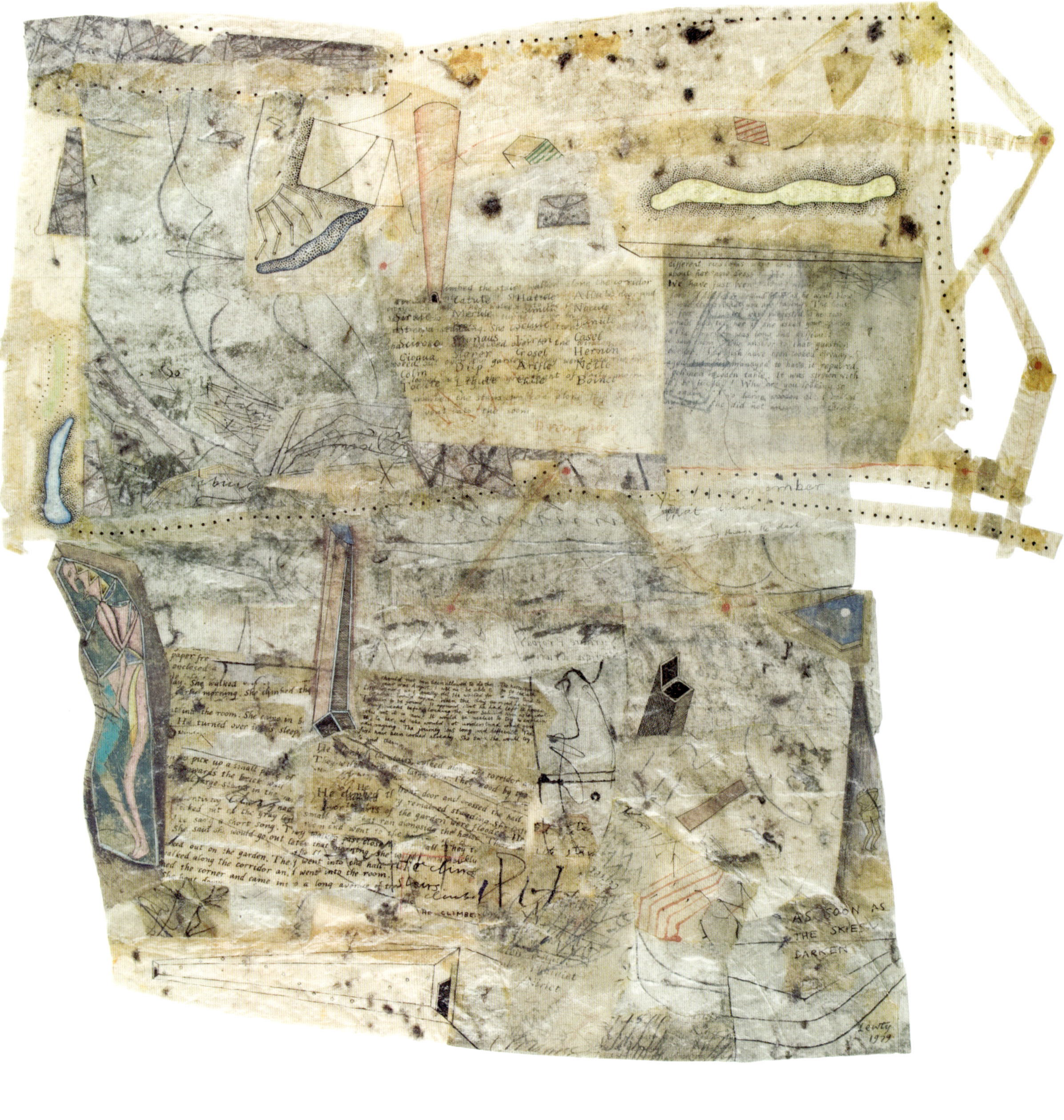

Once a promising configuration emerges, Lewty enlarges the composition onto larger pieces of tissue paper. Now he marks them in black acrylic, crayon or ink. Bounded shapes are gently inflated by the application of dots, graded towards the outline. It's a laborious method but not a mechanical one, for the artist is constantly responding to the contour, shaping and adding nuance to the form. Lewty welcomes the long time it takes, and the rhythmic repetition, finding that while engaged in the work new images propose themselves.

The preparation of the underpaper is in complete contrast to this discipline. Into water-diluted acrylic flooded onto cartridge he does a kind of automatic drawing by pressing hard with a twig or butt of a brush. Only when most of the paint is wiped off with a sponge is the drawing revealed on the mottled cartridge. PVA is then applied to this cartridge and the pieces of tissue paper floated over it. The exact relation between the two layers is in part left to chance. "When the tissue is glued down it becomes transparent", Lewty explained. "You don't exactly know the effect in advance." Out of the collision of the controlled and the free, the final image emerges.

13. *Ochre Triangle*, 1968.

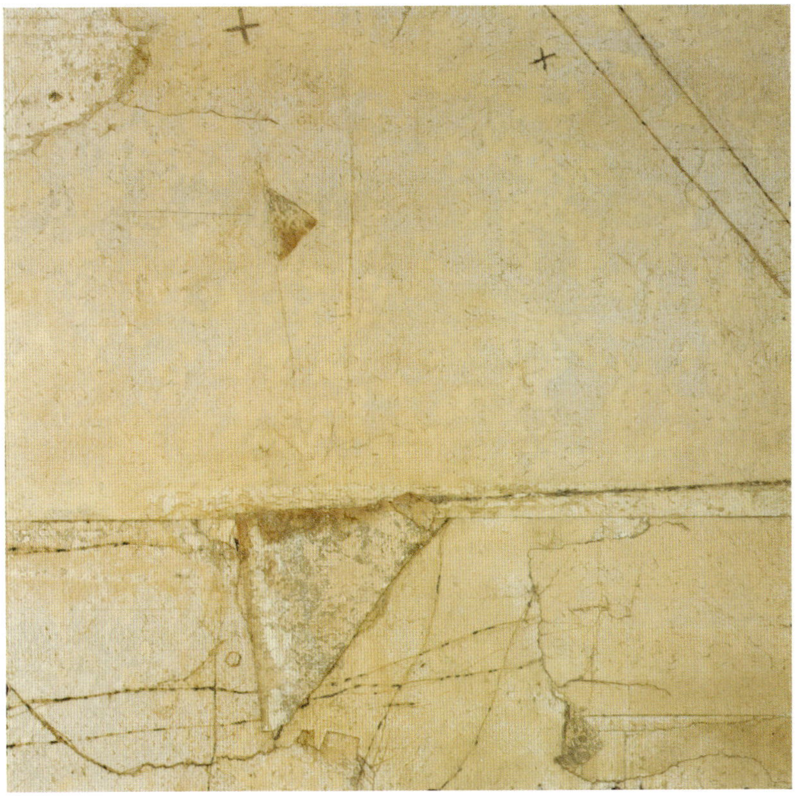

14. *Text On Tissue Paper*, 1980.

VISIBLE WORDS

PAUL HILLS
1991

Lewty's works have been marked by words ever since the late 1970s. They come in several shapes and sizes. Until about 1988 he wrote in large cursive writing on the underpapers. When the tissue paper was overlaid, these runes or lists of neologisms were partially effaced or made difficult to decipher. By his action , working within his studio over a space of weeks, the artist recapitulated the erosion and sedimentation of words that occurs variously according to locality through the far longer phases of historical time. Is it accidental that Midlands-born Lewty's palimpsests celebrate a strangely protean language, in which the known overlaps the unknown, rather than a specific dialect or patois? Writing of Middle English of the fourteenth century Kenneth Sisam observed, "in general the language of the Midlands was characterised by the overlapping of features which distinguish the North from the South". Like so many of his images, Lewty's words speak in contraries, of roots and rootlessness, of continuities and dead-ends.

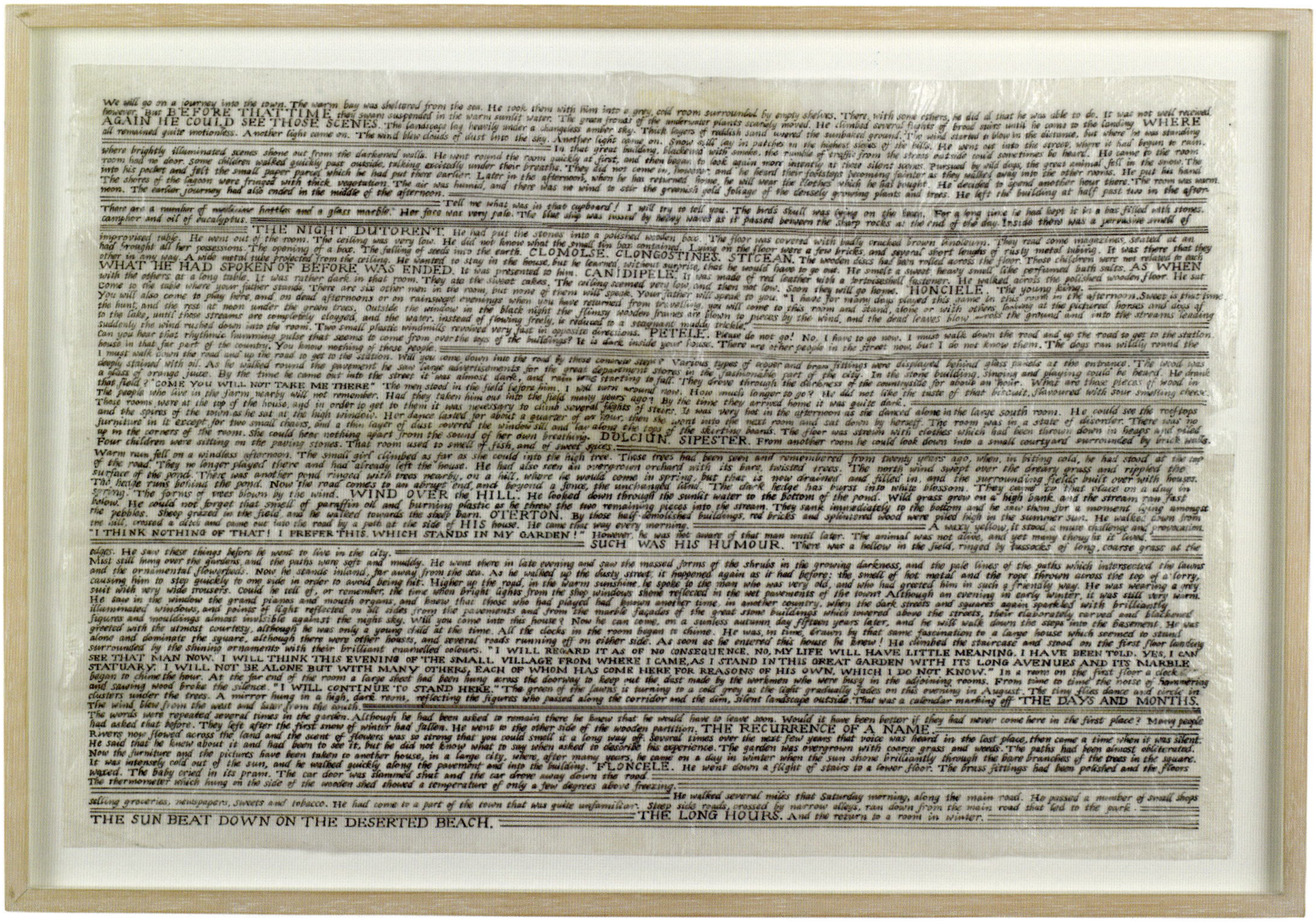

15. *Automatic Drawing*, 1994.

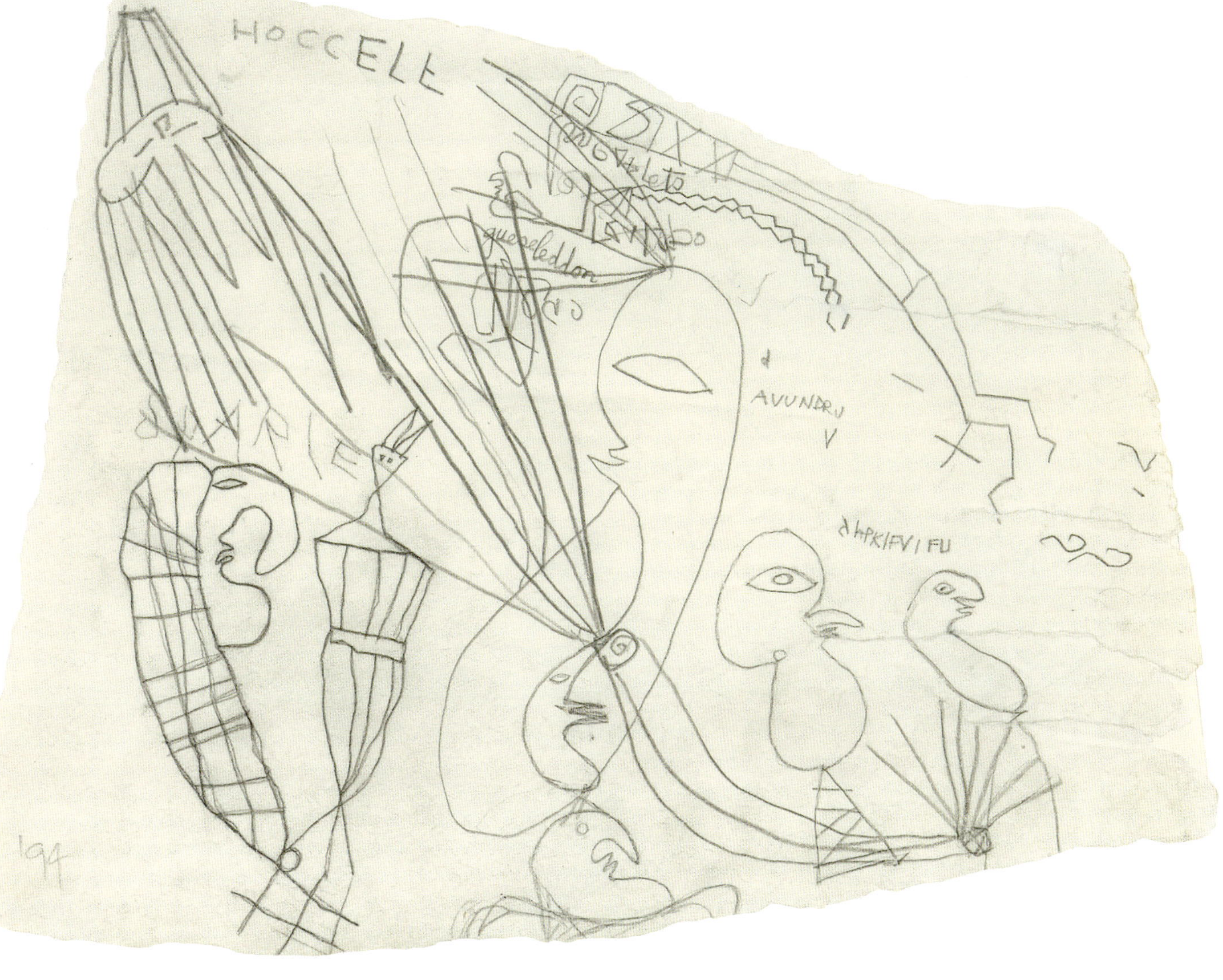

16. <u>Pages From a Notebook,</u> 1990.

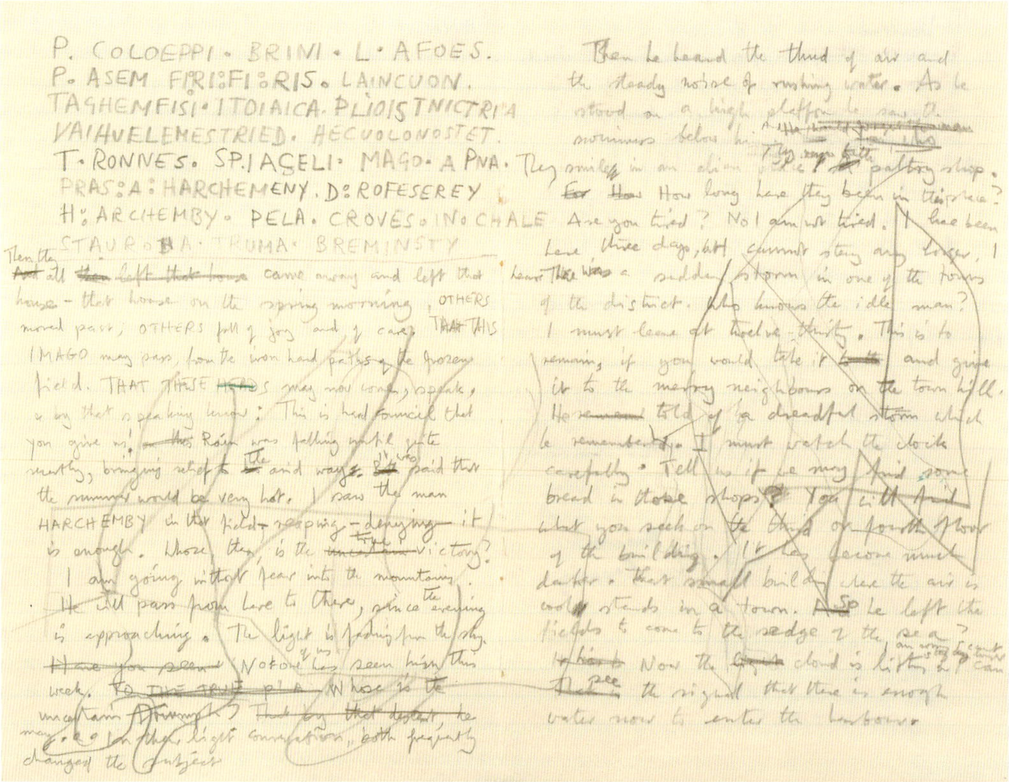

The known words are generally inscribed in black acrylic on the uppermost layer. The texts, taken from the notebooks or dream diaries, were often written down long before the images were made, while the images themselves were not drawn with specific texts in mind. In an unpublished conversation with Colin Hitchmough in 1979, Lewty explained his strategy:

> In the texts words are used in a discursive way, to describe or to evoke an event, or a remembrance, or a sensation, using the word as an adjunct to the image, also to play off the two types of reference—the way that the word functions and the way that the image functions... The word seems to stand half-way between an idea and an image. It's perhaps less abstract than the idea but more abstract than the image. The texts have an oblique reference to the images but they also hint at things which are going on before the images, or behind them, or somewhere completely detached from the images. Invented words come into a lot of these pictures. Nine out of ten people ask if there is a key, a translation. People have seen links with Latin. I am not a Latin scholar and there are no direct links. Somebody was convinced that they were Anglo-Saxon or something similar, but they aren't. To me they are almost images which exist, and which have overtones or associations which often, though not always, relate to the drawn or painted images. It is to give them a name.

One can follow these acts of naming in *Ritual of a Landscape* (plate 17). This pen and ink drawing of 1975 marked a turning point for Simon Lewty. In it he discovered a way of disposing the elements of experience as singled-out by memory, and of conferring names upon them. The images are drawn with exemplary clarity, some in parallel perspective or isometry, all in the deliberately limited repertoire of graphic conventions of outline, stipple and hatching; and the words are inscribed with the same clarity. The presentation is didactic, as though knowledge was being imparted with authority, as in the engraved illustrations to an eighteenth century encyclopaedia or chapbook, yet the invitation leads to a riddle, or to something akin to an alchemical diagram the key to which is lost. In enticing us to attend, the ruse draws us in to look and read, and gives us time to discover some less than habitual mode of feeling or understanding.

By the time of Simon Lewty's show at the Ikon Gallery in 1984 his use of the palimpsest technique of the overlaying of texts had evolved fully. In notes on the texts he explores the idea of words and images almost reversing their roles:

> Words and images are both symbols. The language of images can be almost abstract, as in a diagram or map. The language of words can become almost concrete as it approaches a kind of silent incantation, as in the capitalised sections or in the strings of neologisms. (cf the often declamatory or peremptory nature of dream utterances.) These neologisms constitute a reversal of the usual function of language.... They are an interiorisation of meaning. They are not 'nonsense' as in Lewis Carroll, i.e., a higher form of sense in disguise which is assumed to be coherent and which may perhaps be elucidated; rather they correspond to a kind of mental residue, forming itself spontaneously into words and fragments of words, which are almost like objects, and perhaps could stand in the place of objects.

To isolate any single source for Lewty's fascination with words as images would mislead, since the inspirations and reverberations are manifold. I have already guessed at the importance of words in relation to musical notation. From Surrealism in general, and André Breton in particular, Simon Lewty absorbed the theories of automatic writing. From the Cubists and their followers he learnt how text incorporated into painting can be used to telescope depth: in an interview with Stuart Morgan, Lewty pointed out that, "Text... flattens space—the Cubists knew that." From Paul Klee he learnt how the shapes of letters might become objects in a landscape. Long meditation on William Blake taught him that words and images should share the same strong lineaments, and that, as Paul Nash put it (quoting Gordon Bottomley), "the greatest mystery comes of the greatest definiteness".

None of these would have been potent influences unless they had answered a need. The key may lie in graffiti. A book of illustrations of Medieval graffiti is one of Simon Lewty's prize possessions. Through every age graffiti challenge the polite, the logical, the refined. They are carved or daubed by invisible hands, yet they testify to past inhabitants. Above all they offer the relief of utterance. David Stoker contemplating Lewty's neologisms ventured, cheekily, that "one can't help but entertain the possibility that embedded in these lists is the Albanian for 'Bugger off!'". And Lewty recently confided that while learning calligraphy at Leamington Art School he and his fellow students, "got great amusement out of writing obscene words in chancery script!" More subtle now, the visible words, whether incantation, mantra, psalm or expletive, still act as release.

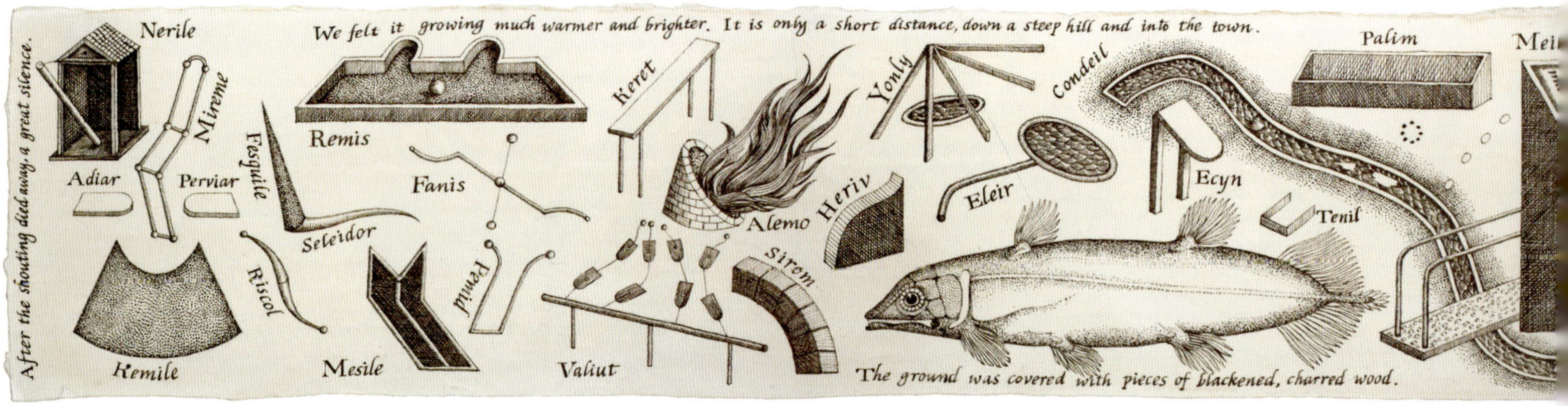
After the shouting died away, a great silence.
Nerile
We felt it growing much warmer and brighter. It is only a short distance, down a steep hill and into the town.
Palim
Mireme
Remis
Keret
Yonly
Condeil
Fesquile
Adiar
Perviar
Fanis
Eleir
Ecyn
Heriv
Alemo
Tenil
Seleidor
Riscol
Pemil
Sirom
Kemile
Mesile
Valiut
The ground was covered with pieces of blackened, charred wood.

17. Ritual of a Landscape, 1975.

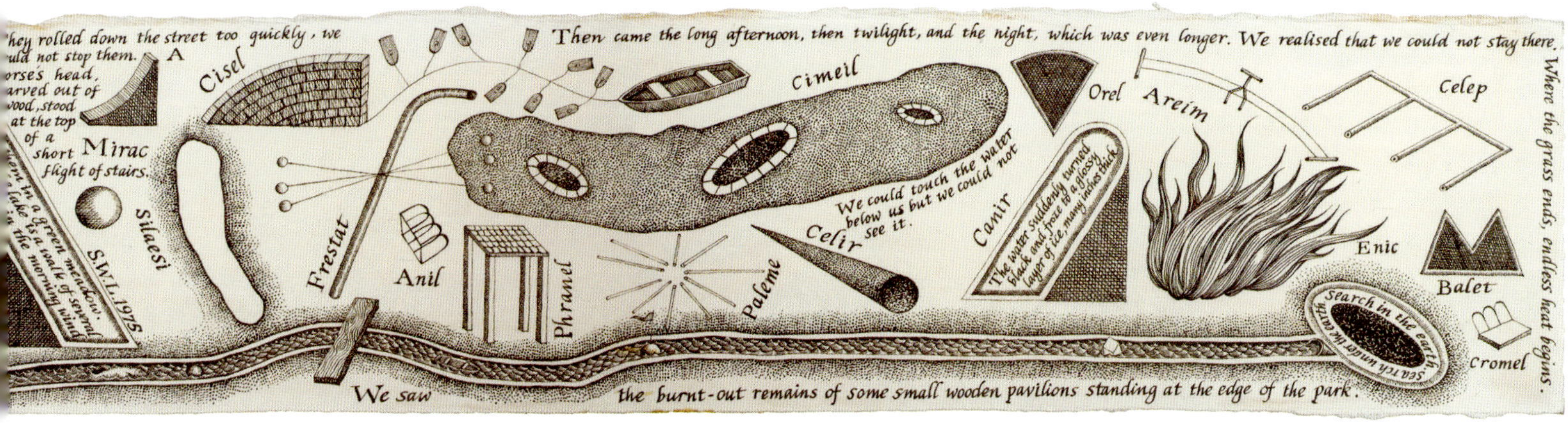

A WALK IN SUTTON PARK

PAUL HILLS
1991

Simon Lewty lived until he was nine at Four Oaks, Sutton Coldfield. Just across the road from his parents' house he used to walk through a gate and find himself in Sutton Park, the last expanse of green belt separating Sutton Coldfield from the conurbations of Birmingham. In August 1991 we crossed the road and went through the same gate.

30 paces brought us into a clearing amongst the trees. It was traversed by paths, the grass irregularly worn back by the tread of many feet. Two women were exercising their dogs. We picked our way through a coppice of silver birch and oak. In the midst of a dark wood I was failing to explain Structuralism. "Here we are in such a beautiful place talking of Derrida!" Simon's rebuke steered us back to the actually loved and known. He picked up a rounded stone, larger than the average pebble but not too big to cup in one hand. It was brownish-purple with green markings. *Pluck the Stone from the Bank*, ran the title of a painting of 1984. Carefully Simon put the stone down in another place.

Our path dipped, then rose to a sandy eminence. Simon knocked with his shoe against some concrete embedded in the ground. I remarked that a bunker wouldn't have been built on this high ground, thinking of what he had told me about his childhood memories of the air-raid shelters in the park. After the war they had remained there disused, and their dark entrances and subterranean chambers fascinated the young boy. Today there was no sign of the barrage balloons that had once been tethered here to protect Birmingham. "No. It's the remains of a war-time lookout post perhaps", said Simon. From here we could see that the park extended for miles. "My sister once got lost in the park. She turned up hours later, very scared. You could go round in circles."

We walked over the heath, gorse growing where the silver birch thinned. Simon breathed in the smells. "I should come back and work here. This is better than Old Milverton."

We headed downhill hoping to find one of the lakes. We skirted a thicker wood with great oaks and some pine; then an expanse of water came into view. Canada Geese were swimming near the sandy shore.

> THESE WATERS ARE
> UNSAFE FOR BATHING
> AND DROWNINGS
> HAVE OCCURRED

Simon looked at the notice; his interest visibly quickened. "I could use that", he said. I thought of the peremptory phrases, the dark warnings, in his own texts. Here too was a narrative that linked past to present, and here was a sign that told of death in the landscape. (Explicating a painting of 1988—*And Told Them of a Story Half as Old as the Field* (plate 19)—Lewty had written of "the many deaths and the perennial rebirth of innocence".)

18. *Hymns to the Sun Misheard,* 1986.

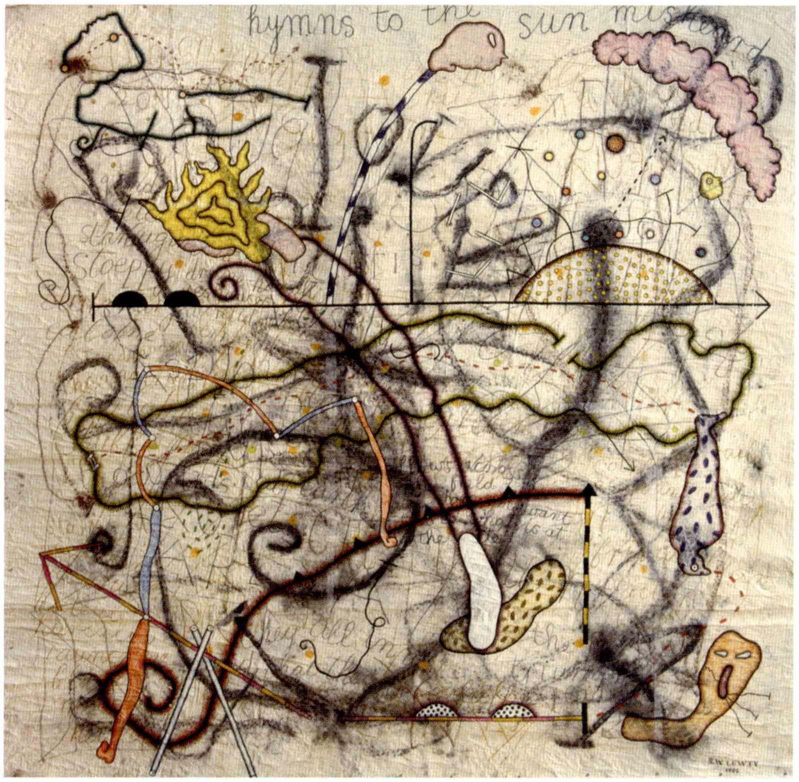

It had begun to rain. We walked up the slope in the lee of the wood. The ground beneath our feet was eroded in channels and rivulets. "I like that", said Simon, pointing to a bridge made of a pair of railway sleepers. The channel it crossed was less than a foot deep, barely two feet wide; any child could jump it. Now that the stream was dry, the bridge was like a marker on a trail, a sign. Long ago those sleepers had lain elsewhere. Simon pointed out that a little to the west a Roman road, the Icknield Way, traversed Sutton Park.

Further on we paused by a wooden bench. Its seat was covered in graffiti. The largest read MATTHEW, its freshly cut capitals breaking across older, spikily carved names, now blackened. Simon deciphered "1924". The line from David Jones' *In Parenthesis*—"Scratched out dates measuring the distance back to antique beginnings"—came to mind. Strange to think that this bench had pre-existed us. Its supports were rough-hewn logs with the stumps of branches sticking out. "Seeing names carved on trees may have started me off in my interest in graffiti", said Simon.

Later we lunched in Sutton Coldfield and lost our way looking for the car in a multi-storey carpark. Driving back I remembered the warning in one of Simon Lewty's paintings: "After you have returned, you will have to decide what you will tell."

19. And Told Them of a Story Half as Old as the Field, 1986.

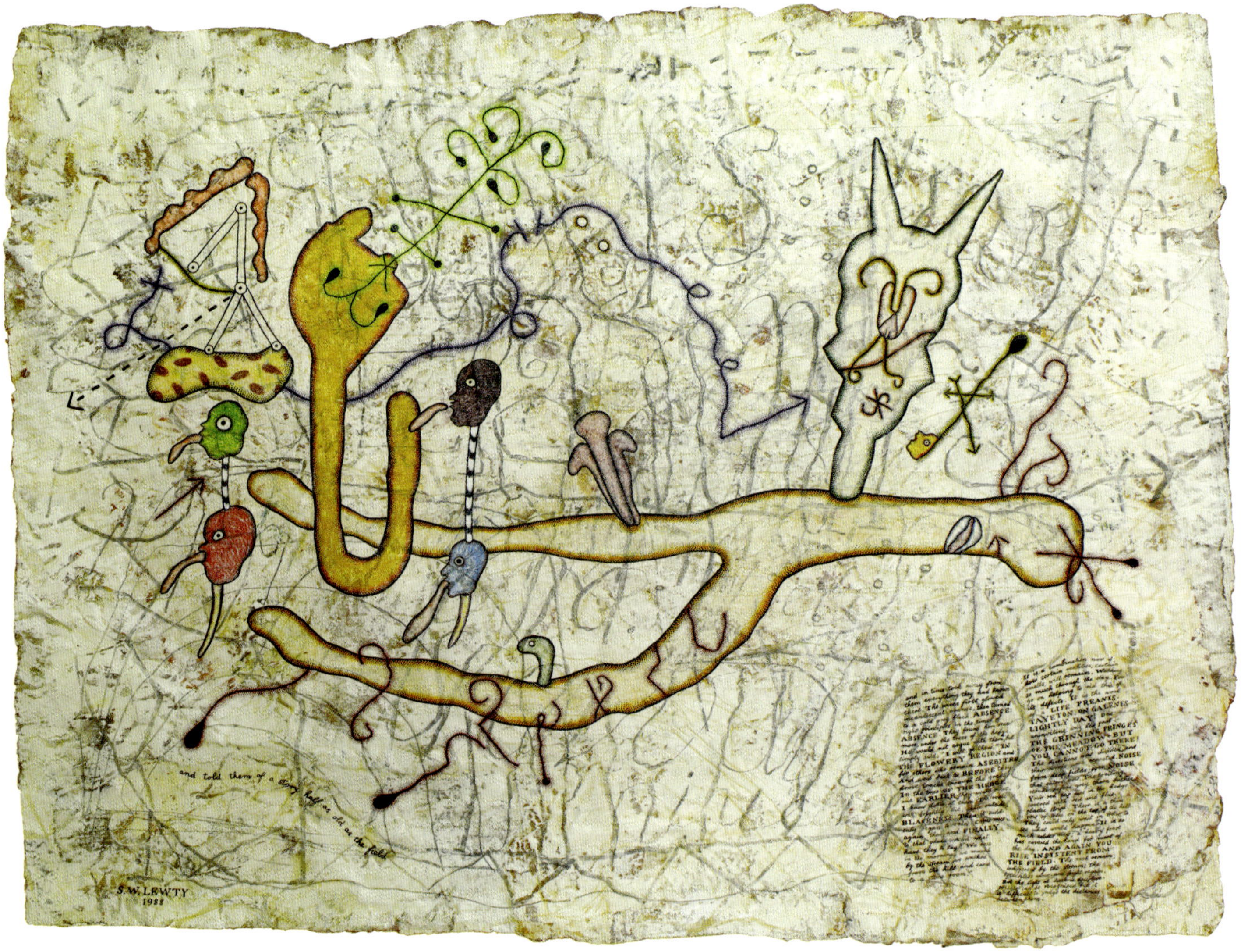

20. Beyond the Field, 1988.

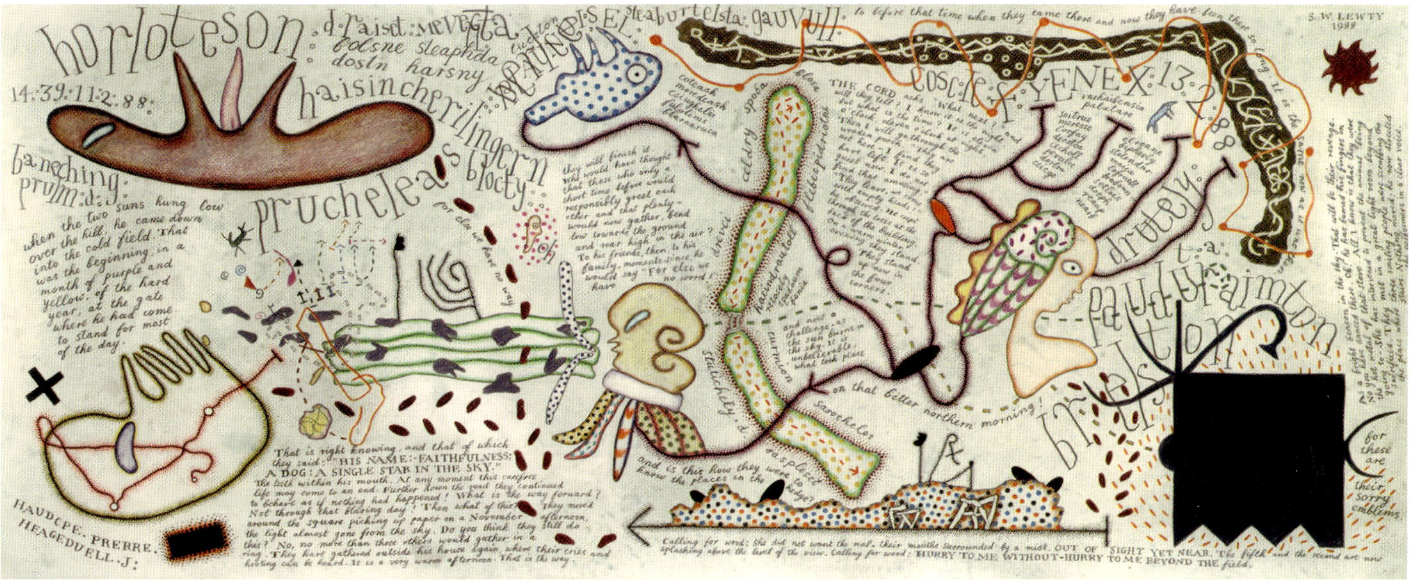

21. But Who Tried Without Success, 1986.

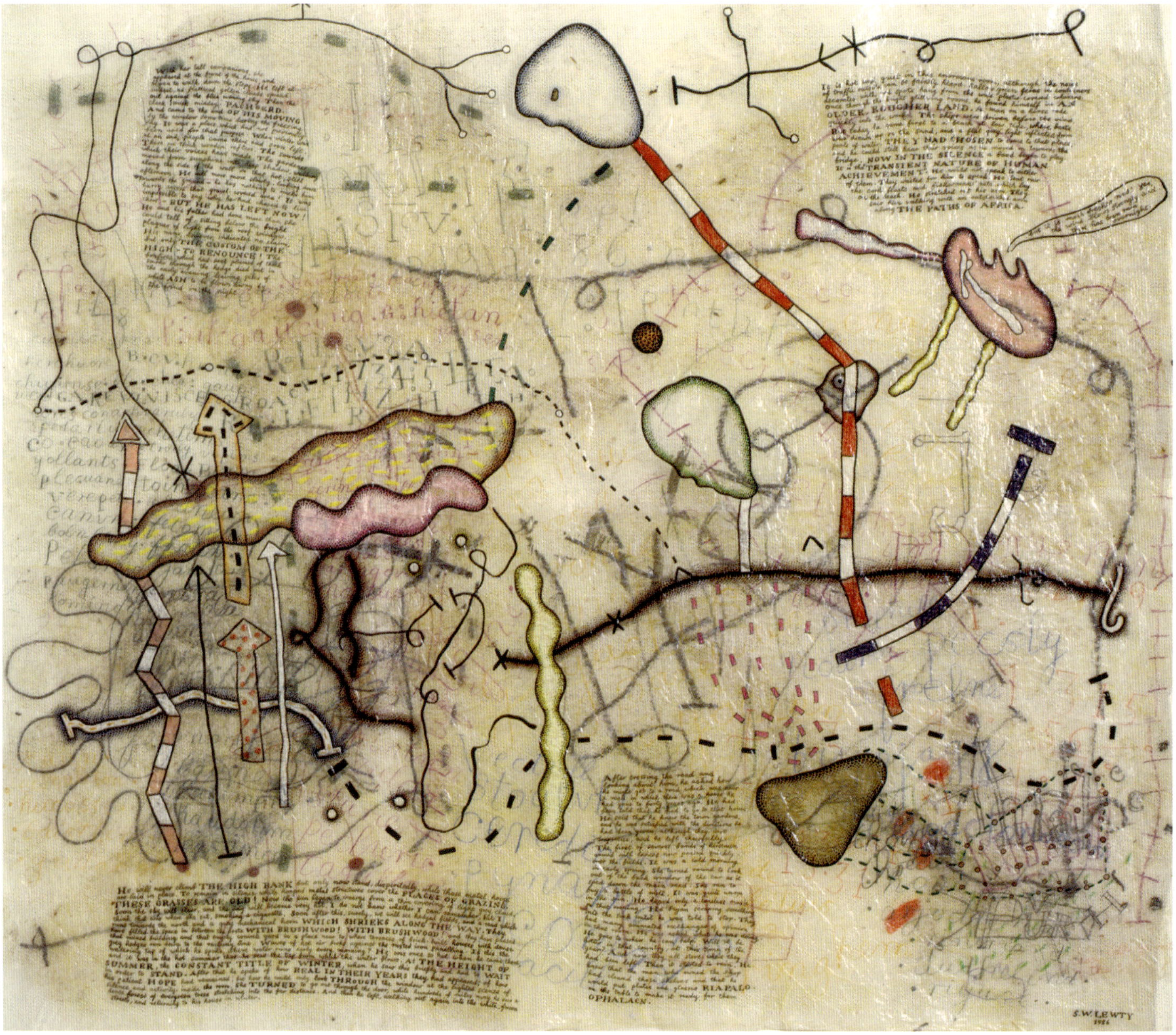

22. *Over the Bay as Across Fields*, 1986.

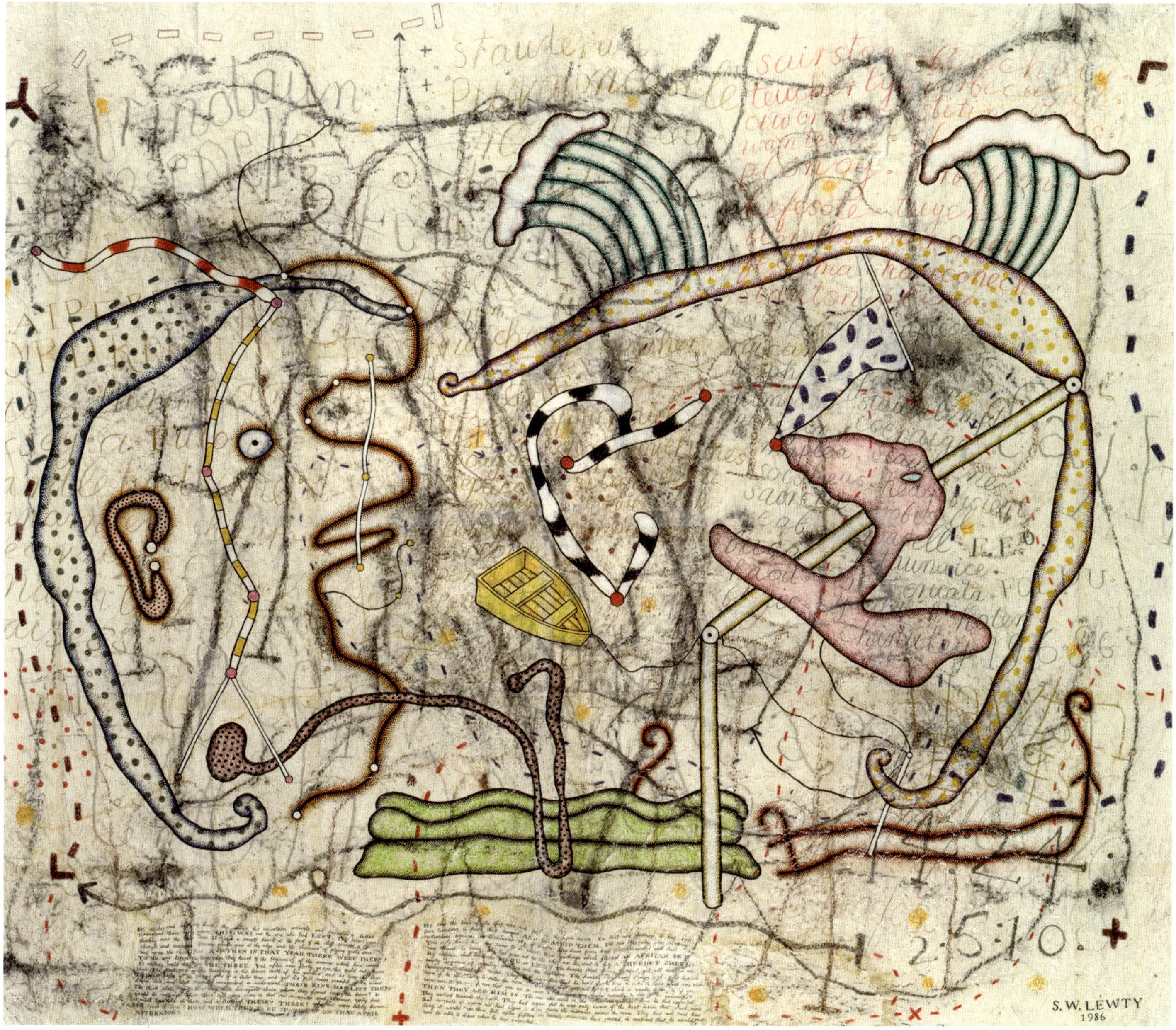

23. Garden Plan and Room, 1986.

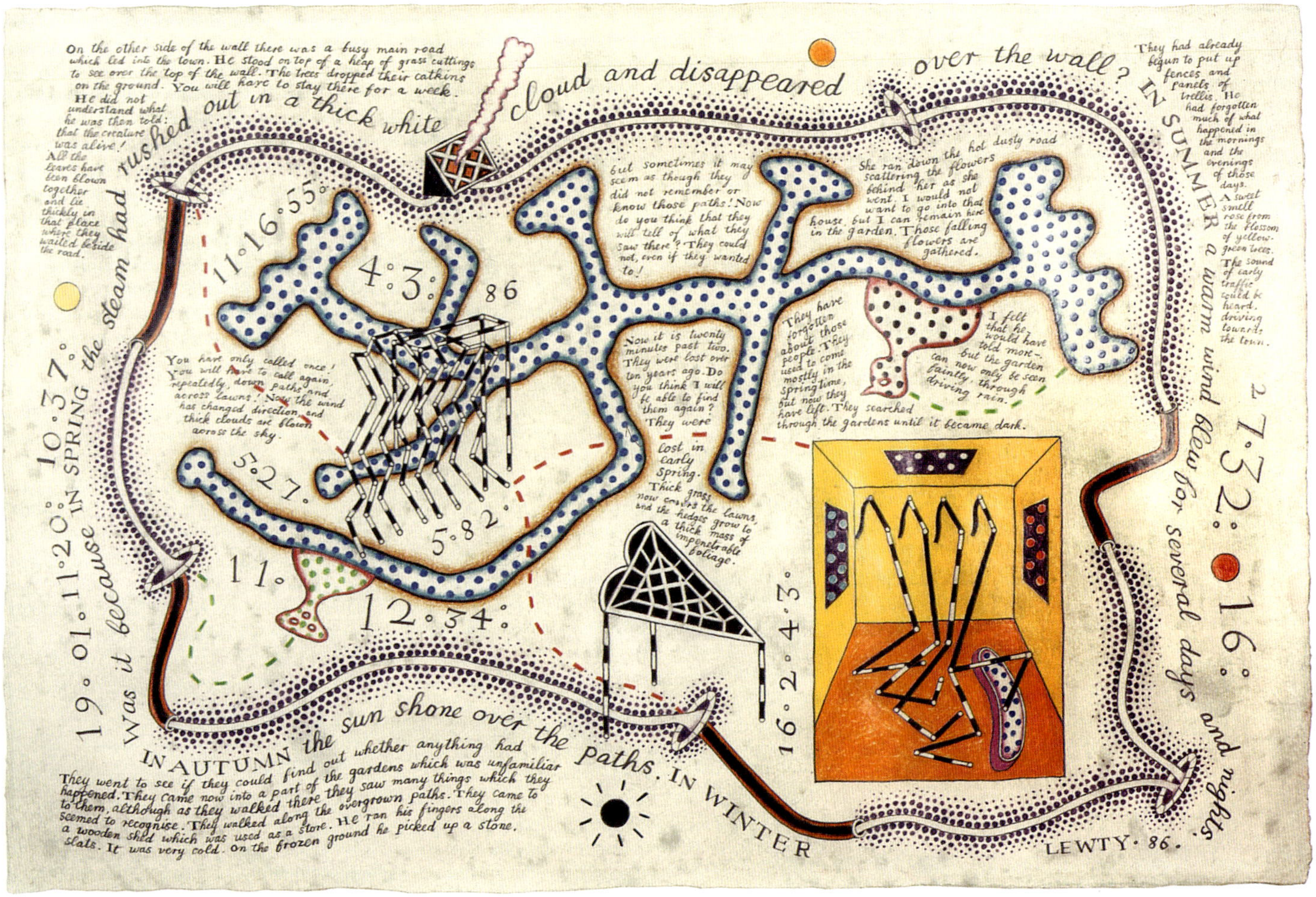

24. *Out in the Open Air*, 1989.

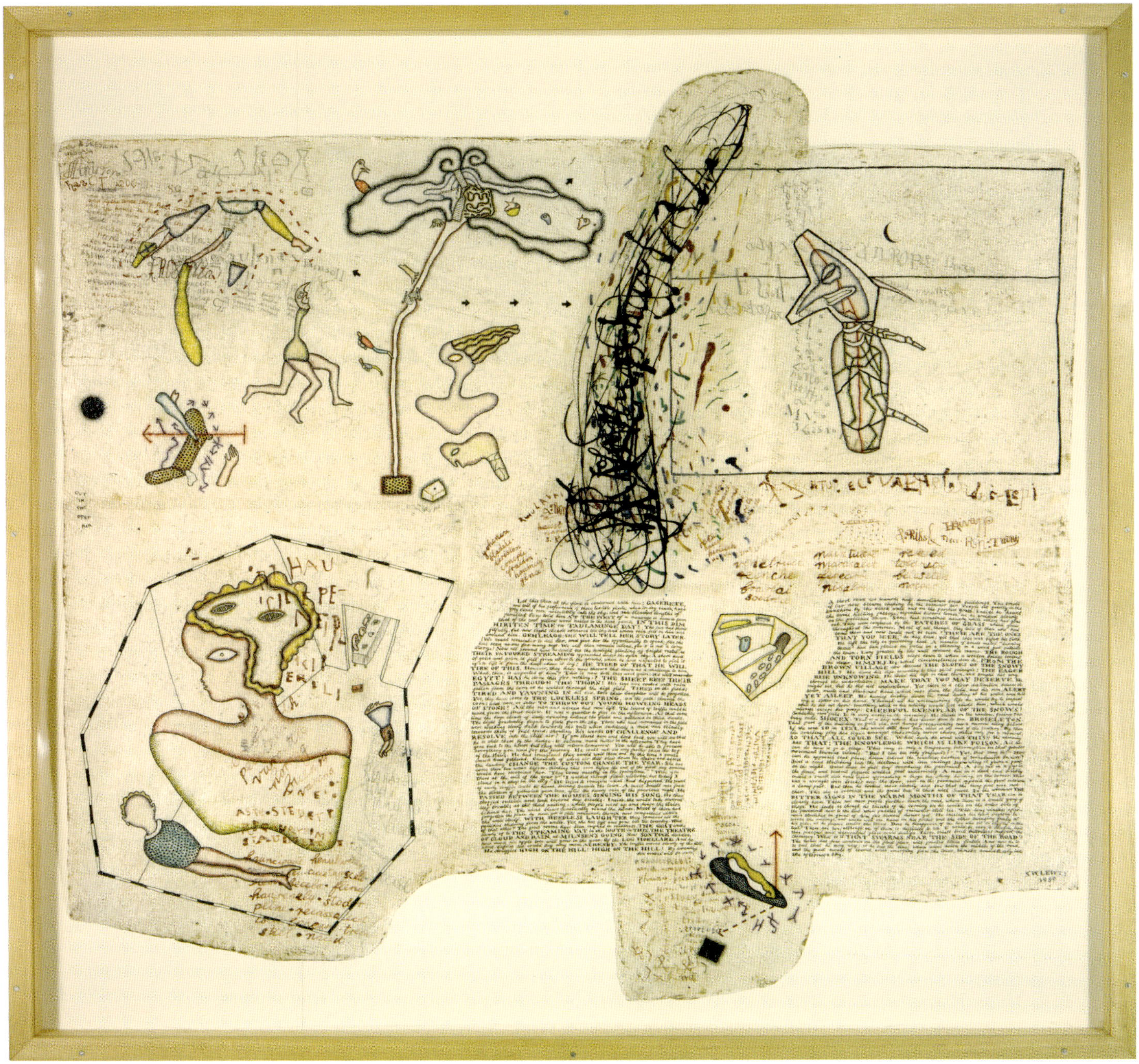

25. *Where Have You Come From?*, 1991.

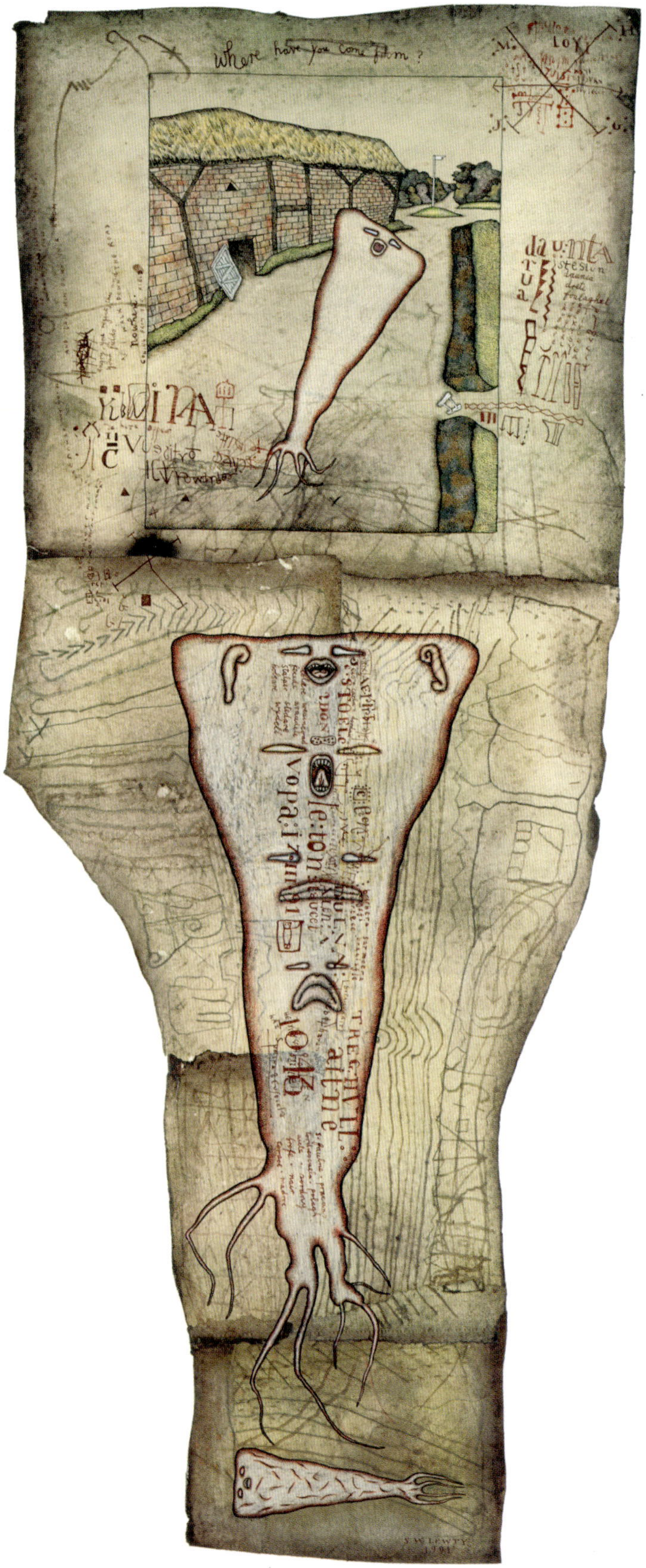

SIMON LEWTY

PAUL HILLS
1991

The wayfarer or pilgrim, disguised by many metamorphoses, is a recurring image of Simon Lewty's recent paintings. In *A Dull Fable* he is harried by dogs, while his head, soul-like, sleeps cocooned within the great burden upon his back. In *Why Worry?* the burden is transformed more fully into the chrysalis shape: here rebirth is a hope, but no certainty. *In Life Without Name* (plate 26) the pilgrim has become a lumbering monster, an exile who can find home in no habitat.

Often stacked like the narratives of the life of a saint on a thirteenth century altarpiece, these scenes of the travails of life's journey are marked by a kind of hieratic, almost totemic formality. Occasionally, as in *Where Have You Come From?* (plate 25) the T-shapes recall the format of a crucifix. Calligraphic signs in brownish-red ink, the colour of dried blood, cut across the images like some devilish rubric. But, as in the *Resurrection* by Stanley Spencer, the unseen is set in the context of the local and the particular. The barn in *Where Have You Come From?* is a barn at Old Milverton, close to where Simon Lewty lives, and known from countless walks. What lies athwart this barn, is set up again below it, and again buried like Adam's skull at its foot, is not the icon of the slain god revered by Christian tradition but a root with many mouths and even the semblance of a face. It is the mandrake root. Fabled for its resemblance to the forked human form, and believed to utter a shriek when pulled from the ground, the mandrake root haunts Simon Lewty's recent work.

Why is Lewty gripped by the folklore of the mandragora, the magic root? It may be because it symbolises a marriage of heaven and hell, embodying those contraries without which, as William Blake prophesied, there can be no progression. The shriek of the mandrake can make men mad, yet the root also has beneficent powers; it can induce pregnancy. In Lewty's paintings the recurrence of the penis-like tongues suggests both procreative energy and primal fears. They tell of a world compounded of good and evil, the world of which John Donne sang:

> Go, and catch a falling star,
> Get with child a mandrake root,
> Tell me, where all past years are,
> Or who cleft the Devil's foot.

Simon Lewty's recent work dares to face ancient darkness, as well as to hope for perennial rebirth. The savagery that Hogarth showed to lurk beneath the polite surface of eighteenth century society, Lewty recognises in our world of Barbie dolls and Pit-bull terriers. Cerberus roams abroad, even as on the streets of London young men sleep rough on pavements with, if they are lucky, a sleeping-bag for a chrysalis. "What's under works up", David Jones foretold. And Simon Lewty explores these strata, unsure as to what roots may be brought shrieking into the light of day. Well may he ask, both of himself and of his creation, *Where Have You Come From?* Any answers must be provisional.

26. Life Without Name, 1989.

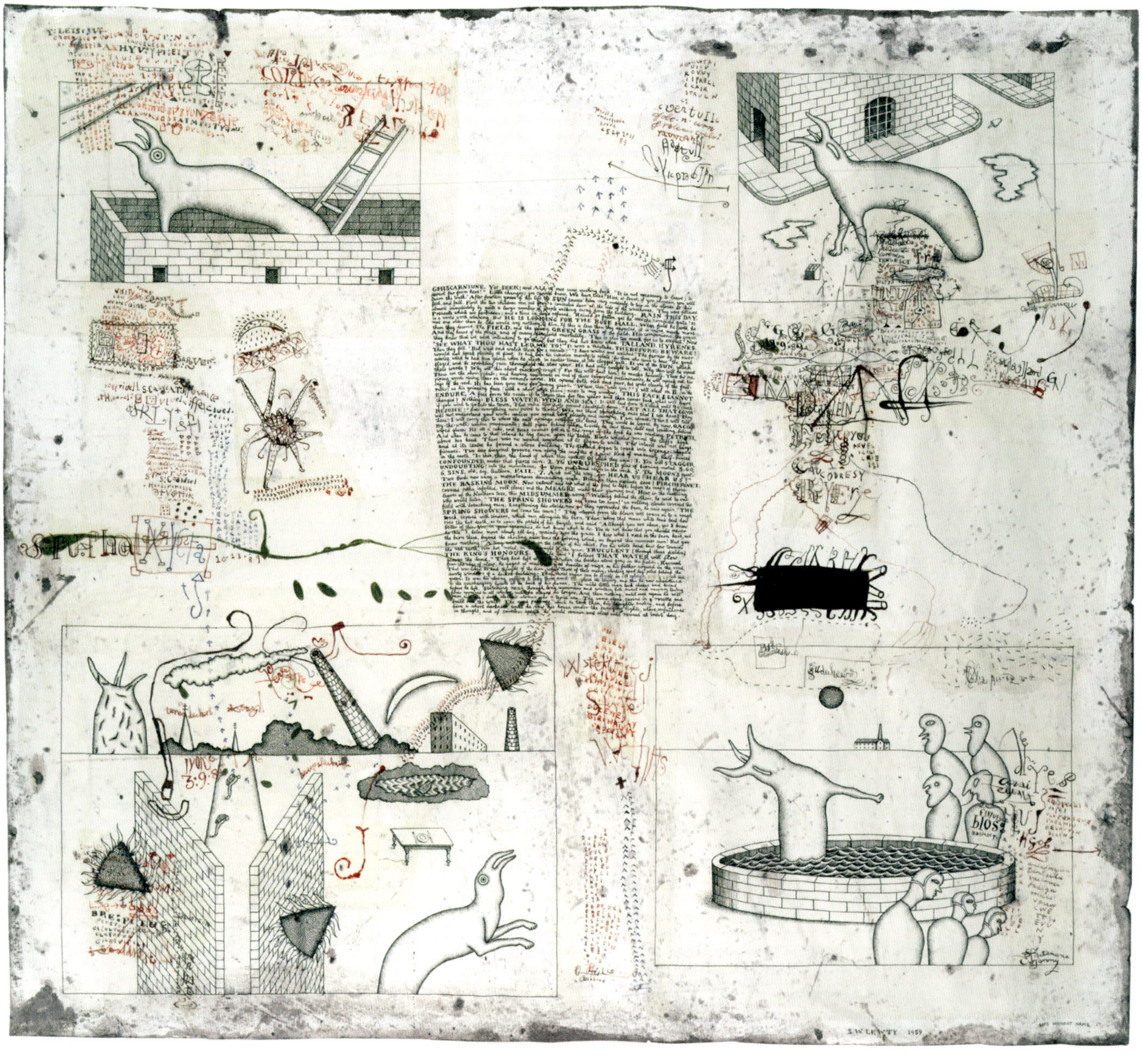

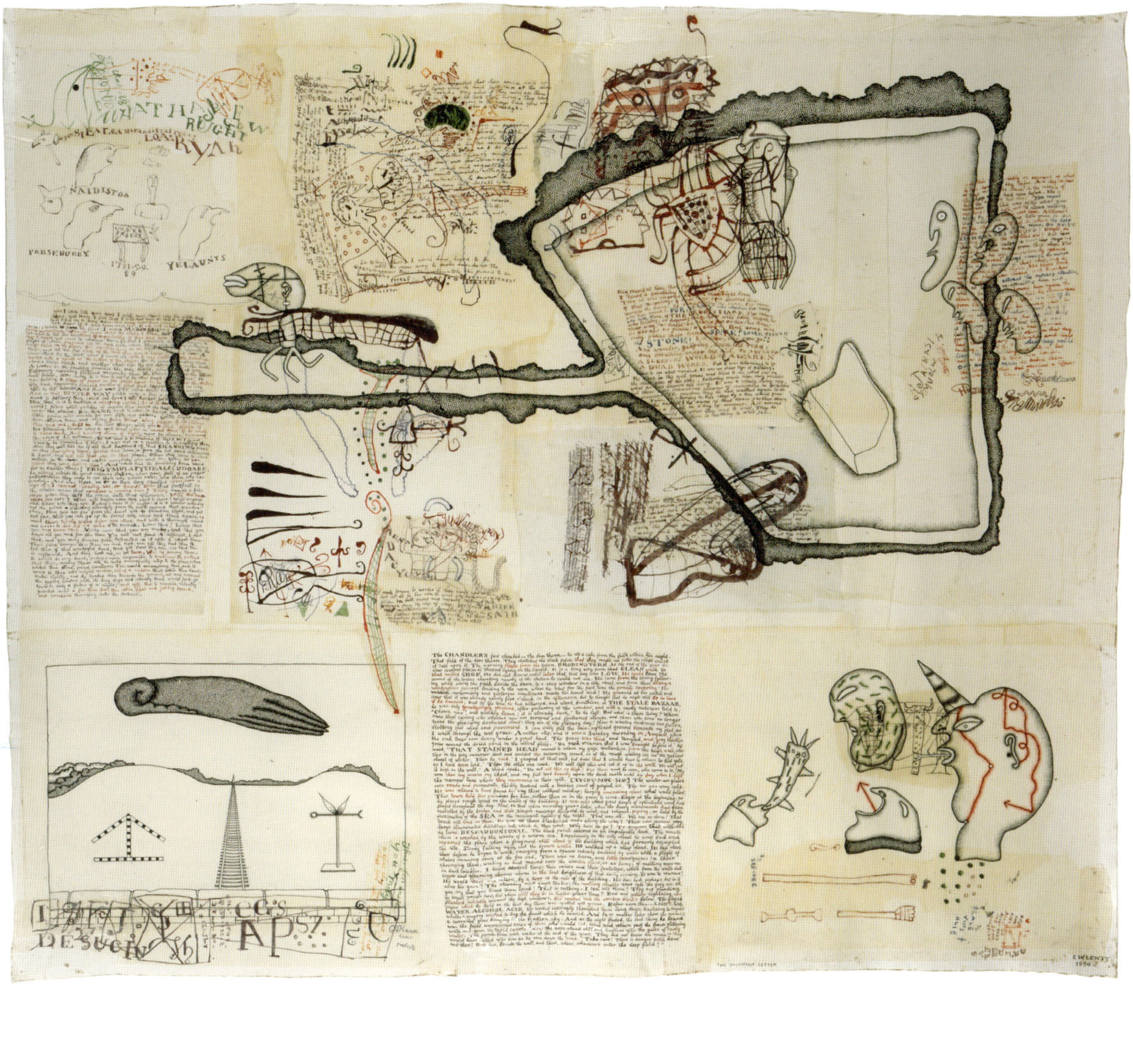

27. *The Palimpsest Letter*, 1990.

28. *Voices in the Close Country*, 1991.

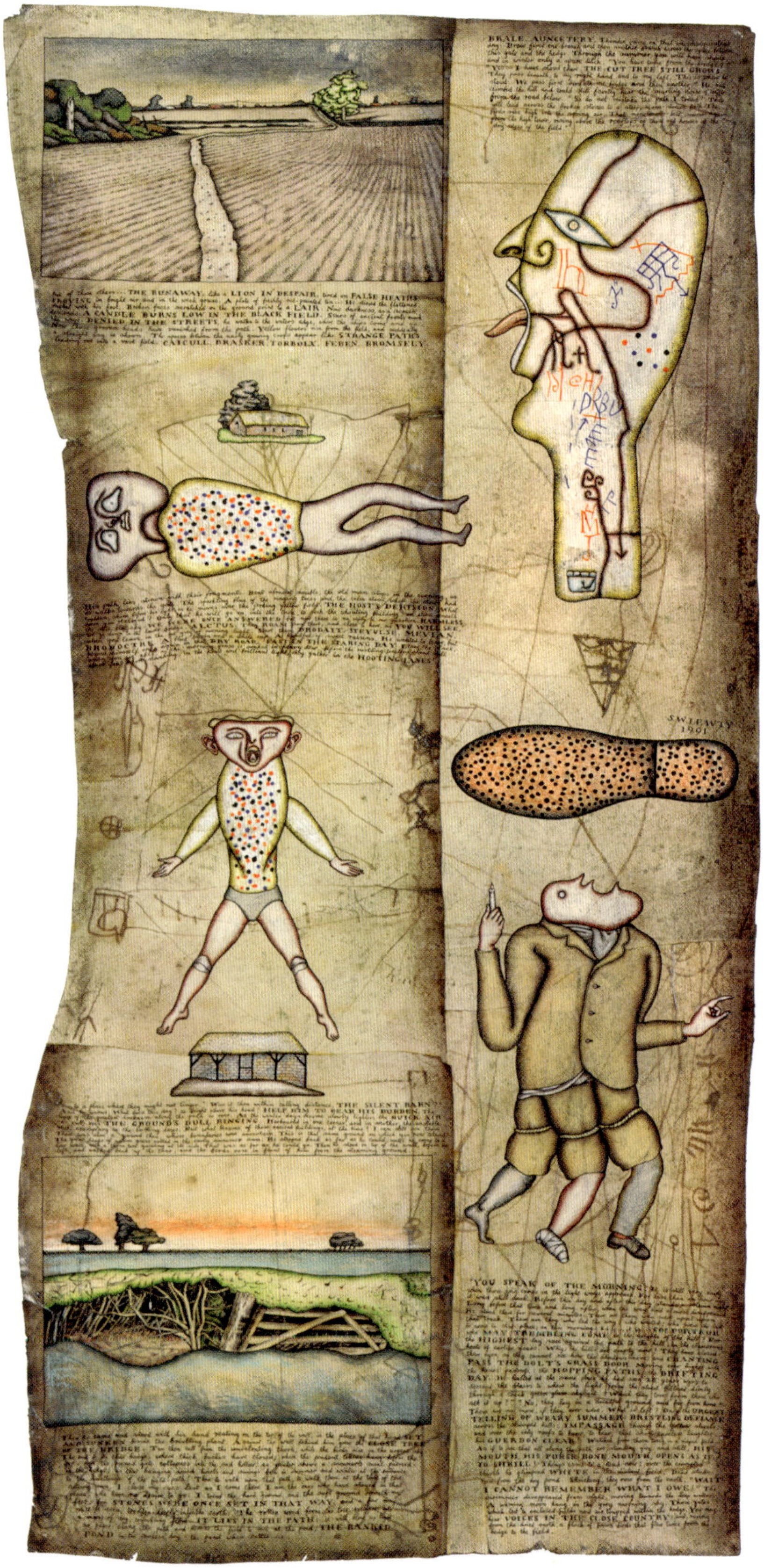

29. *The Lured King*, 1989.

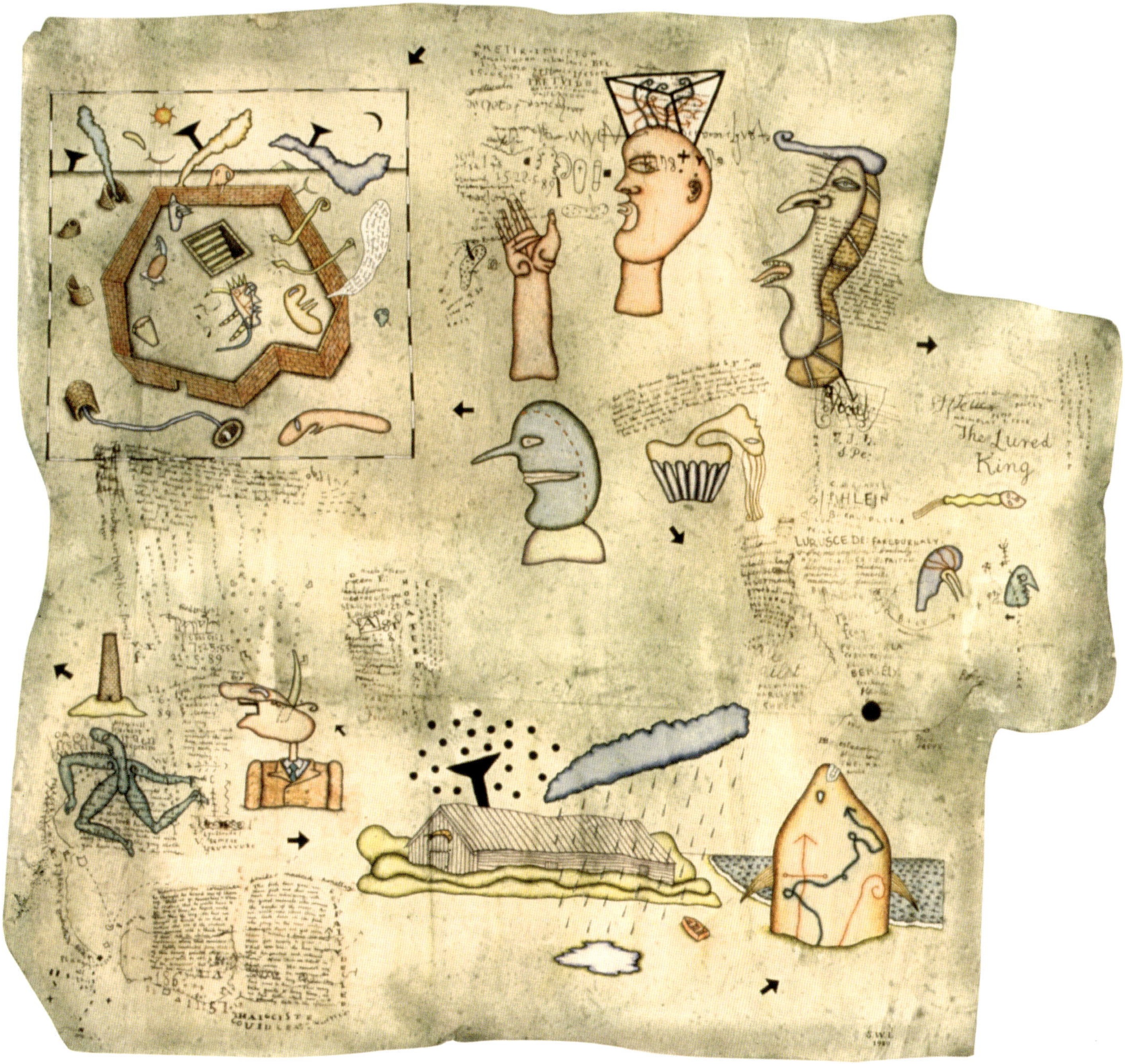

30. In the Lost Town, 1992.

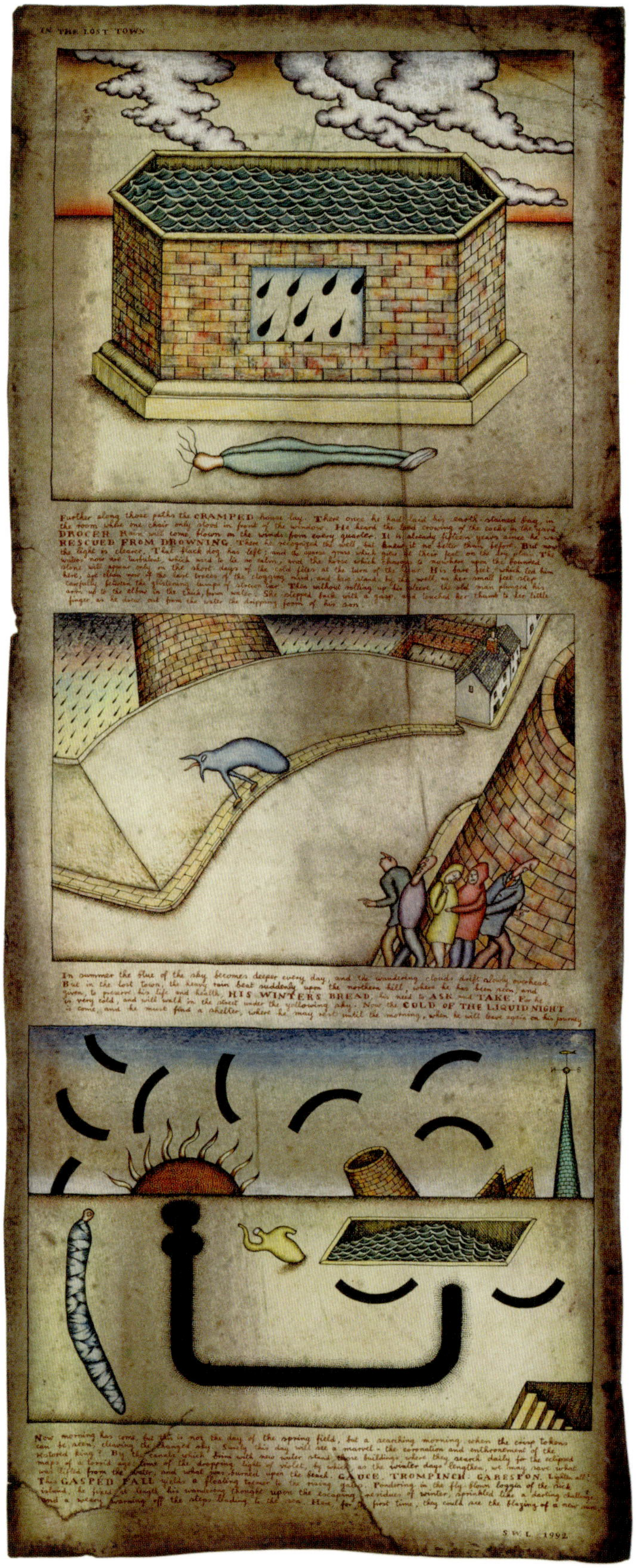

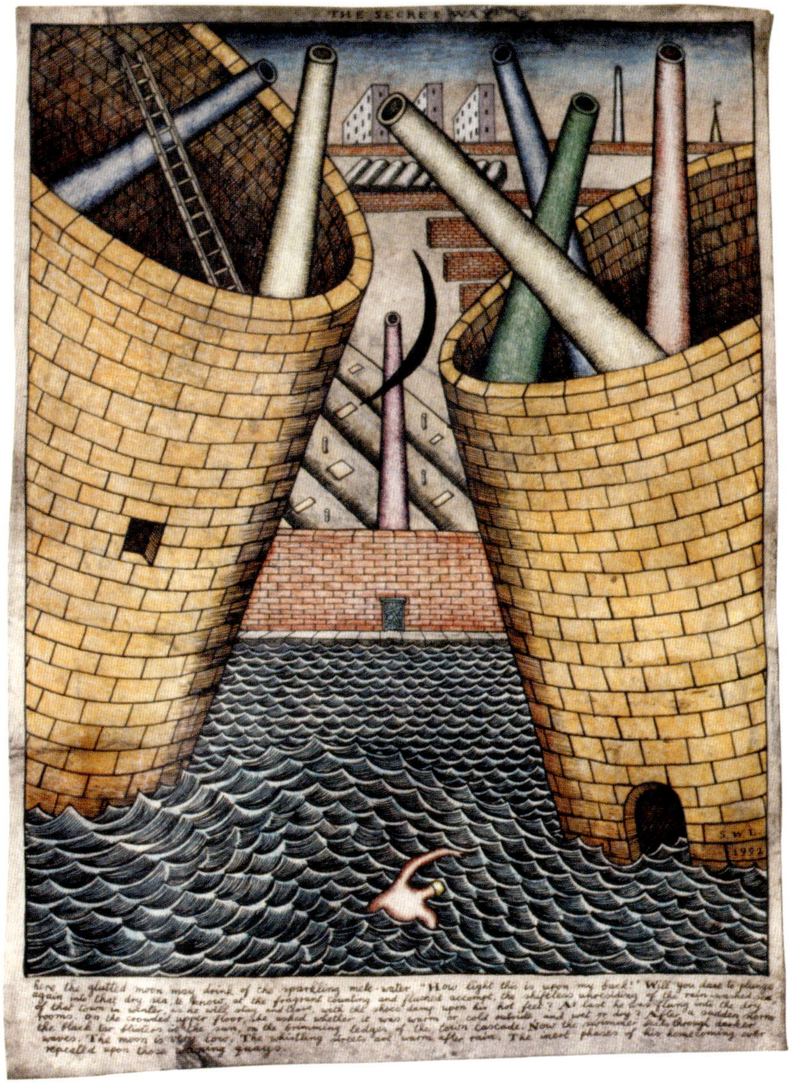

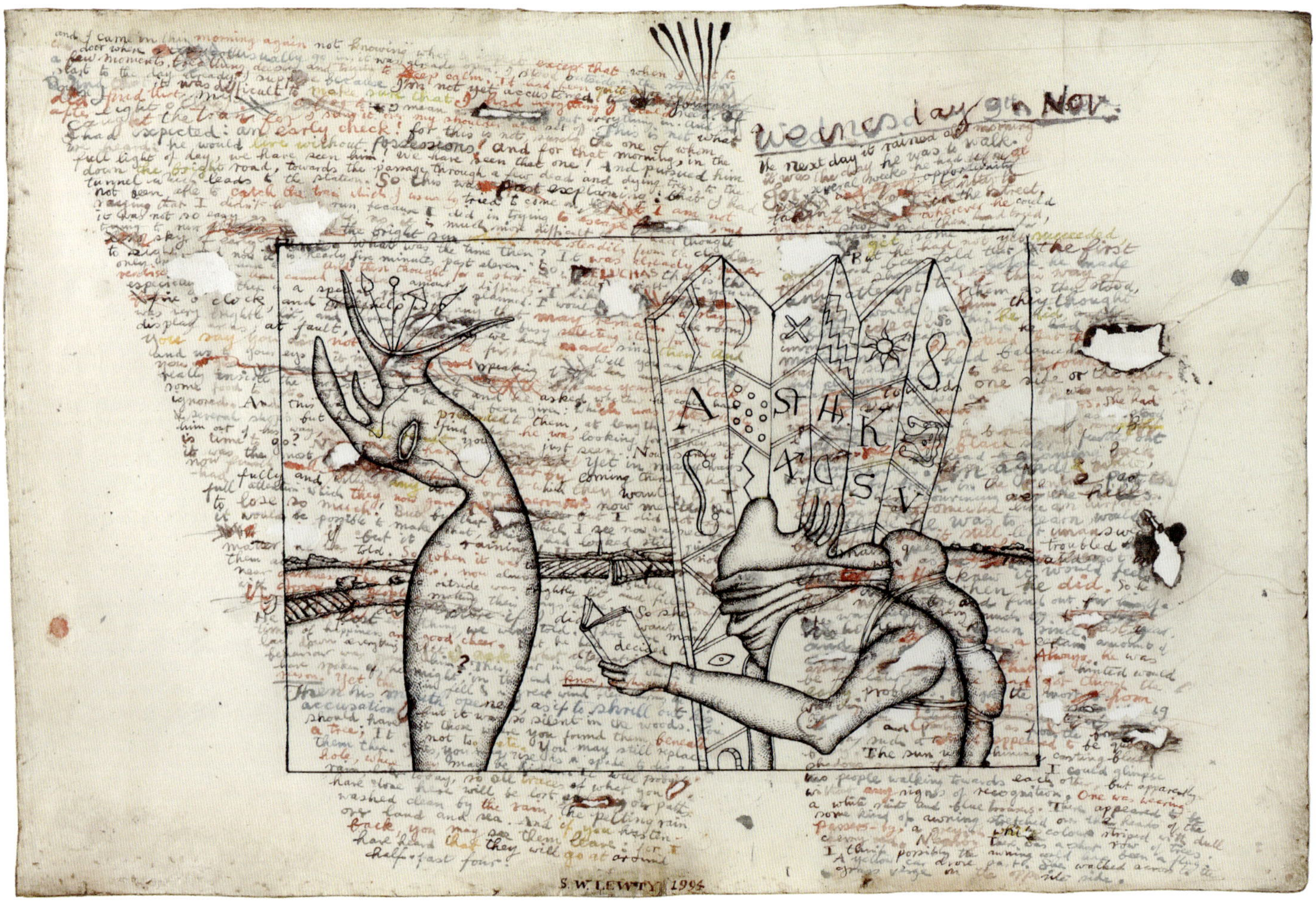

32. *The Question*, 1994.

VOICES FROM LOST FIELDS

PETER LARKIN
1995

Why does Simon Lewty persist in treating with the unknowable within today's cultural predicament? If his techniques serve to sift mental residues, he also relishes the recklessness and occasional savagery with which such reserves, once disturbed, promise to mock the experimental ingenuities of our time. However bizarre the bricolage, the marks he makes seek to win their way through a sort of necessary parody towards a region in which our singularity reattaches itself, so that we skitter among burdens, play with repetitive but scarcely liberated persistencies. We remain unsure what roots are involved, or whether such lost integrations are anything more than the treacherous graininess of soil creasing soil. Our scarified contemporary surface may launch its own wars on the depths, bringing up shards which had never sought the light or are actively eroded by it. But in the process what might be taken for an upper floor slips between many other layers and is displaced amid what it had (and has) surpassed.

Pure loss, Lewty's work seems to conclude, cannot be shown: the sense of deficit directs itself at and as the figure of residue, so that loss can be seen and interpreted as a something, something under working up. Are we left with a hopeful token or a curse, this tracing of lost voices, abandoned fields, a residue on the way itself to becoming a voice or figure of voice, thicker and more globose as it continues to recede, echoing from one plane to another, murmuring its mutation through one layer after another? If there is nostalgia for a younger time here, with this artist it typically turns towards hunger for a density of *warning*, for a grotesquerie surprising only as it may deliver apt admonishment.

For many years Lewty's output has been a process of, and figure for, palimpsest. Everything can be a potential surface for inscription, each site itself a source for, as well as the impression of, a making of marks, much as the body makes tracks across the earth but is refigured within the earth after death. This modulation of surface, both written on and writing for itself, is what constitutes the figure of layer for Lewty. Commenting on another artist, David Jones, Lewty offers a further clue: "The question of the relationship between layers remains. Does mystery evolve from myth? If it does evolve, to what extent is myth changed or erased in the process?" The search for mythic origins cannot be called off; it is this very endeavour which sheds enough light for loss to retain at least a penumbral, rather than purely numbing, quality. Lewty's marks may not refer directly to origin, but they do not remit the distance *from* origin. His artistic conscience forbids any side-stepping move dismissing a supposedly empty past in favour of a ludic or carnivalesque present. Rather, he continues to explore what possible fidelity (however mordant) might be sensed among the corrosive versions of past upon past. He is not seeking a conventional illumination of that relation; his researches from the present remask the past just where they rifle through it. This remasking, as art, does offer itself as a rememoration, however.

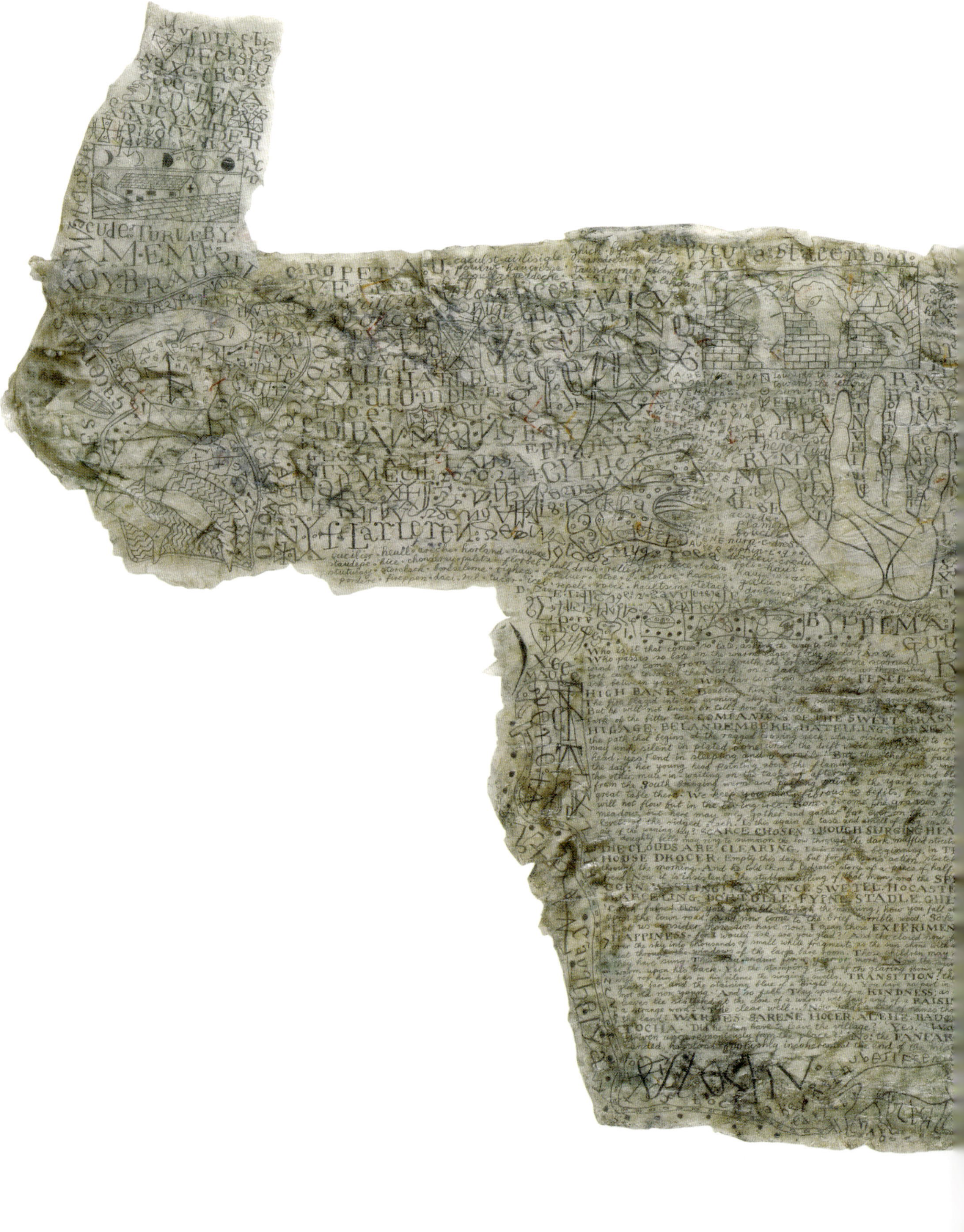

33. _He Departed Like A Stranger From His Own Habitation_, 1994.

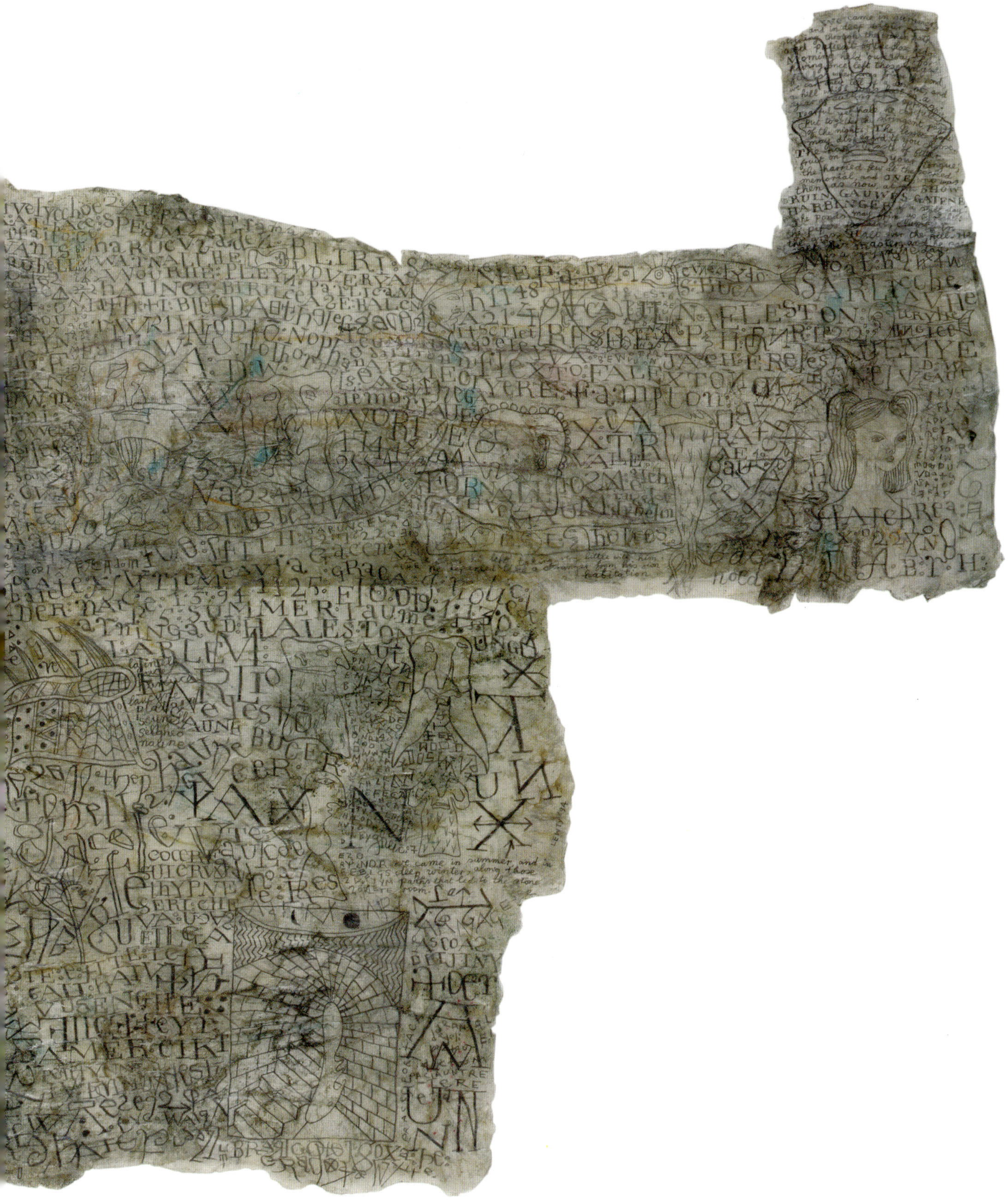

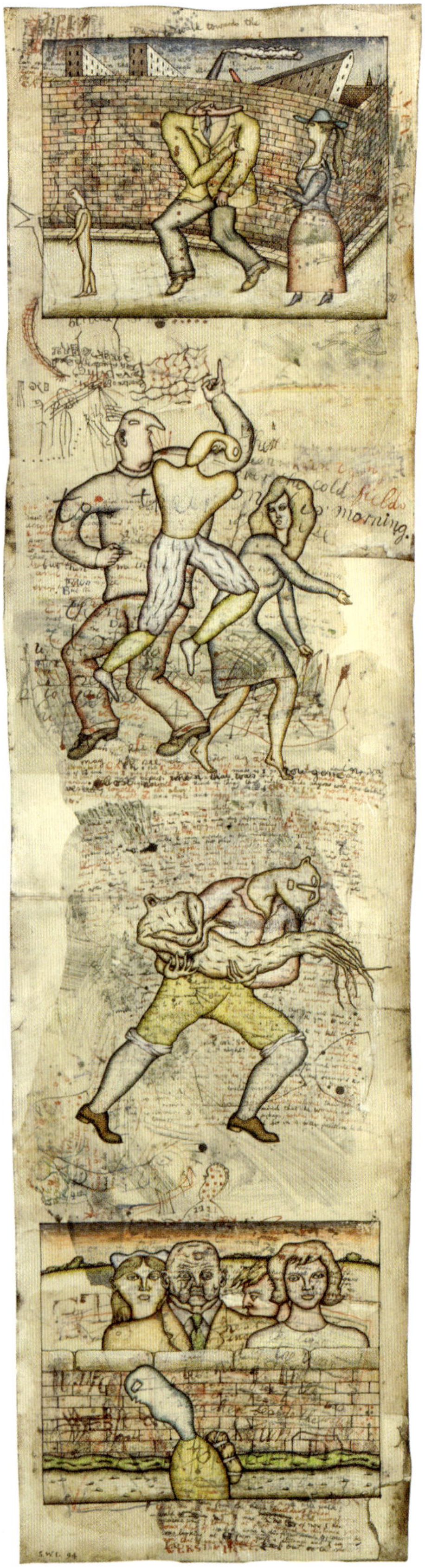

34. *The Guide,* 1994.

We are presented with an art of *disturbed* embedding, where fragments both press down on, and lift up through one another, i.e., what is embedded is the opposite of static. Voices and messages reduced to common but unfamiliar mark project from the medium which partly obliterates them but may also offer the possibility of shelter. We can imagine them growing more healed and reconciled, but also becoming less readable, less in need of our decipherment. But we cannot imagine them at all without a sense of loss, we resent their silence. And in Lewty such voices are doubly silenced, speaking in codes we can no longer reassemble, or regaining a degree of concretion that renders them inscrutable. If voice is reduced to what Lewty has called "silent incantation", it reawakens as the mysterious image or figure of voice, which does indeed speak from its field, from the layering itself. This oblique, visual speech is not suavely naturalised or randomly liberated: the mark which is the figure of voice still bespeaks loss, still mourns its erased presence and curtailed horizon, is still bound by the old insistencies, rituals and trials.

Figure of voice is delineated by the deliberate, graphic nature of Lewty's work. The technique varies according to the needs of each picture, but one constant is the use of embedded layers of paper, each sheet or fragment bearing its own particular messages, patterns or icons, until a complex set of strata is arrived at. Five levels of the graphic appear put to work here: a scrubbing back of a previously flooded surface; rune-like or graffiti-type marks strongly suggesting lettering; unknown words or phrases but in a recognisable script; readable though riddling blocks of phrases seemingly part of an interminable narrative; finally, a possible macro-reading of the purely animistic forms as moving towards a rebus, towards one overall but unknown letter. Within the graphic there is always the characteristic split between figuration and writing, writing included here as worthy of visual representation in its own right, whilst the purer figuration remains caught in the struggle of form towards abstract codes of representation. These graphic trails, as they could be called, both abstract and animistic, might be compared to the linear clouds or contrails left by an aircraft. Lewty's art seems to engage a linear zone or spiritual wake of low pressure, into which shapes condense and elongate, at once discards but free to mutate further, though strictly along the line of their origin, the deposit of their tradition. These are not random forms secreting their way into a symbolic and cultural vacuum, nor do they simply represent an after-life of symbols. We should think of them more as *after-symbols* continuing to bear the burdens of the psyche but currently emerging from within the margins and by-products of a life interminably renewing itself without ever surrendering or cancelling its defeats and losses. What is renewed will re-cover again and again.

35. *Inner Sea*, 1995.

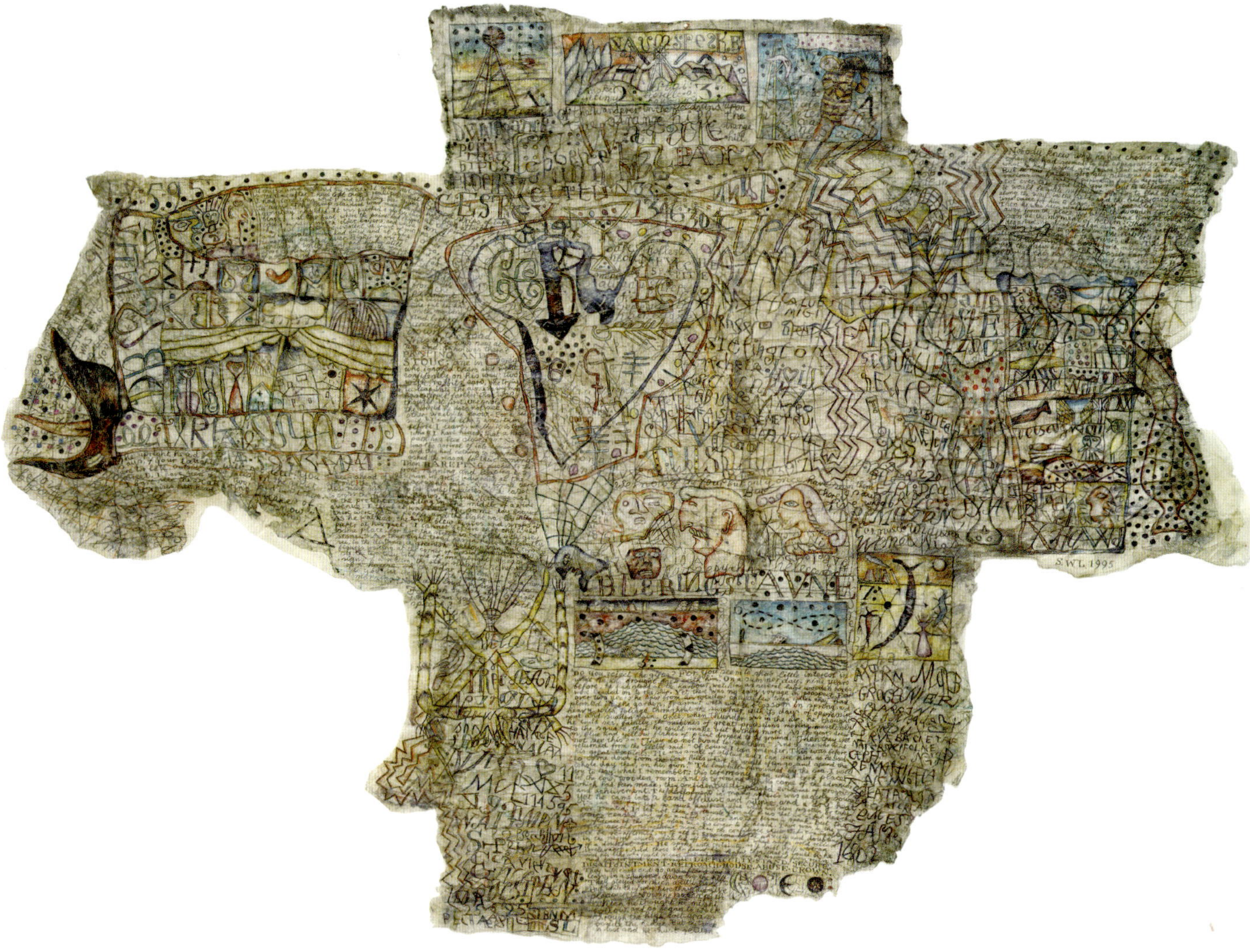

below and right 36. *Rebuke Of Light*, 1999.

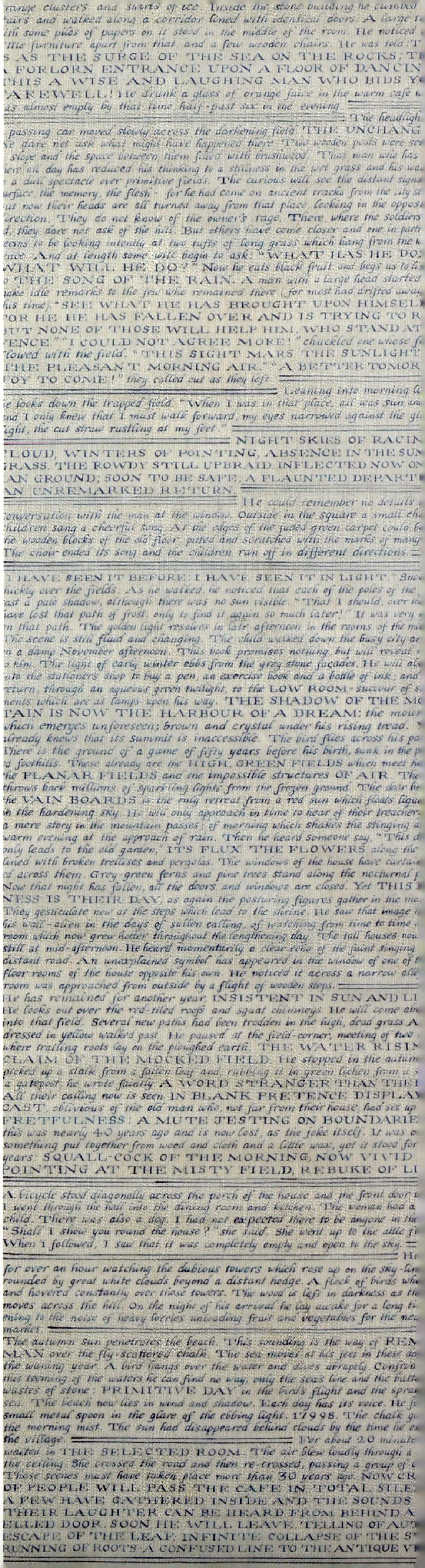

EPISODES

PAUL HILLS
2000

Who speaks these lines, who writes them, who makes them visible? And to what present, past or future do they belong?

Their formality mimics print. Blocks of text, with margins justified and alignment true, stand four-square before us, mighty fragments, bulwarks shored against time's ruin. The look of the epigraphy, alternating between majuscules and a cursive hand, recalls legal documents or public proclamations, bye-laws pasted at the park gate. Yet in all but the most recent works these formal blocks of text are infiltrated, ambushed, encircled, overlaid or underlaid by freehand markings, rogue letters, runes, loops, scratches, tripping flecks and dashes of colour, deposits of blackness. Civilised order encounters primeval energy.

To move closer, to turn from looking to reading, partially undoes this contrast of the civilised and the free. The Roman gravitas or authority of the calligraphy is mocked by many voices. The texts are epic in scale and tenor. They tell of dramas, exhortations, rebukes, threats, uncanny premonitions, memories of places known before birth and perhaps revisited after death. Always the narratives are shot through with episodes, interjections and interlocutions. Whereas much visual art today can be registered at a glance, Lewty's rewards sustained attention, indeed it challenges us and lures us to move close and to look, read and listen. The time this takes, slowing us as we read the lines, sometimes jumping from line to line as changes of colour divert attention, invites us on a meditative if not always tranquil journey. Ear and eye are both engaged. In *Day of Heat, Day of Storms* (plate 39), we read of: "Rusa, whose eyes are painted blue; Boniore, whose telling is merely an echo, whose voice will fade at the singing yard and the stained house." As in a folktale or Arthurian legend, sensory perceptions are reshuffled, magically displaced. Time and again visible words are stained with sound or the echo of things seen.

In Simon Lewty's earlier paintings the inscribed texts were often accompanied by figurative imagery, homunculi with vegetable-like heads, roots that clutch, surreal city chimneys, tree-stumps, hedges and enclosures. Now that these creatures and locations have gone, it is as though—as the artist recently remarked—he has translated his imagery back into words, texts which in turn are made visible, given a unique habitation and a name.

Why, we may ask, has the artist, for the moment at least, banished the lure of the figurative? I would suggest that it is to forestall an inclination to read the paintings in terms of illustration, thereby bringing us forcibly back to the work as an object, to the look of the whole, to the matter of the text and its material presence. It calls us to attend to the imaginative vision of silence and sound—the possibility, as one line puts it, of *Perpetual Silence Amid Intrusive Noise* (plate 41). By renouncing illustration, Lewty deepens the play on regarding and disregarding. So in *Whispers from a Mysterious Revolt* (plate 40) our eyes may—or may not—alight on the words: "... and the unregarded message flutters on the wall. Beyond the wind and Lenten snow: a retribution in the lists you see and heed or disregard." This is an

37. *Drift Of Days*, 1999.

art which holds contraries in suspense: the indifference of the world, its unknownness, is set against its penetration by mind, feeling and memory.

Essential to Lewty's strategy is the removal of the personal trace and agency of the artist. Just as the texts themselves appear to emanate from a deposit of shared experience laid down over many centuries, rather than from a single authorial voice, so too the freehand markings evoke a palimpsest of worn and weathered graffiti rather than an individual handwriting or signature. In *Whispers from a Mysterious Revolt*, Lewty uses photocopies of his automatic drawings to lend his markings unity and detachment. Incorporating photocopies masks the agency of the creator, giving to the finished work an air of inevitability.

The result is a beautifully resolved sense of presence, of weight and dignity, of ritual order, of stability and yet also of energy and rhythm. As in Giorgio de Chirico, a strong architectonic structure sustains their mystery. After prolonged contemplation Lewty's latest works afford an extraordinary plenitude. It springs in part from the way the blocks of text dwell in the white field. In *Day of Heat, Day of Storms*, the text, consisting of no less than ten thousand words, fills the rectangle from edge to edge with the inevitability of a stream of water filling a beaker to the brim. In *Rebuke of Light* (plate 36) the double columns of sky-blue words have come to rest low in the field, the whiteness above intimating the substance of the light referred to in the title; and this blue of sky and white of light is stretched, held in tension, by the little squares of red.

The play between the material presence of the works as objects and their immaterial subjects is understated and hardly to be defined. Of course the fabulous shuffling of the senses, the magical synaesthesia, points beyond the sensory to the unseen and unspoken. Many of the inscribed narratives are set out-of-doors in some primordial field and tell of cloud, of shafts of light, of wind and gathering darkness, of *Season of Sun and Rain* (plate 38). None of these encounters with the elements are literally figured yet we may occasionally or fleetingly apprehend their equivalents in the misty layered whiteness of tissue or the dashes of sunny yellow lying over the dark words. To go further than this would be to mislead, for such associations are never deliberately set up; indeed the artist renounces any obviously descriptive deployment of colour.

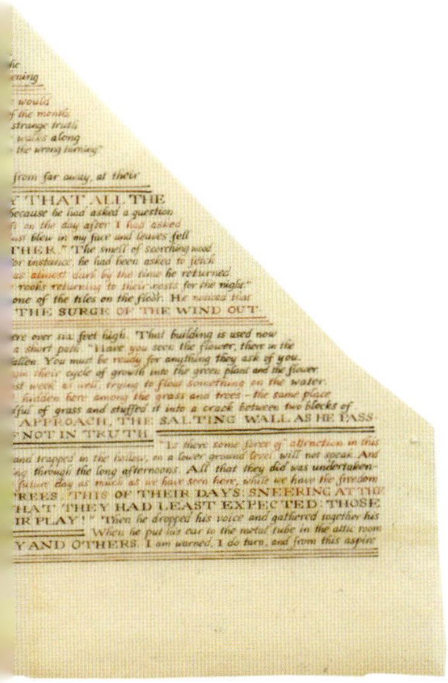

While Lewty's texts excavate ancient worlds of light and darkness, and show forth the persistence of the disregarded, they also belong to now. Without indulging in any trite or obvious topicality, from a deep perspective they invite reflection upon our present situation. The connection to now is all the more powerful for being oblique, perhaps even unintentional, but Lewty's works remind me of how we are immersed by electronic and other media in a flood of disembodied words, messages or signs beamed to us without apparent human source or agency. These ghosts in the machine today intrude everywhere upon our lives, bleeping and commanding. To our peril they are obliterating place, time and history, drowning out ancestral voices. In the face of this contemporary leavening and loss of meaning, the need to inscribe, to give shape to utterance, to dwell with the incomprehensible, is all the more urgent. In this sense Lewty's latest works invert and redeem the disembodiment which threatens us. Against the *Drift of Days* (plate 37) stands a bulwark.

38. *Season Of Sun and Rain*, 1999.

39. *Day Of Heat, Day Of Storms*, 1999.

below and opposite Extract and detail from 39. *Day Of Heat, Day Of Storms,* 1999.

OUR RESPITE: TWO came over the sunset hill. She opened her mouth to yawn. Her hair blew out behind her head in the wind of the twilight field. Our diversion: feats of jumping and leaping, of high springing and a fall. He had come to tell them of what he has found in the hedge. His hand, feeling among the closely woven branches, had touched a small bundle, tied with paper and hanging from a twig. On pulling it out he tore the damp paper and its contents were revealed: a few seeds, a rust stained glass jar, several disintegrating pieces of paper covered with writing and a small piece of burnt wood. It was too dark by then to see if there was anything more in that hedge. He could only guess at who had put the package there and why. It must have been there much earlier in the year. DRIFT-NEED, SEAT OF THE CENTURIES, WINTER REPETITION OF THE HEDGE AND THE SEA. He climbed the stone stairs and walked enthusiastically about the room, boasting of the objects he had collected. I DO NOT KNOW HOW TO SAY THIS. The pipes were still lying in a corner but now SIX rise, the whole of the FRESH ARRAY mounts, A SNAPPING RISER and FLASK OF SIGNS. Two were SCARE-STICKS, one with a looped leather strap, one with the head of a blade. 'So he would leave this bundle by the side of a dusty road where any passer-by could pick it up and examine its contents?' 'Yes, that is where it was found. It seems to show that he no longer cared what happened to them.' The overlapping plates part, only to reveal two tiny mouths, fixed in soundless shouting. You ask what it means—what does that rain means, which falls on the dry earth? The emptied cloud lifts from the bank, the black fish plunges into deeper waters, 'All this has been heard.' Is it possible that he might have read the book and then forgotten, or come to the wrong conclusion entirely? That the RETELLING may become THE UNTOLD, as harsh tides of winter break on the lost beach, as flies gather round the dew-ponds in the summer field. So that he may return to those PASSING DAYS, EPISODES OF A LOST LAND.

ivided. The determined messengers IN URGENT FAITH float low over the hot land
is to stir up various runs which have been made over the years by rabbits and other small
where you walk." For THE BRISK have declared: there is no need to look further into that
ND. And these will arrive tomorrow: ——— RETE
E, WHOSE TELLING IS MERELY AN ECHO, WHOSE VOICE WILL FAD
n the street outside, surrounded by a noisy, gabbling crowd. They stretched out the twisted skin
——— He looked down at sunlit tracts of country. He went into a build
place of blown spume. It forms tenuous enclosures, articulated by the wind and the sea, in the

estions he put to them. "Is this the far coast? That land I can see, that water I can glimps
TIME OF THE DESTRUCTION OF COURTIERS" Small ships ply in these coas
d deserts, their rivers flowing towards the south. A VOID APPEARS, WHITE IN T
OAST. FOR THIS IS WHERE WE MAY FAIL. THE FAVOURED DEPAR
——— OUR RESPITE: TWO came over the sunset hill. She opened her mouth to yawn
he closely woven branches, had touched a small bundle, tied with paper and hanging from a twi
if there was anything more in that hedge. He could only guess at who had put the package
alked enthusiastically about the room, boasting of the objects he had collected. I DO NOT KN
with a looped leather strap, one with the head of a blade. "So he would leave this bundle by the si
mouths, fixed in soundless shouting. You ask what this means - what does that rain mean, which
n entirely? That the RE-TELLING may become THE UNTOLD, as harsh tides of win
aid anything to you yet?" "No, although I think he is trying to." At length his presence may be
e wooden fence. They seemed shocked and astonished, yet surely his words may save his ground, HIS
ss telling under leaning trees. Two laugh openly, one casts about to swear, one has come only to s
t both his hands to show them what he has brought with him. For in that house he was with
TREET." There was no-one in that street at the time. It was only later that the trenchant man
rishment is a bidding, in his time, of that dark source WHICH MAY FAIL and of the circlin
embling square as the SKIPPING MAN approaches concrete reservoirs sunk in the wet grass. =

we are left... He barely brings himself to see. He barely brings himself to know. Pursued by
rs Their nodes and pinnacles will capture this, the only GIFT OF SCANTY DAY. Hig
clear-land.) COMBAT OF AN INDIFFERENT DAY, (in full sight of his choking a
, the better to see the prospect of his way across the hills, yet remains, venting his unheeded sow
alls and the great concrete buildings. FLIGHT TO THE BRIDGE, IMAGO OF THE N
mly to a flight of stone steps, leading nowhere. A dark door serves as both entry and exit to these g
ect of days, watchful of the path beyond the bridge which leads both to city streets and squares by a
clear of the STUNNED ALMANACS OF THE TURNING YEAR. Light spores
t against the clear horizon of the surging plain." Here a plant is falling in flames There is

a friend, he will choose to go to the station at the far end of the city. He did not know the exact
F UNCERTAIN DAY, SWOON OF THE EMPTY TOWN. Now he tells: HUZ
AND THE SPENT ACORN ROLLS AT MY FEET?" There was FROST FO
d by the bank of a dark, fast-flowing river. FALSE SHAME! So to fill their heads with his
EY ARE COMING OUT OF THE GREY WOOD. WILL YOU TAKE THEIR H
old man did not answer, but passed him on the beach, with moist eyes. The younger man climbed high
floor under the concrete walls. When the treading mounts to the upper floors you will go out b
n and pink clovers rise from the misty grass on a morning, hundreds of years before her birth. As h
of water. THE IMMENSE HILL is quite silent. In the still hour THEIR FRETTED
n the shining sea and to one sorrowing amid the anxious, questioning crowds. The door opened i
AT NIGHT, HE WILL CLIMB TO HIS BED AND SLEEP. They are BEYOND
e of that first winter, of his arrival in snow and rain, and yet compared his life there favourabl
OOR FARING, ALONG LIT AND UNLIT STREETS. ———
to the noise of heavy lorries unloading fruit and vegetables for the nearby market. FACES A

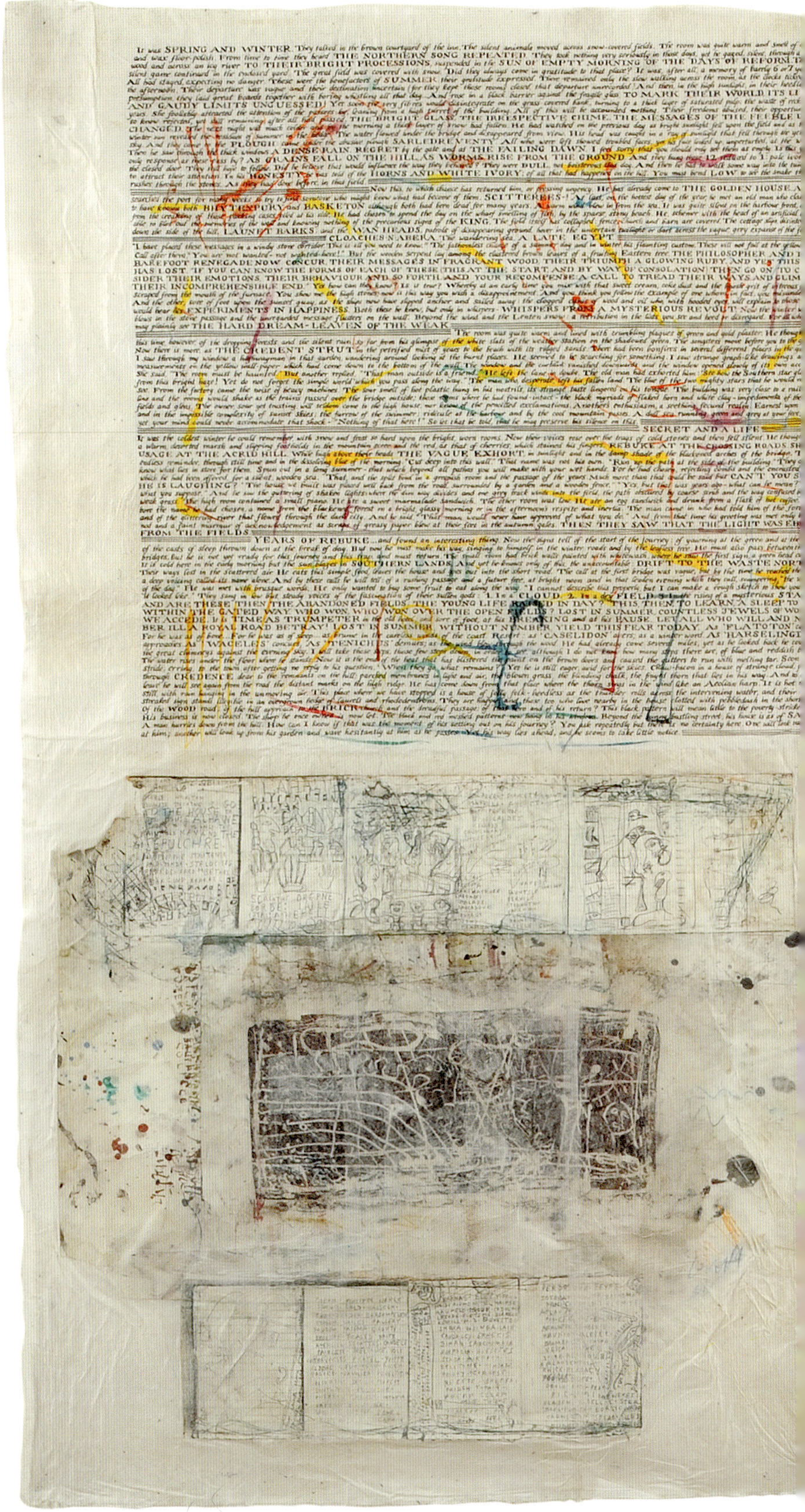

40. Whispers From A Mysterious Revolt, 1998.

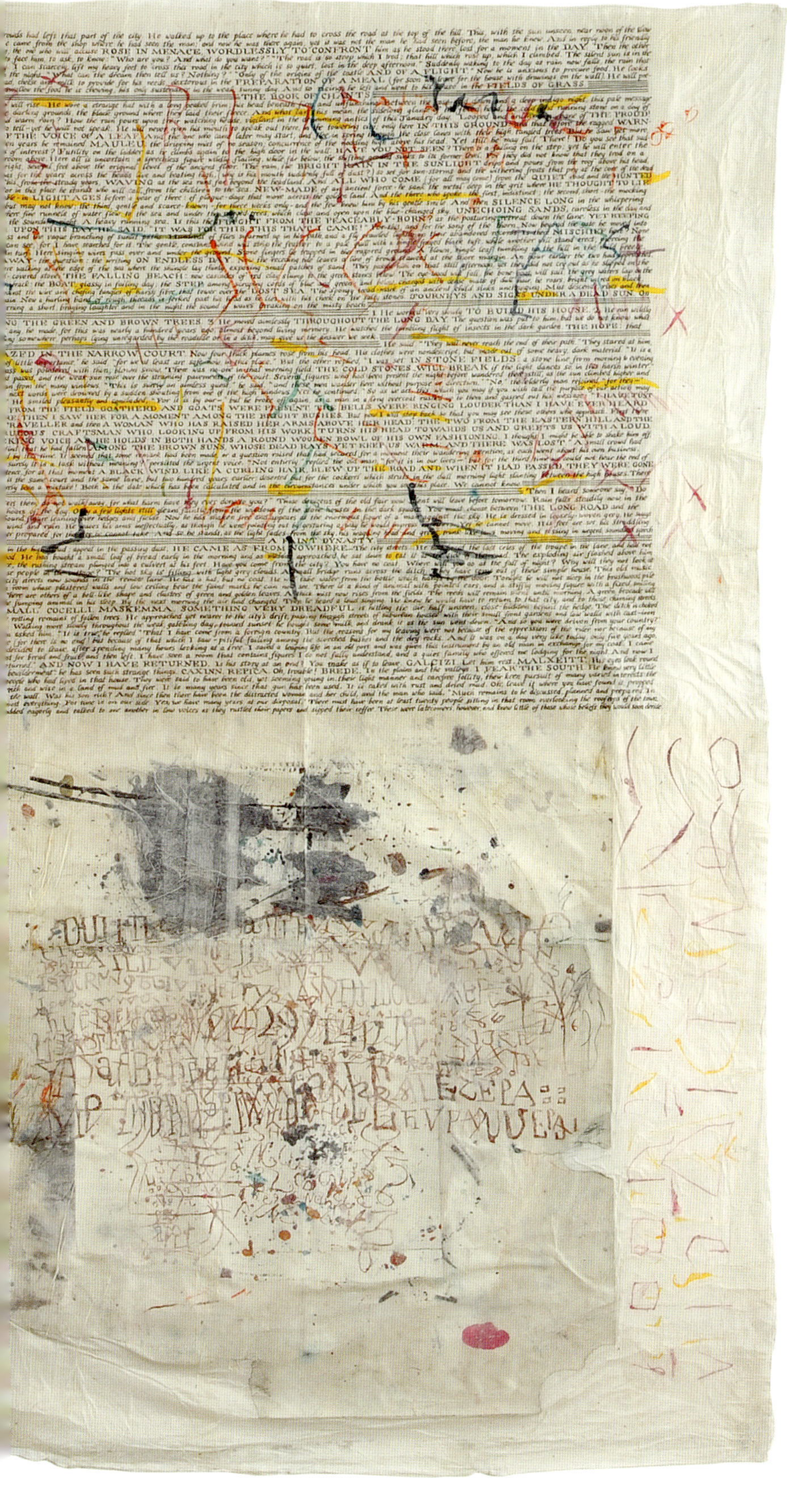

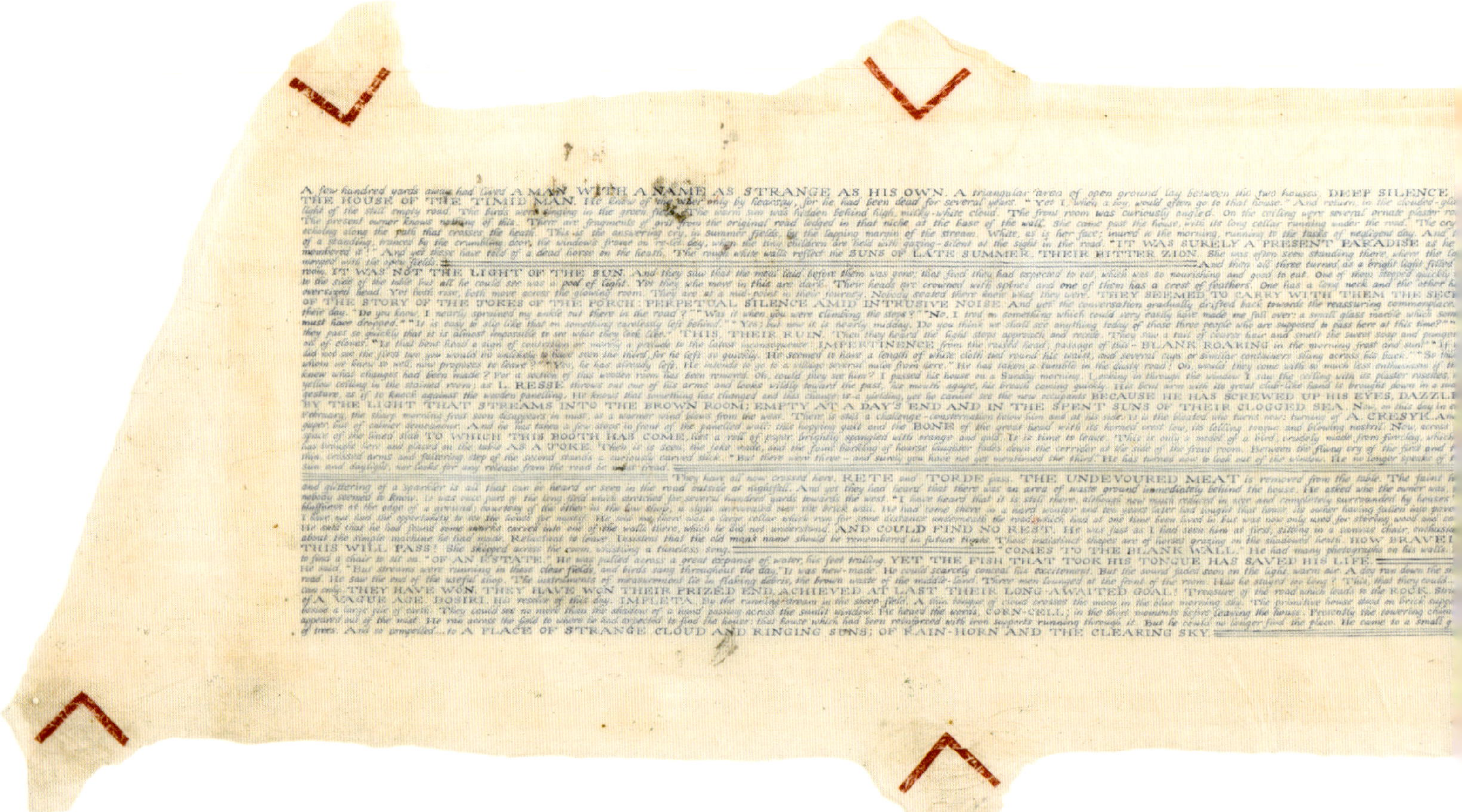

41. *Perpetual Silence Amid Intrusive Noise*, 1999.

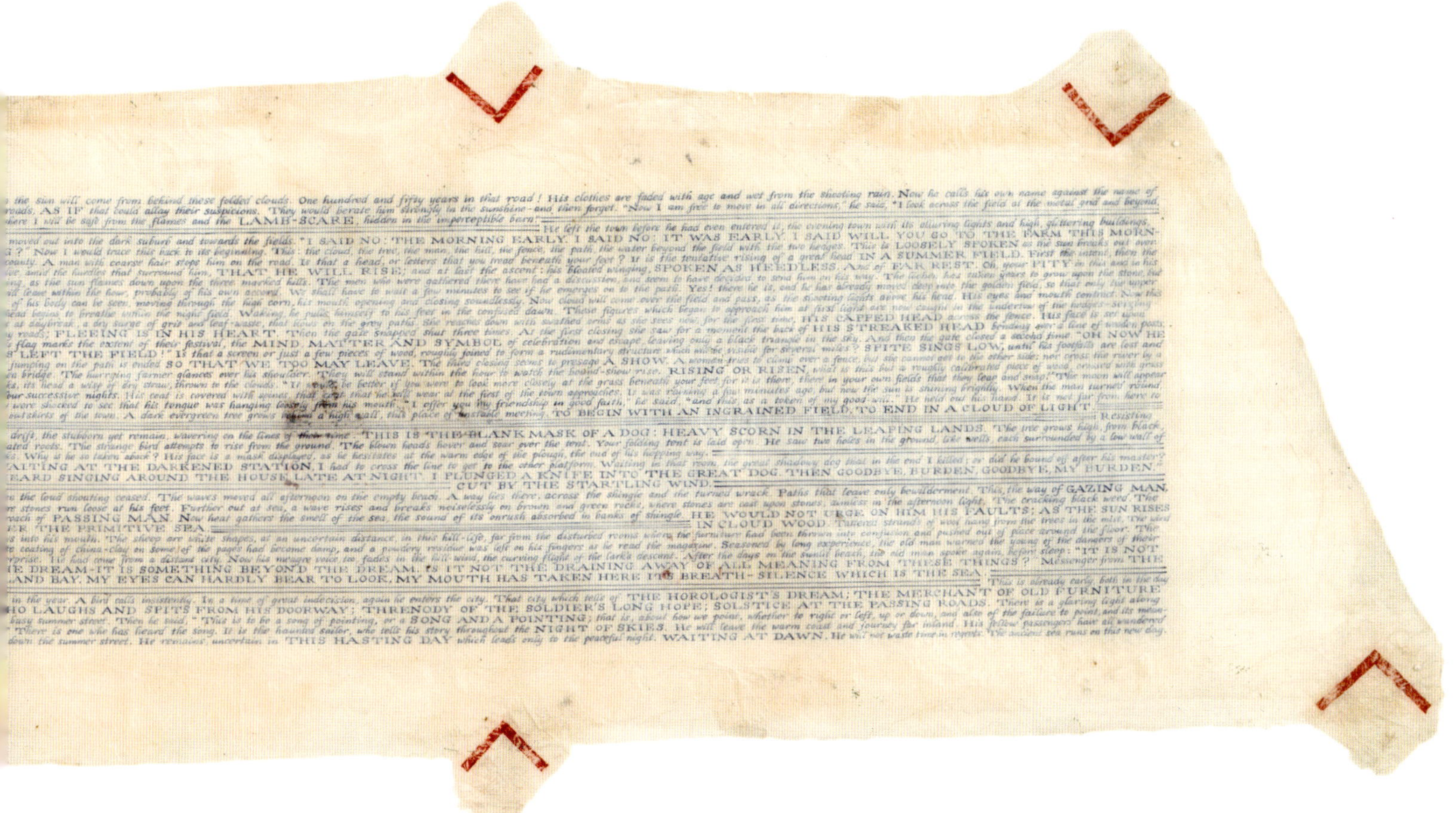

ECLIPSES: A RESPONSE

JESSICA DUBOW
2004

... they seemed uncertain which of the small streets leading off the main thoroughfare they should take. Simon Lewty, *Variant from a Book of Rain* (plate 45), 2002.

The map is a generalisation, a theorisation, a reduction. Its paradox is that it is both nowhere and everywhere. A utopia. Like the drawing of a straight line, or the gridding of a city, to map a space means to clear the way for rational advance: to eliminate the natural breach, to abstract the inconvenient particular. It is, in short, the product of a will that elects the ideal over the material and the mental over the manual.

Lewty's work is not about the map. It is, rather, about what precedes the map and what the map forgets: not the systemic regulations of the route but the minute, material act of passing by; not the vacua that exist between nodal point and nodal point, but the peripatetic passage between them. It is an art that shows in concreto how the lived body and lived landscape entwine to make and remake each other. It is about the active in-dwelling of space....

Curiously, tellingly, it is through his written texts that Lewty's peripatetic sight is given form. [His] writing serves less to represent a space than to speak of a certain way of inhabiting it. It is a mode of observation and occupation that eludes immediate legibility as it is shaped by the contingencies of the route, by fragments of trajectories, by splicings of space. Such textual descriptions are myriad, but they do not compose a series. They do not constitute a narrative because each phrase, like each momentary sight, has a singularity, a density, an opacity all of its own. Indeed, like the mobility of a hand-held film camera, Lewty's texts visualise movement through space; the words do not settle but "act out" the walk: not retroactively, but "during the time the feet perform it".[1] In much the same way, the alternating rhythm of reading and looking, the fragmentation of phrases, their detours and driftlanes, all play a part in the ambulatory nature of Lewty's vision: the sense in which his sight originates in space and lives its movements from the inside.

And Lewty challenges us to accompany him on his walks. For unlike a map we cannot read Lewty's work from a distance or assume a stance of inert contemplation. We are compelled, instead, to move in close so as to focus the telling detail, follow the curve of a calligraphic letter, or the loop of a sinuous line. We are attuned, in fact, to the same perceptual delicacy that attends the body when it traverses a strange space for the first time: the awareness of how a foot might angle itself to accommodate an obstructing stone, how a head might dip to negotiate an overhanging branch... To look at Lewty's work, then, is in a sense to constitute the vectors and arrests of actual movement.

And more than this. For along with this topological understanding of visual perception comes a kind of meditative state that leaves thought behind, or better yet, that allows it to follow the pathways of least resistance. To say this is not simply to note that Lewty's texts exist halfway between memory and

42. *Repetition and Dream I*, 2003.

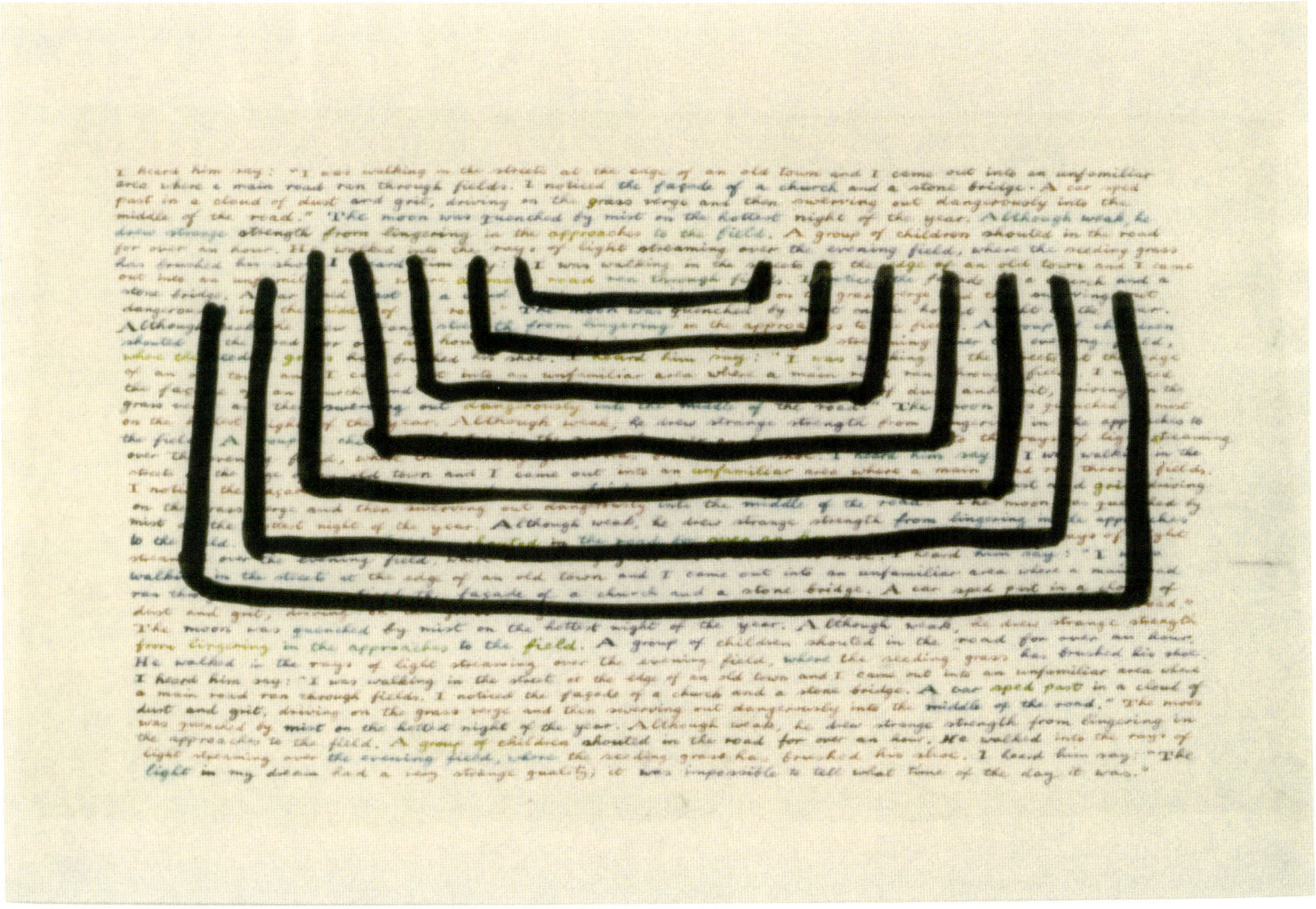

myth, elliptical sense and fanciful non-sense. It is also to recall that psychic state in which time and thought give over to space and sensation, when the topology of one's surrounding—its moods, its affectivities, its shape, its style—immerse the body in a make-shift itinerary, allowing it to store up rich silences, wordless stories, or follow the durational flows of an inward history. One might also see it as a kind of geometaphysics furnished by the leftovers from measurement and estimate. By those extra and other things—relics, legends, desires—that turn the table on sedentary sense.

If this 'other' and 'extra' realm is part of what we mean by the artistic imagination, in Lewty's case it is one that begins on ground-level; with a concrete practice that, step by step, redraws the eye into the physical environment as into the body of the seer.

1. Michel de Certeau, *The Practice of Everyday Life*, Berkeley: University of California Press, 1988, p. 116.

43. *Inscriptions Without Blame*, 2002.

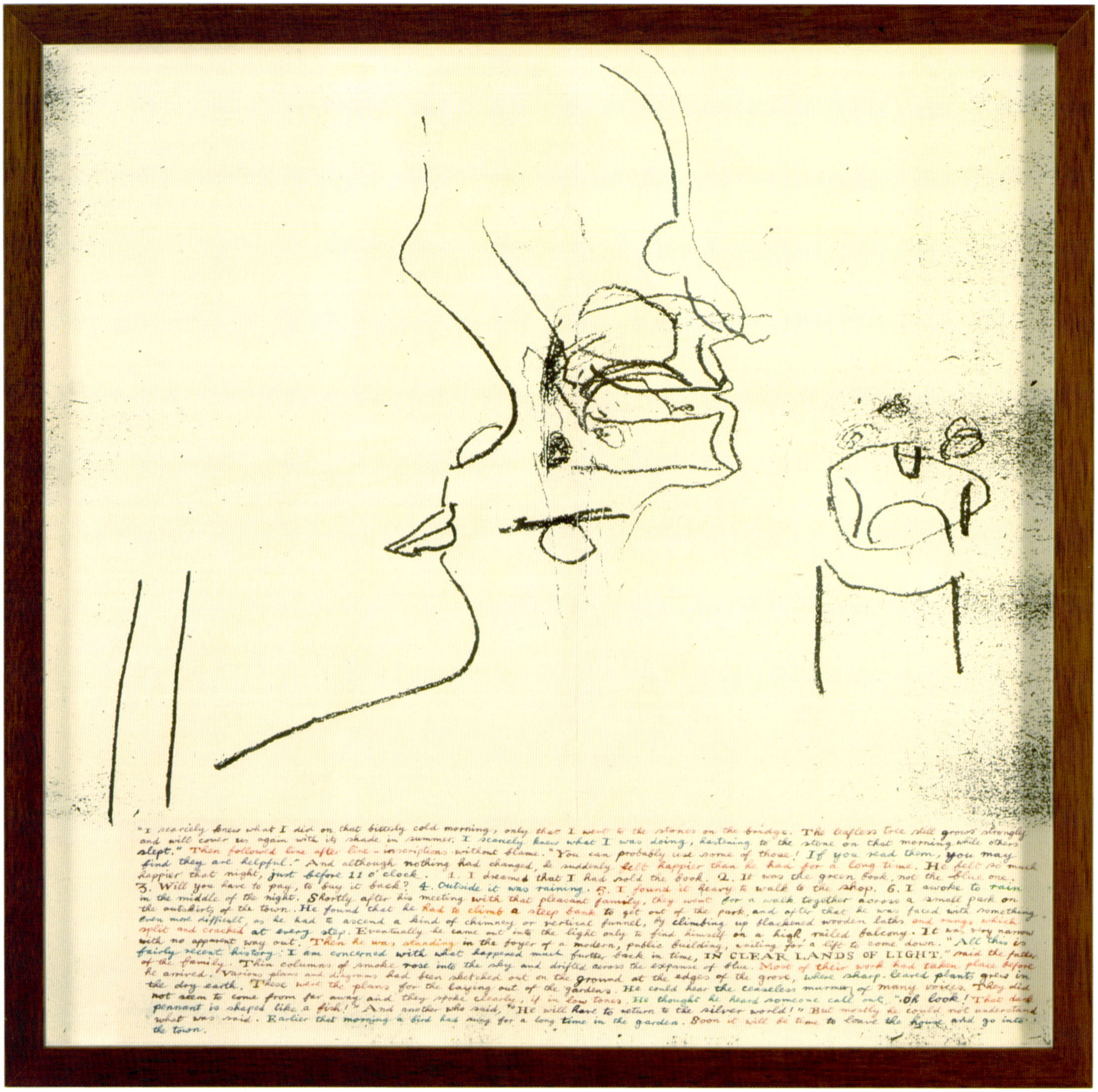

44. *Diagram From A Dream*, 2002.

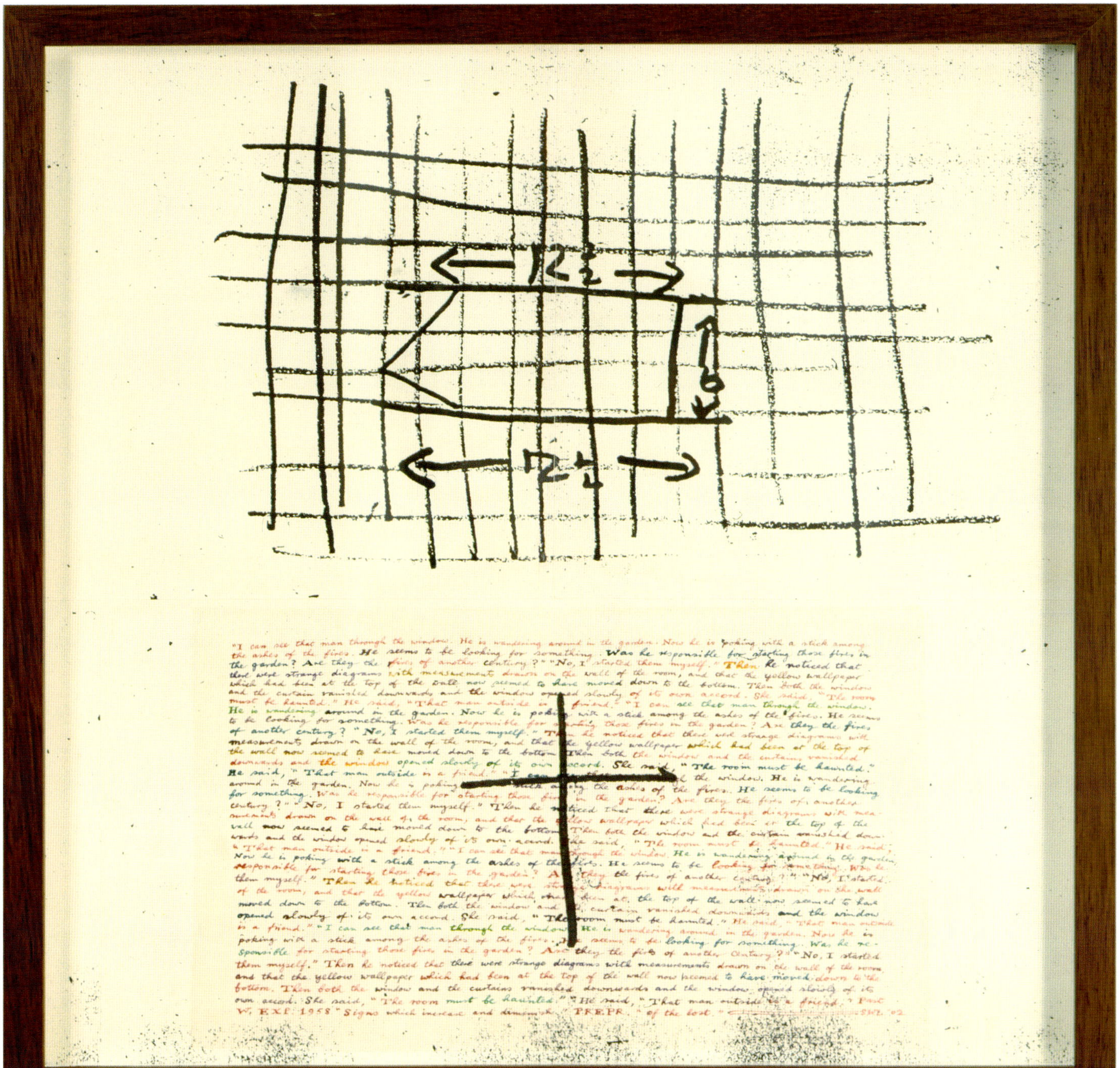

"I was in a cellar among worn and pitted stone columns. There was an eroded seat or throne. Some of the lights in the house were on, and others off. The fence is still his property."
The TONGUED MAN stands in the pretended 'street' of the saturated village. PHILEAN is standing in rain. BAUCERY is standing so still by the pond. "Is this the food
that you have given me? Such food as I have never seen before!" The CHILD'S VOICE speaks. Several people had approached by that time. Sometimes he dreamt that he was being
swept along by crowds of people dressed in the costume of the eighteenth century.
stands, his calm sustained in light and heavy rain, and in the TRAMPLING CHANTS as this day moves towards an unmoving evening. Now that the hard wind has subsided, he
his ungainly body at rest, yet poised. His ever-stirring feet tread out silent paths, green beyond the grit of the new roads which cuts in THE SOUNDING FIELD. A blackbird
flies into the tree, shaking droplets of rain from the wet leaves, while higher, in the same tree, the head of a grotesque bird is formed in four leaves. Doubt is in your hooded eye, a proposition
to your vapid mouth quivering loosely in the radiant sky over wet gardens in MAY. Now BRAPESON droops HUGE against WESTERN SKIES, HIS WARNING DIS-
REGARDED, HIS ROLLING TONGUE DEPLETED BY HIS ATTEMPTS TO TELL: "THE NORTHERN NODES WILL BREAK HIS STAFF"
"I SAW HIS STAFF WAS BROKEN!" "THE DRAIN OF SUNLIGHT BOWS HIS HEAD, UNFLINCHING SUMMER'S TOKEN." But the morning
wind now pushes masses of cloud across the sky. His PALE RIBS rise and fall, his SET HEAD faces full into the wind as, with hair streaming, he raises his voice to shout out the
few sections of his argument that remain intact – LOUD ON THE MORNING AIR! For here there was once a system set in strange blocks of words. Can we learn it once again?
Even as he silently hangs his head, those word-frames are loosed to dispersal, and all seems lost in the wind, but you may be able to see them again from time to time – to find them once more at
the return of evening. "The words, when set down, were difficult to follow." There seemed to be much repetition of MAN, ESTATE, WOOD, HILL. He said: "I came only to tell
you this: RAIN SPITS IN THE TINY STREET – I TRACE THE PATHS OF THE RAIN."
wall, their metallic tendons braced in the SHORT CLEAR SUN OF NORTHERN SEAS. The sharp profiles of beaked and armoured heads appeared late on the white
with splayed paws and sunken heads. Their rotting membranes are stretched taut over the shingle until within a few weeks they are absorbed into the bruised beach or washed out to sea
again on the high tide. A bird called towards the sea as the sun sank behind the hill and the harsh grass settled TO NIGHT. He will live through those nights before the sea. He has
faced the beach for twenty years, a strong return, though born of weak resolve: his life amid the driftwood and the mottled stones, the tiny crab and the sand-flies that swarm at his feet.
RETURN AT EVENING.
He returned late in the day and came at nightfall to a strange, high city. Soon it was very dark. He heard the washing of waves, although the city was far from the sea.

45. Variant From A Book Of Rain, 2002.

46. *Strange Eyes*, 2007.

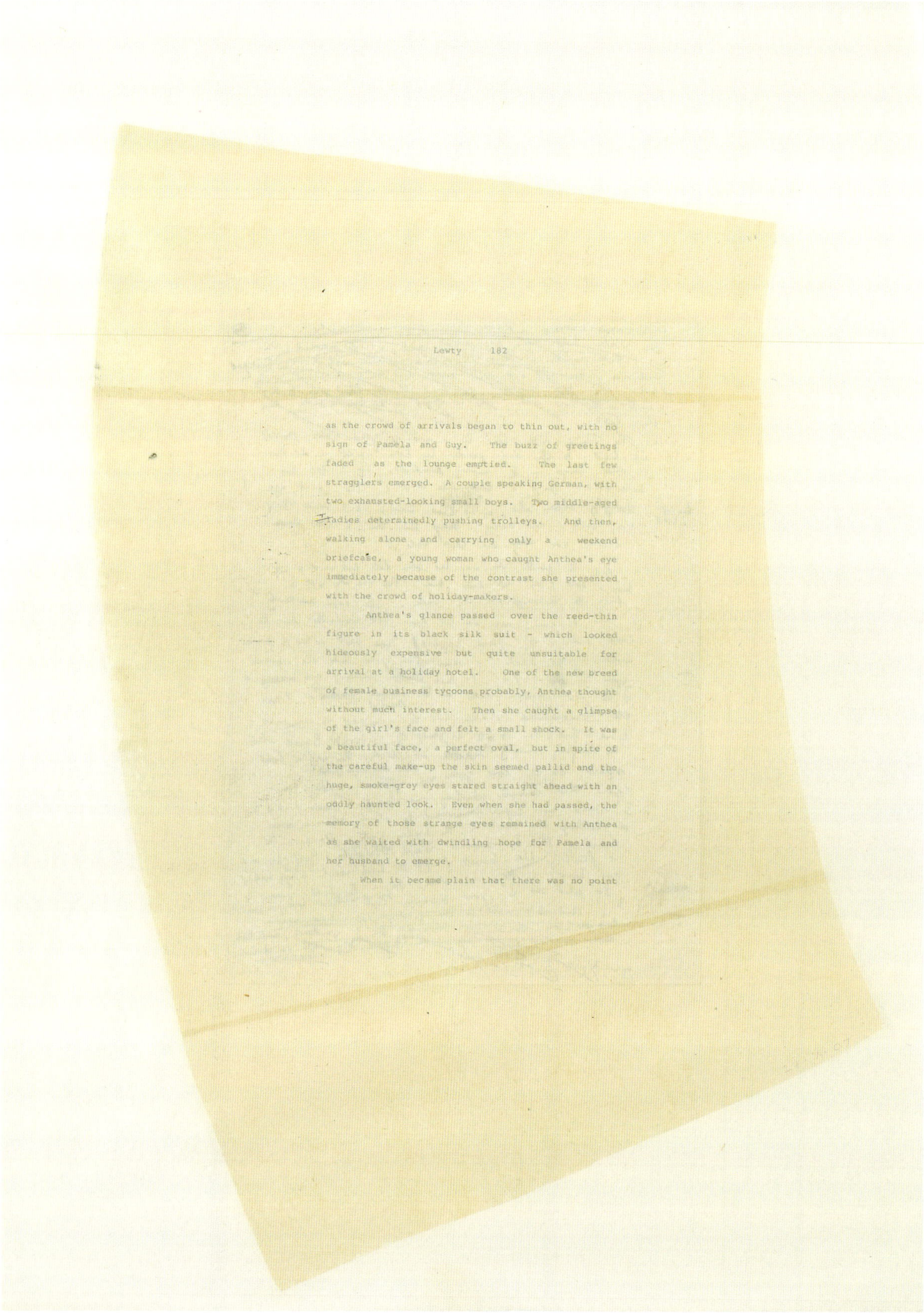

Lewty 182

as the crowd of arrivals began to thin out, with no sign of Pamela and Guy. The buzz of greetings faded as the lounge emptied. The last few stragglers emerged. A couple speaking German, with two exhausted-looking small boys. Two middle-aged ladies determinedly pushing trolleys. And then, walking alone and carrying only a weekend briefcase, a young woman who caught Anthea's eye immediately because of the contrast she presented with the crowd of holiday-makers.

Anthea's glance passed over the reed-thin figure in its black silk suit - which looked hideously expensive but quite unsuitable for arrival at a holiday hotel. One of the new breed of female business tycoons probably, Anthea thought without much interest. Then she caught a glimpse of the girl's face and felt a small shock. It was a beautiful face, a perfect oval, but in spite of the careful make-up the skin seemed pallid and the huge, smoke-grey eyes stared straight ahead with an oddly haunted look. Even when she had passed, the memory of those strange eyes remained with Anthea as she waited with dwindling hope for Pamela and her husband to emerge.

When it became plain that there was no point

47. _Far From The Town And Yet Not Far_, 2001.

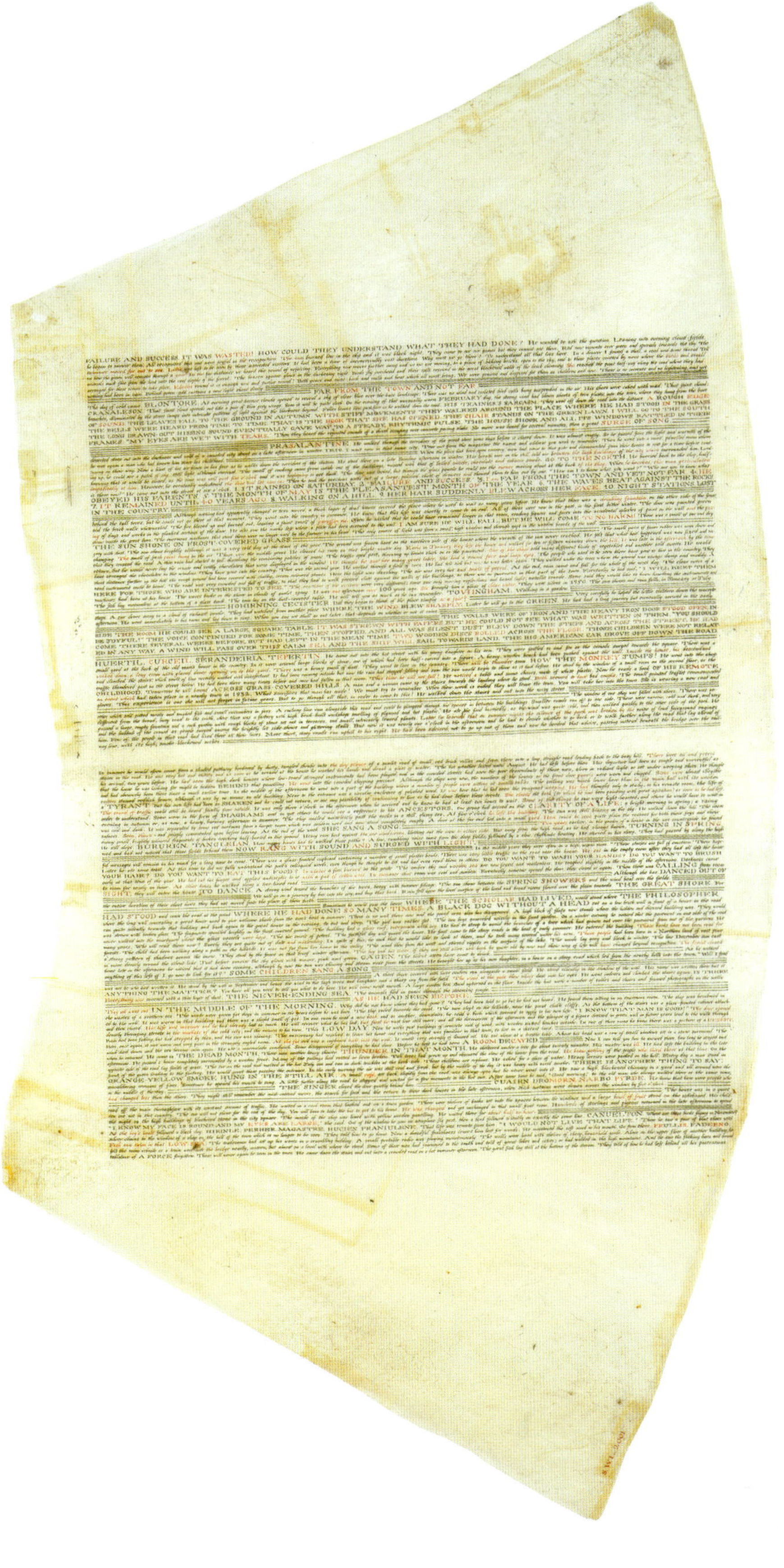

he would often come from a shaded pathway bordered by dusty, tangled shrubs into the dry silence of a sunlit
he road. He was very hot and thirsty and as soon as he arrived at the house he washed his hands and drank a gla
two years before. He had seen the high, dark houses where low-toned stringed instruments had been played; a
use he was looking for might be hidden BEHIND that panelling. He went into the crowded shopping precinct.
viously been there since a much earlier time. In the middle of the afternoon he went into a part of the building wh
ined reddish brown, although it was by no means an old building. Near to the entrance was a circular enclosure of
ANT. But his own life had been so SHAKEN and he could not return, or see any possibility of continuing
of traffic could still be heard faintly from outside. It was only three o'clock in the afternoon when he arrived
nderstand. Some were in the form of DIAGRAMS and in yet others he could see a reference to his
n autumn or, as now, a heavy, burning afternoon in summer. The ship sailed noiselessly past the rocks in
d dark. It was separated by some red curtains from a larger room which was seldom used and now stood complete
een, shown – and crisply commented upon before leaving. At the end of the week SHE SANG A SONG.
ll, brightly coloured fragments of broken crockery half-buried in the ground. Heavy rain beat against the car windscree
pt. BURUREN. TANGLEIAN. How many times had he walked those paths? A low, rumbl
ad not noticed that those fields behind them NOW RANG WITH SOUND AND SURGE

es will remain in his mind for a long time to come. There was a glass-fronted cupboard containing a number of sma
ate some toast. At this time he did not fully understand the poet's colloquial words, even though he thought he did, a
AIR? DO YOU WANT TO EAT THIS FOOD? In winter a fire burned in the grate. T
at time of the year. He had cut his finger and applied antiseptic to it with a pad of cotton wool. In summer t
r nearly an hour. At other times he walked along a tree-lined road.
, they will enter the house TO DANCE. A strong wind tossed the branches of the trees, heavy with s
We will go on a journey by bus into the city, and buy that book.
duration of their short lives they had not moved from the place of their birth.
Sometimes he would pass the house
STOOD and cross the road at the point WHERE HE HAD DONE SO MANY TI
ng wall concealing a great house used to give welcome shade from the sun's heat in summer. There is no wall there
silently towards that building and back again to the great house in the evening, to eat and sleep. The girl was
with broken glass. The fragments sparkled brightly on the frost-covered ground. The building had a glass roof, overgr
ed into the courtyard where the glass vessels were kept. The air smelt of petrol. The faithful dog will guard t
. Who will read them now? Surely they are quite out of date and misleading. In spite of this, he said that he
e child had been walking along a path on the hillside. It was not far from her home in the valley. The wind blew
ttern of shadows across the snow. They stood by the fence on that brief winter afternoon. The boy and his siste
nsely around the silent lake. Just before sunrise the sky glows with mauve, pink and green. GAGEN. T
the afternoon he noticed that it had been raining, although by now the sun was shining and steam rose from the
this left if I go now to look for it?" SOME CHILDREN SANG A SONG.
A short drive
who had written it. He stood by the wall in September and heard the wind in the high trees and laughter and a sharp
HING THE MATTER? You have all you need to tell you what to do here. He will come next month.
was covered with a thin layer of dust. THE NEVER-ENDING SEA. The animals fled in
AS HE HAD
ent out IN THE MIDDLE OF THE MORNING. Why did he not know where
of a southern sea. The woods were green for days in summer in the years before he was born. The ship sailed towar
all. It was warm in that building and there was a slight smell of gas. In one room he read a new book and in anot
sed. His life was insecure and he had already lost so much. He will recover what he has lost, but first he must los
nging streets in the markets of the cold city, and the return to his room. This LOW DAY. Now he walks p
en falling, but had stopped by then, and the sun was shining. The missionary had resolved to leave his home and ever
gain, it was warm and very quiet in the strangely angled room. At the far end was a cupboard built into the wall. It sm
own and the sea became calm again. He ate a marmalade sandwich. Some disapproved of everything he had done. Befo
rned. He came in THE DEAD MONTH. There was another heavy shower. THUNDER IN T
He passed a house completely surrounded by a wooden fence. Many of the palings had rotted or been broken. Tall tr
of the road lay fields of grass. The tar on the road had melted in the hot July sun and ran in dark trickles at the kerb
gates leading to the factory. He would greet those passing the entrance. In the early morning the air was still cool a
GE-YELLOW SMOKE HUNG IN THE STILL AIR. A small café, set back sligh
remains of fires. Sometimes he opened his mouth to sing. A little further along the road, he stopped and waited f
e of the day. THE SINGER closed the door quietly behind h
d less than the others. They might still remember the mist-covered moors, the search for food and the return to

opposite Detail from 47. *Far From The Town And Yet Not Far*, 2001.

below Detail from 46. *Strange Eyes*, 2007.

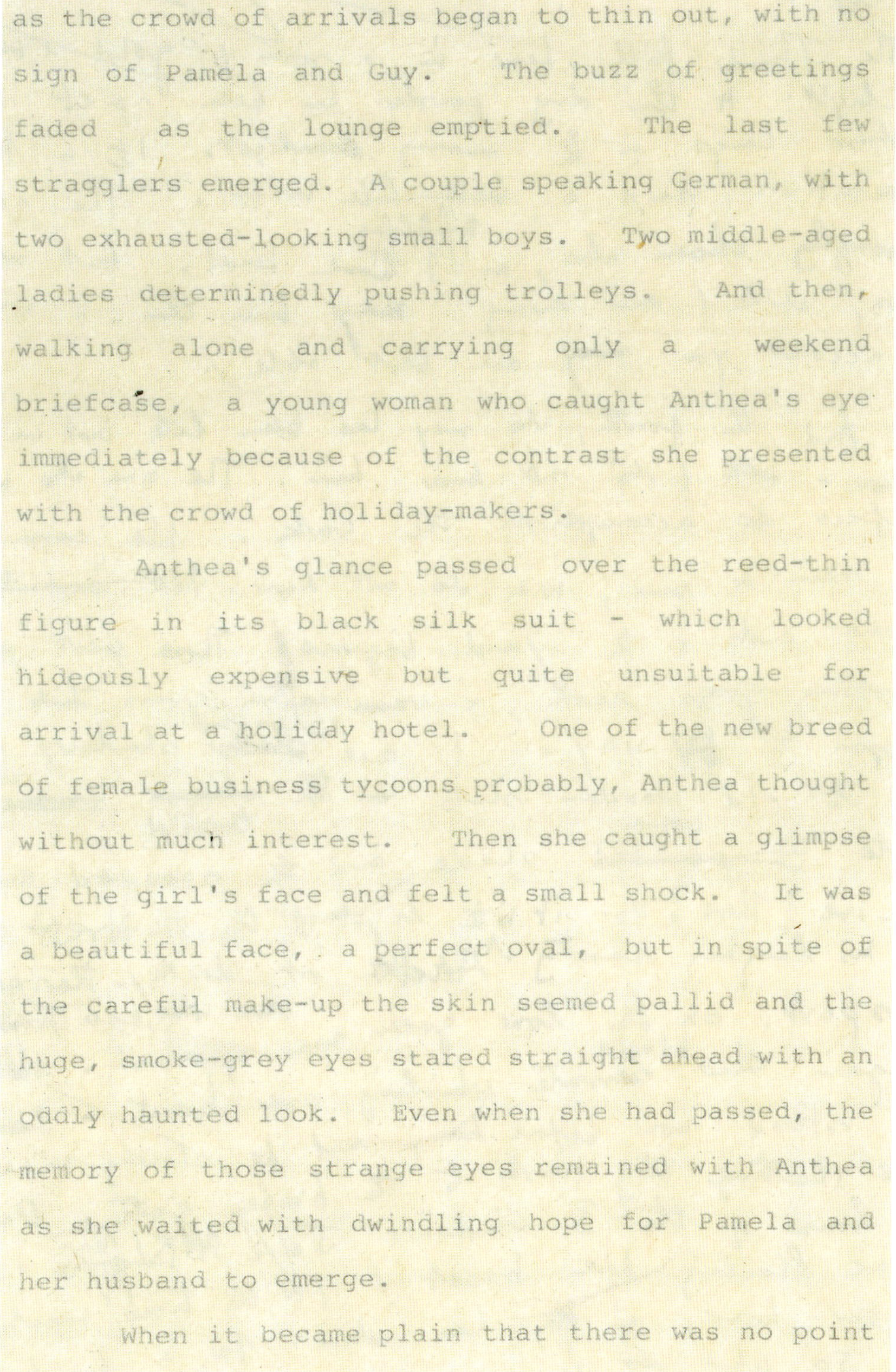

as the crowd of arrivals began to thin out, with no sign of Pamela and Guy. The buzz of greetings faded as the lounge emptied. The last few stragglers emerged. A couple speaking German, with two exhausted-looking small boys. Two middle-aged ladies determinedly pushing trolleys. And then, walking alone and carrying only a weekend briefcase, a young woman who caught Anthea's eye immediately because of the contrast she presented with the crowd of holiday-makers.

Anthea's glance passed over the reed-thin figure in its black silk suit - which looked hideously expensive but quite unsuitable for arrival at a holiday hotel. One of the new breed of female business tycoons probably, Anthea thought without much interest. Then she caught a glimpse of the girl's face and felt a small shock. It was a beautiful face, a perfect oval, but in spite of the careful make-up the skin seemed pallid and the huge, smoke-grey eyes stared straight ahead with an oddly haunted look. Even when she had passed, the memory of those strange eyes remained with Anthea as she waited with dwindling hope for Pamela and her husband to emerge.

When it became plain that there was no point

1. A Person in Love

2. A Married Person.

3. A Lawless Person.

4. An Erring Person

5. A benevolent person.

6 A protecting person.

7. A person of ideals

8. A person influenced by an obligation.

9. A person subjected to adverse conditions.

190 A Resentful person.

LL A person swayed by pretence.

12 A subtle person.

13 A person influenced by the occult and mysterious

14 A normal person.

15 Any person.

1. Engaging in a difficult enterprise when promised a reward for high achievement.

2. Falling in love at a time when certain obligations forbid love.

3. Seeking to demonstrate the power of love by a test of courage

4. Suffering an estrangement due to mistaken judgment.

5. Seeking by craftiness to escape misfortune.

6. Falling into misfortune through the wiles of a crafty schemer.

7. Falling into misfortune through mistaken judgment.

8. Seeking to save a person who is accused of transgression.

9. Facing a situation in which the misfortune of one greatly esteemed calls for courage and sagacious enterprise.

10. Living a lonely cheerless life and seeking companionship.

11. Seeking to conceal identity because of a lofty idealism.

12. Committing a mistake and seekin in secret to live down its evil results.

13. Forsaking cherished ambitions to carry out an obligation.

14, Seeking to overcome personal limitations in carrying out an enterprise.

15. Seeking retaliation for a wrong either real or fancied.

16. Finding (apparently) an object greatly coveted and obtaining (apparently) that object.

17 Being impelled by an unusual motive to engage in crafty enterprise.

18 Becoming involved in a mysterious complication and seeking to make the most of a bizarre experience.

19. Becoming aware of an important secret that calls for decisive action.

20 Being impelled by inordinate fancy to exercise mistaken judgment in a love affair.

21 Becoming involved in a hopeless love affair and seeking to make the best of a disheartening situation.

22 Confronting a situation in which courage and devotion alone can save the fortunes of the beloved

23 Finding a sustaining power in misfortune.

24 Being delivered from misfortune by one who, in confidence, confesses a secret of transgression.

25 Following a wrong course through mistaken judgment.

26 Secretly seeking to preserve another from danger.

27 Aiding another to hide from the world a fateful secret.

28 Resisting secretly from an honorable motive a mandate considered discreditable.

29 Embarking on an enterprise of insurrection in the hope of ameliorating certain evil conditions.

30 Embarking upon an enterprise in which one obligation is opposed by another obligation.

31 Seeking by unusual methods to conquer personal limitations.

32 Assuming the character of a criminal in a perfectly honest enterprise.

33 Devising a clever and plausible delusion in order to forward certain ambitious plans.

34 Seeking to test the value of a mysterious communication and become involved in strange complications.

35 Seeking to unravel a puzzling complication

36 Becoming involved in a love affair that encounters unforseen obstacles

37 Confronting a situation in which wealth is made conditional upon a certain course in a love affair.

38 Falling into misfortune through disloyalty in love

39 Bearing patiently with misfortunes and seeking to attain cherished aims honorably.

40 Rebelling against a power that controls personal abilities and holds them in subjection.

41 Becoming involved in a complication that has to do with mistaken judgment and suspicion.

42 Refusing to betray another's secret and calmly facing persecution because of the refusal.

43 Enlisting whole-heartedly in the service of a needy unfortunate and conferring aid of the utmost value.

44 Becoming involved in a complication that challenges the value of cherished ideals.

45 Finding an obligation at variance with ambition, inclination, or necessity.

46 Seeking to forward an enterprise and encountering family sentiment as an obstacle.

47 Assuming a fictitious character when embarking upon a certain enterprise

48 52 Encountering a would-be transgressor and seeking to prevent a transgression.

49 53 Engaging in an enterprise and then mysteriously disappearing.

50 54 Engaging in an enterprise and becoming involved with the occult and fantastic.

51 55 Being put to a test in which love will be lost if more material fortunes are advanced.

52 56 Meeting with misfortune and being cast away in a primitive environment.

53 57 Becoming involved with conditions in which misfortune is indicated.

54 58 Becoming the victim of mistaken judgment in carrying out an enterprise

55 59 Undergoing an experience that results in a remarkable character change.

56 60 Seeking against difficulties to realize a cherished ideal.

57 61 Falling into misfortune while seeking honorably to discharge an obligation.

58 62 Opposing the plans of a crafty schemer

59 63 Becoming involved through curiosity aroused by mystery in a strange enterprise.

60 64 Becoming involved in any sort of complication.

1. Pays a grim penalty in an unfortunate undertaking.

2. Emerges happily from a serious entanglement.

3. Foils a guilty plotter and defeats a subtle plot.

4. Undertakes a role that leads straight to catastrophe.

5. Emerges from a trying ordeal with sorely garnered wisdom.

6. Makes the supreme sacrifice in carrying out an undertaking.

7. Reverses certain opinions when their fallacy is revealed.

8. Achieves a spiritual victory.

9. Achieves success and happiness in a hard undertaking.

10 Meets with an experience whereby an error is corrected.

11 Discovers the folly of trying to appear other than as one is in reality

12 Rescues integrity from an entanglement

13 Comes to the blank wall of enigma

14 Meets any fate good or evil.

15 Achieves a character transformation

opposite 48. *Character, Situation, Outcome,* 2007.

CAPTURING A CONSCIOUSNESS

The making of an oral history life story recording with Simon Lewty
CATHY COURTNEY
2009

In his essay, "The Sadness of Dreams", Stuart Morgan says, in relation to the separate entities that made up the drawings in Simon Lewty's 1985 Serpentine Gallery exhibition, "no single rationale connects them". Whilst this may be true, it is equally the case that the shapes and figures were and are connected by a single consciousness, that of the artist. An oral history recording (however lengthy) is at best partial, incomplete and, to some extent random—the way a person speaks of the past on a glittering day when no mishaps have befallen them will be different from their delivery on the same subject in a drab light when they have a headache and have spent the morning trying to sort out an error on their income tax demand. Taking these qualifiers into account, a detailed life story recording made over a series of longish sessions spaced out over several years can nevertheless provide a unique insight into the mind—its constants and its changeability —of a single person.

I made recordings with Simon Lewty between 2006 and 2009 as part of an on-going project, *Artists' Lives*, which is based in the oral history section of The British Library and run by National Life Stories in association with Tate Archive. With the exception of two sessions that took place in the British Library, a pattern emerged whereby I would travel from London by train to Leamington Spa, where Lewty was based for part of the year. Mostly I arrived so that we could record for a stretch before lunch and then resume after a short break; usually I came away with four or five hours of 'conversation'. I place the word conversation in speech marks because, although the life story approach favoured by National Life Stories (which was founded in 1987 by the social historian Asa Briggs and the oral historian Paul Thompson) is *conversational* in character it is not, of course, a conversation as the word is usually understood. It is a controlled, and to some extent artificial, interaction between two people one of whom ideally says very little and the other of whom ideally says a great deal. The presence of the interviewer necessarily shapes the dialogue and influences the responses—oral evidence of a quite different kind would have been laid down had Lewty sat alone with a tape-recorder and, *pace* Samuel Beckett's *Krapp's Last Tape*, proceeded to speak a version of his life in whatever sequence and degree of completion he chose. The material would have been altered had he been interacting with an interviewer other than myself, and the fall of the kaleidoscope pattern would have varied again had the sessions been undertaken and completed, for instance, on consecutive days over two weeks at his other home and workplace which overlooks the seafront in Swanage.

There were many reasons for establishing *Artists' Lives* within the context of National Life Stories (NLS). One was a desire to ensure that artists were

49. *Mythe*, 2006.

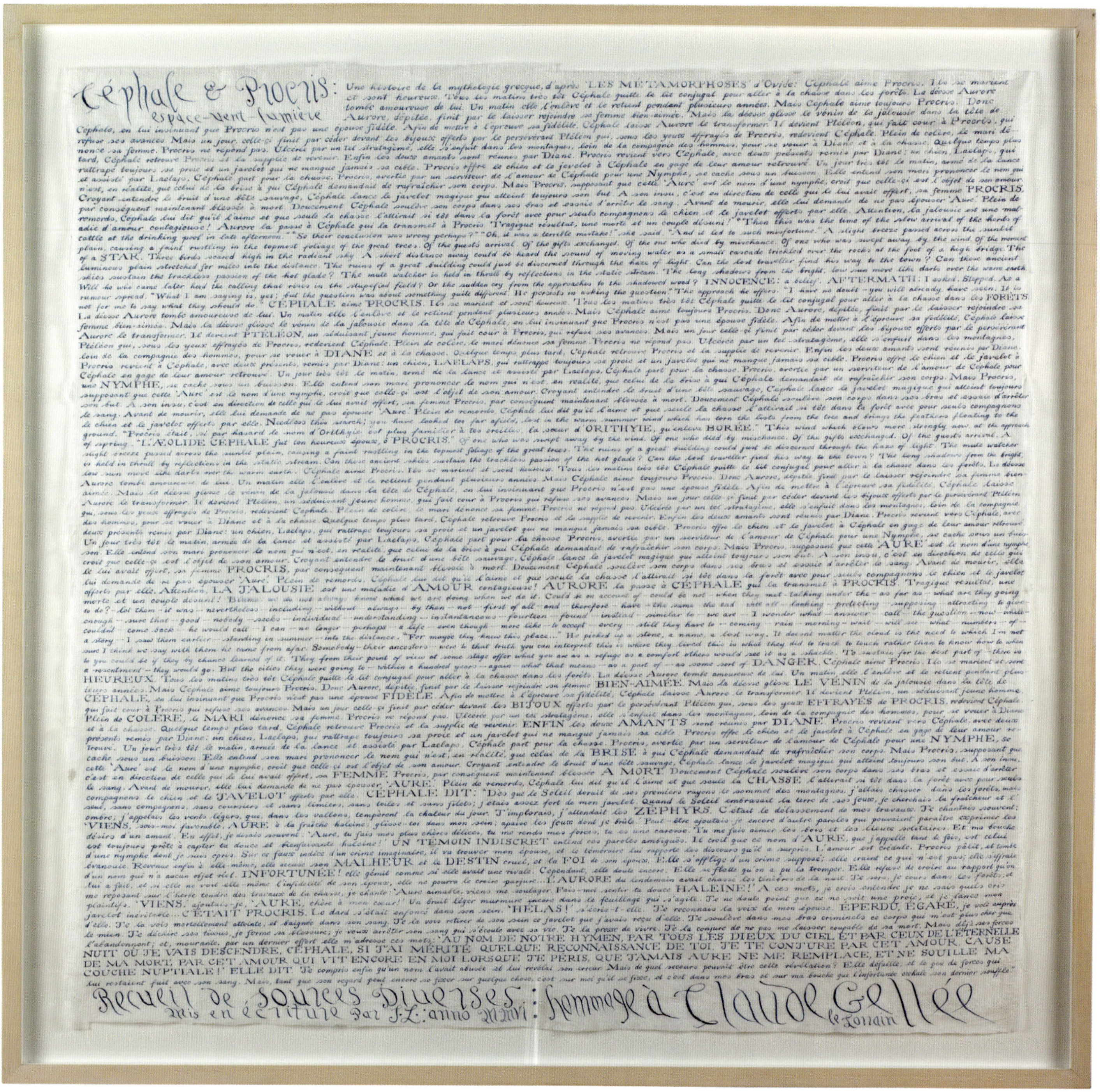

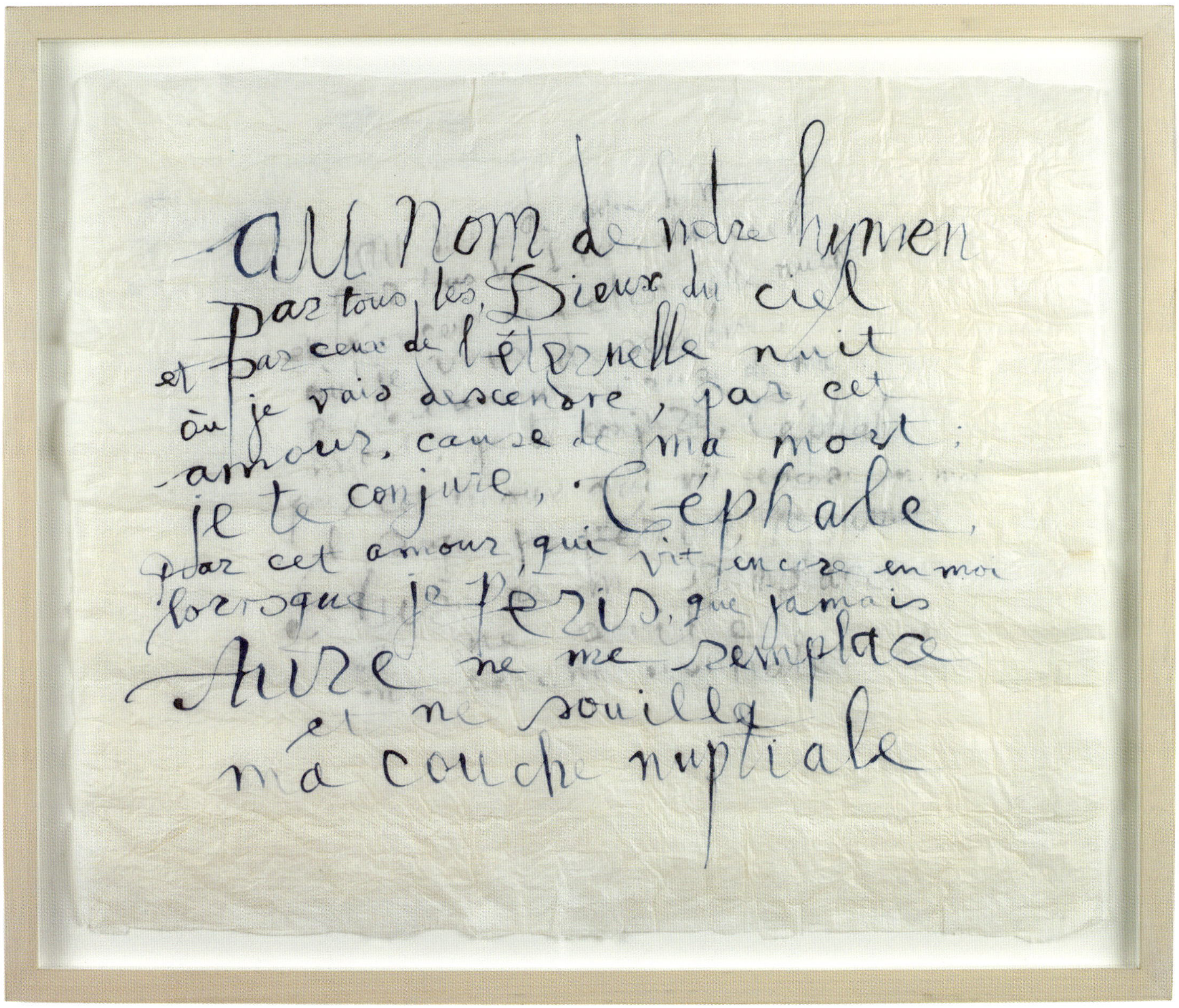
au nom de notre hymen
par tous les Dieux du ciel
et par ceux de l'éternelle nuit
où je vais descendre, par cet
amour, cause de ma mort ;
je te conjure, Céphale,
par cet amour qui vit encore en moi
lorsque je péris, que jamais
autre ne me remplace
et ne souille
ma couche nuptiale

50. *Echo*, 2006.

given a platform in which to lay down *in their own vocabulary* an account of their lives and work so that their use of language, their emphases, concerns and omissions could be publicly accessible alongside commentaries on them by art historians and other writers and broadcasters. Another aim was to pluck the artists from the tight enclosure of 'the art world' and to encourage them to tell their stories in the more truthful context of their place in the mixed society with which they interact in their day to day lives. NLS aims to make life stories with as broad a span of British society as it can within the constraints of its budgets (it is a charity) and the size of its team of interviewers; projects to date include *Living Memory of the Jewish Community*, *Lives in the Oil Industry*, *Food: From Source to Salespoint*, *An Oral History of the Post Office*, *Book Trade Lives* and *Architects' Lives*.

Although the content of every recording is singular and specific to the individual, the intended structure is broadly similar for all the projects, little different for an artist than for a steel worker, a postman or postwoman or a publisher's rep. The interviewer will aim to cover the marking points along a chronological spine which runs from before the subject's birth (by means of handed-down memories or other knowledge of forebears) and through childhood and schooling before the focus moves to training and the person's working life and adult relationships. Imaginary and emotional landscapes are every bit as important as geographical and physical manifestations. No topics are out of bounds—religious beliefs, attitudes to death, to sex, to money, to politics, property, clothes, food and football are all among the myriad topics likely to occur but, as in reality, these will be woven into and inseparable from the main thrust of the narrative which, in the case of the artist nearly always centres on his or her work.

To guard privacy, to encourage frankness and to protect against accusations of slander, everyone making a recording for NLS can close their material during their lifetime or for longer. (Lewty has chosen to do this and I have no intention of breaking this confidence; the details included in this essay are here with his blessing.) NLS' ambition is to lay down an unparalleled resource for future researchers, and the quality of captured discourse is as far from the sound bite as it is possible to reach. One of the great advantages of the life story is its willingness to encompass diversions and anecdotes—the chronological spine may often be near invisible to listeners and it is the interviewer's job to ensure that all the gaps are filled even if they do not occur in the expected order of the logical progression from birth to whatever age the interviewee happens to have reached. The flow might be interrupted by the need to follow a topic in especial depth or by something apparently haphazard. One vivid sequence in Lewty's recording, for example, concerns the passage of a diamond of sunlight as it moved slowly over the work in progress fixed to the wall behind the artist's seat in the room where we were talking. Whilst this might seem to some an irrelevance, it not only triggered a new level of discussion on a recurring theme concerning Lewty's fascination with time and its inherence in his work but also conjured an exceptionally vivid feel of Lewty's environment and his sensitivity to delicate changes within it. A potent sense of 'thereness' and of 'being in the moment' was evoked which, for the majority of listeners not invited or able to visit Lewty's studio, offers an exceptional substitute just as the whole recording permits entry into areas otherwise considered off-bounds in the normal flow of social interaction.

left 51. *First Spiral*, 2005.

middle 52. *Emerging Spiral*, 2005.

right 53. *Second Spiral*, 2005.

A recording made over the timespan of Lewty's contribution to *Artists' Lives* is able to elicit comment on the development of new work as well as a much more detailed account of the past oeuvre than is usually otherwise available. Even if the artworks under discussion are visible, the interviewer will try to elicit a description of each from the artist to ensure that a listener has not only the best chance of envisaging the work in question through the medium of words but also learns as much as possible about how the artist first perceived it and how it was constructed. (Inadvertently, these passages are often of enormous benefit to conservationists seeking to repair and maintain the artworks in question.) Sometimes, when describing the evolution of a particular piece, an artist will exclaim—"I hadn't realised that myself until I had to tell you," an exciting moment when the immediacy of the recording *becomes* history as well as *recounting* it by force of the speaker having to articulate a thought which until that instant had lain dormant and untouched by the tools of communication. These are instances of revelation for both speaker and listener, and the manner in which the artist 'recovers' and continues the narrative can sometimes be a subject of equal fascination.

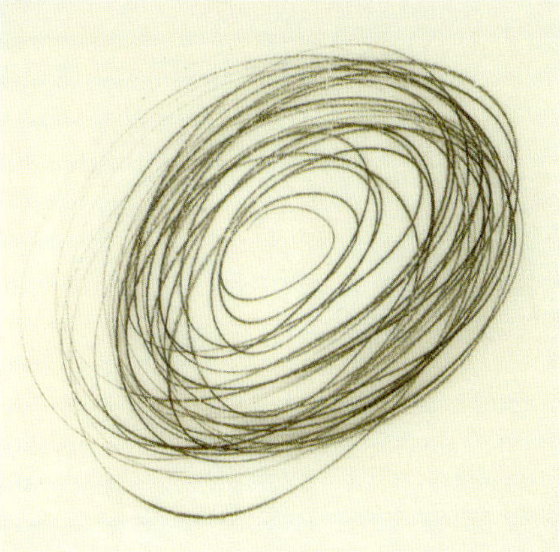

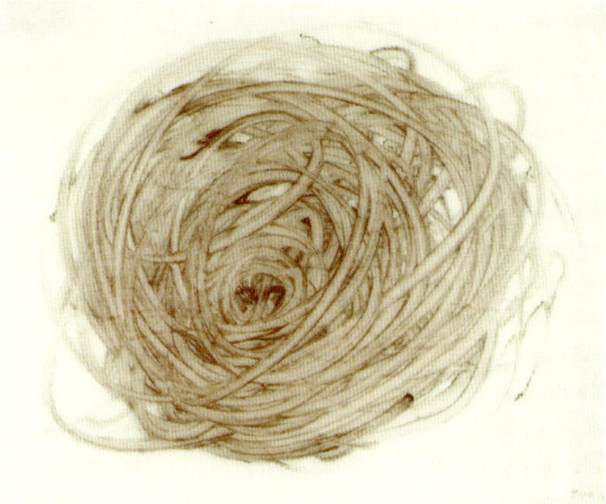

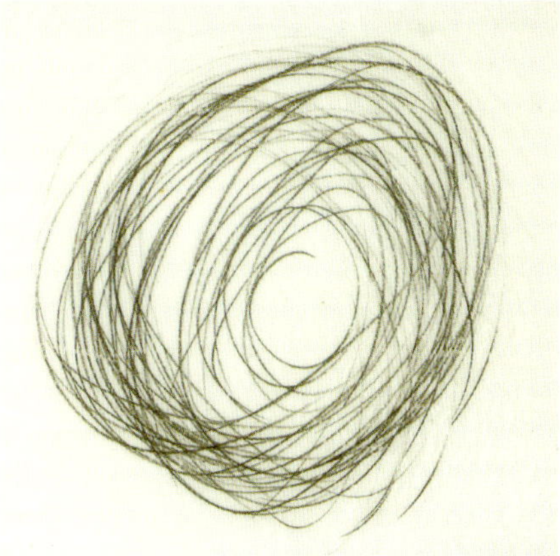

As well as the main phases of Lewty's development from his days as an art student onwards, each recording session picked up on work in progress including preparations for forthcoming shows with the Atrium Gallery, Bournemouth, one-man and group exhibitions at Art First (his London gallery since 1994), and several with Lacerta (an initiative started by Susan Michie which at various times has instigated out of London exhibitions and which is, according to Lewty, less of a formal grouping than "a manifestation of something—in its latest manifestation it's a publishing house with ISBN numbers" for which he has contributed a long essay on Michie's work, *Writing Silence*). At various points, the recording also captured Lewty's sudden re-acquaintance with works of his own which he hadn't seen for decades, when they resurfaced in the gallery or at auction, occasions when the interviewer could explore both the story of the picture being created and its impact on the maker on meeting it again. So that listeners can have the opportunity to compare the artist's words with the works themselves, care is taken to ensure that examples found in public collections are discussed in the recording and, where appropriate, the interviewer will take photographs of the studio to illustrate its state during particular sessions.

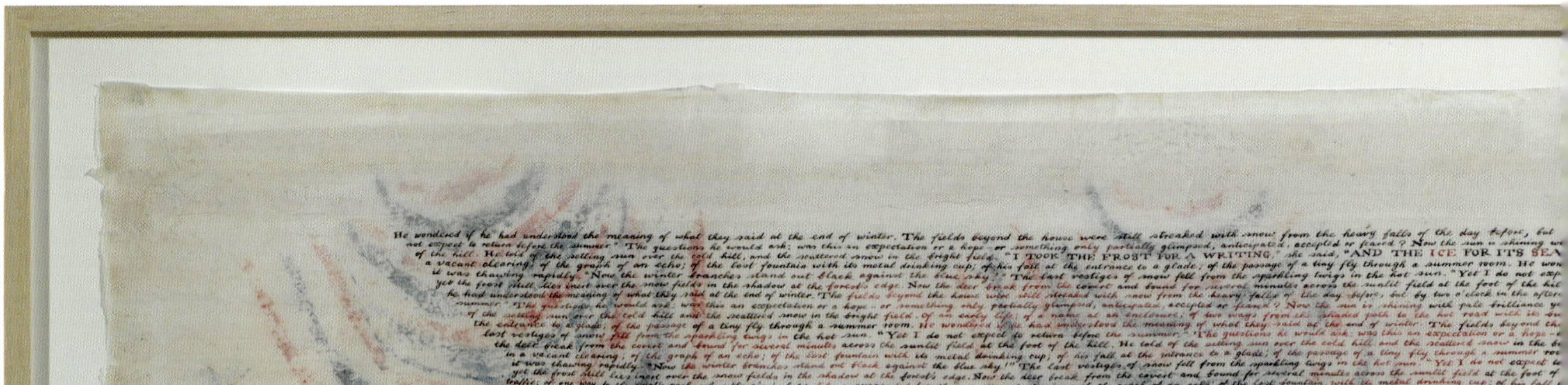
"I TOOK THE FROST FOR A WRITING," she said, "AND THE ICE FOR ITS SEAL."

54. *I took The Frost For A Writing, And The Ice For Its Seal*, 2004.

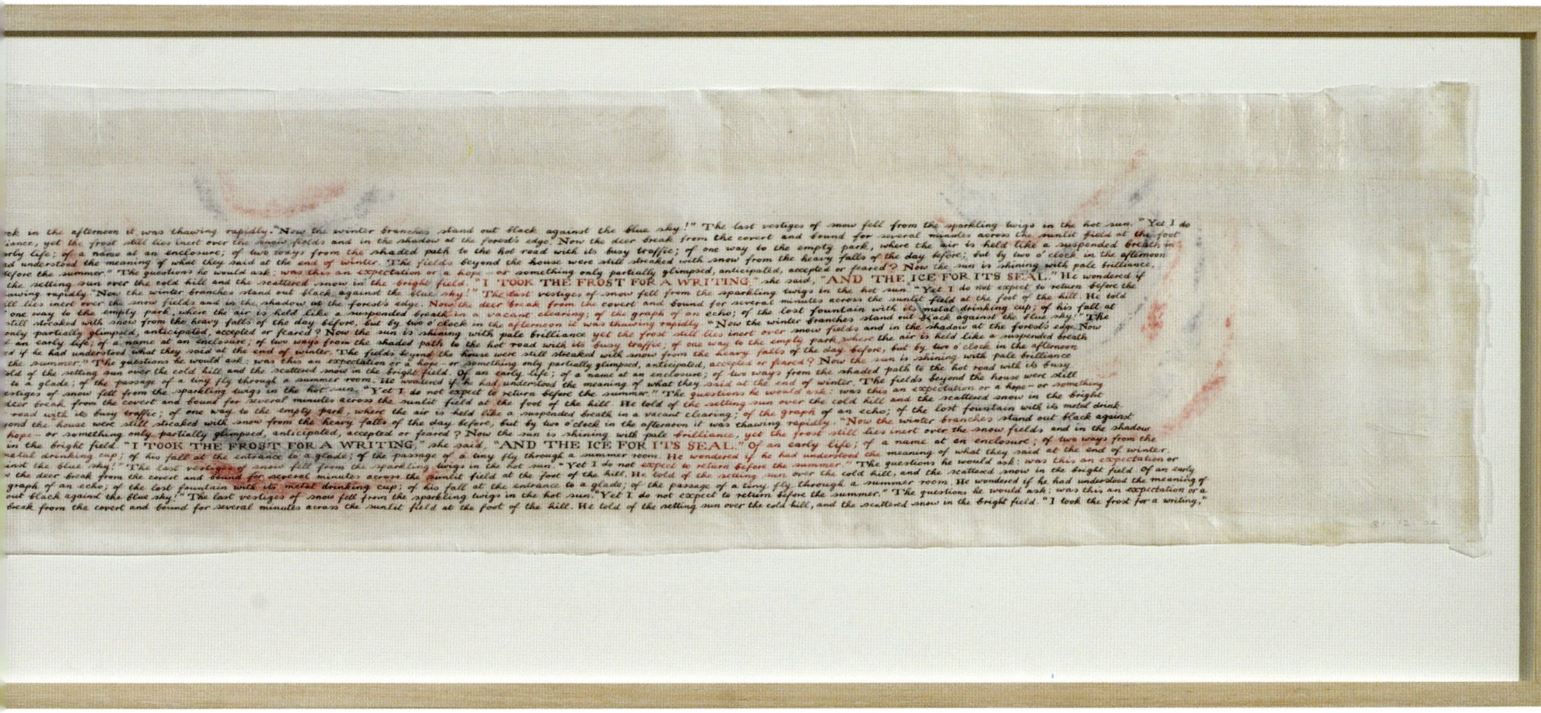

As Lewty is an artist known for the deployment of fragmentary and dislocated texts and visual allusions it may be a shock to some future researchers to discover his fluency and exceptional clarity as a speaker. His response to questions is unusually well structured, free from false starts and stumblings and, typically, complete. In addition to its many other facets, his recording suggests what a very fine teacher he must have been, given his ability to cut to the heart of the matter, whether the topic is his own work or that of another artist. Frequently our discussion would veer to a subject impossible for Lewty to anticipate—perhaps a long dead artist, perhaps a contemporary, or a writer or broadcaster—and he would be unfailing in offering an informed, intelligent, distilled, undogmatic response. His teaching, like other strands of his life, is otherwise largely undocumented but nevertheless was his main salary earning activity until he made the brave decision to stop completely at the age of 40 and risk the life of a full time artist. Thus there is a clear division between his earlier professional life —when he wrote a review for *Art Monthly* in 1978 the magazine described him as "a teacher and art historian"—and his resignation from Mid-Warwickshire School of Art in 1982, a topic which, naturally, is covered by his life story recording, but there are at least a dozen other turning points—whether a crucial discovery made accidentally through using a particular material, a suddenly perception of the connection between two things, or a line of thinking triggered through reading—which would be even more difficult or quite impossible for a future investigator to unearth were it not for Lewty's own testimony. In this way, the recording, whilst not in any way claiming to provide simplistic 'keys' to unlock meaning, can go a long way in stemming misinterpretation as well as in offering pointers for those who wish to follow them.

There is a disturbing sense of portent in some of Lewty's early work and in the themes which recur later on. Not only do the bursts of flame in the impacted, strangely related and detailed images of the early 1970s (plate 55) have an eerie foreboding of the 1988 fire at Anne Berthould's gallery that devoured an important body of his work, but the powerfully intimated presence of part-known, part-heard, off-stage voices seems directed forward to the loss which Lewty faced in 2004 when the untimely death of his only sibling, his sister, Deborah, two years his junior and his last surviving close relative, occurred within a short time of the demise of his mother and his brother-in-law. Unfashionably for a man (there seem to be frequent articles in the press about women actively choosing to remain single, but few about their counterparts) the artist, when not within his family household, has consciously opted to live alone. There are, therefore, no witnesses who could speak to a future biographer with first-hand intimate knowledge of Lewty's formative years, making it all the more urgent that his own recollections be preserved. Whilst he has long-lasting, important friendships with, amongst others, a circle of artists, writers and academics linked with the University of Warwick, and, as the recording recounts, adds new friends to this company when he encounters someone with whom he has territory in common, he is careful to establish boundaries and I suspect few have more than a hazy notion of the totality of his existence, let alone the intricacies of his intellectual world.

In case this sounds bleak, I should emphasise that one of the delights of making the recording with Lewty is the infectious way in which he conveys his intense excitement about life and his hungry enjoyment of the zones of existence with which he chooses to engage. He is a great *noticer* and responder—to ideas, to landscape, to light, texture and absurdity—and this bubbles through his life story. It's quite easy to understand why he chooses to remain within a tight geographic boundary—London, the Midlands, Dorset—and declares himself "allergic to travel" (a single trip to Chartres was enough to extinguish further *wanderlust*), needing silence and space to process his reactions since it is abundantly evident that he was full to bursting with the experiences he'd had by the time he was ten years old let alone with anything that's occurred in the more than five decades which have followed. His mode of living is a deliberate, creative solitude, and he is the most expert person I have come across at discarding what he doesn't need and protecting what is crucial to him. On the surface the rhythm of his years has been steady. In physical terms the most dramatic outward changes have related to a degree of restlessness in terms of exactly where he lives both in Leamington Spa and in Swanage and in the balance of time he spends in each, (which has been mutating back and forth like a private tide for nearly 30 years)—but the force of his considerable energy has been conserved for his internalised world. It is an atypical twenty-first century way of life, and all the more remarkable for it.

Just as Lewty's flair as a speaker permits the listener to imagine the images eaten up in the Anne Berthoud Gallery fire and thus fills in a vanished section from the jig-saw a future researcher may seek to complete, so he brings his family on stage in the recording. He does so with a generosity of spirit and an attitude of affectionate respect that ensures each person becomes a stand-alone figure rather than being viewed only in relation to himself, and does not presume to answer for them on subjects they didn't share with him, according them a proper complexity and dignity. His parents—Richard and Marjorie Lewty—are portrayed as three-dimensional human beings, each with their own past histories, battles and triumphs and not primarily in terms of whether they were a good or a bad father or mother. Indeed the figure of Marjorie, to whom Lewty was close until her death at 96, is one of the most intriguing characters to emerge, a woman who found herself in difficult circumstances and quietly and independently took responsibility for her life, reading and thinking her way towards a new way of being whilst all the time remaining outwardly in the same position as she had started. A practical and self-contained woman, part of her solution was to teach herself to become a writer and she turned herself into a successful Mills & Boon author without reneging on her role in the household, bringing in a welcome income (her books still earn royalties) at the same time as forging a largely private but nevertheless significantly redrawn fresh identity.

One can't help feeling that the example of Marjorie's disciplined commitment to her own field of creativity must have influenced her son and that there might be a connection between growing up with the sound of industrious typing and the fact that Lewty has always preferred to have his studios within the houses he has lived in and quickly gave up an attempt at an external workspace. This close binding together of work and home is another aspect that made a life story recording an appropriate medium for encompassing something of Lewty's world. When he works today in the modest rented home he keeps up in Leamington, the muffled sounds he is

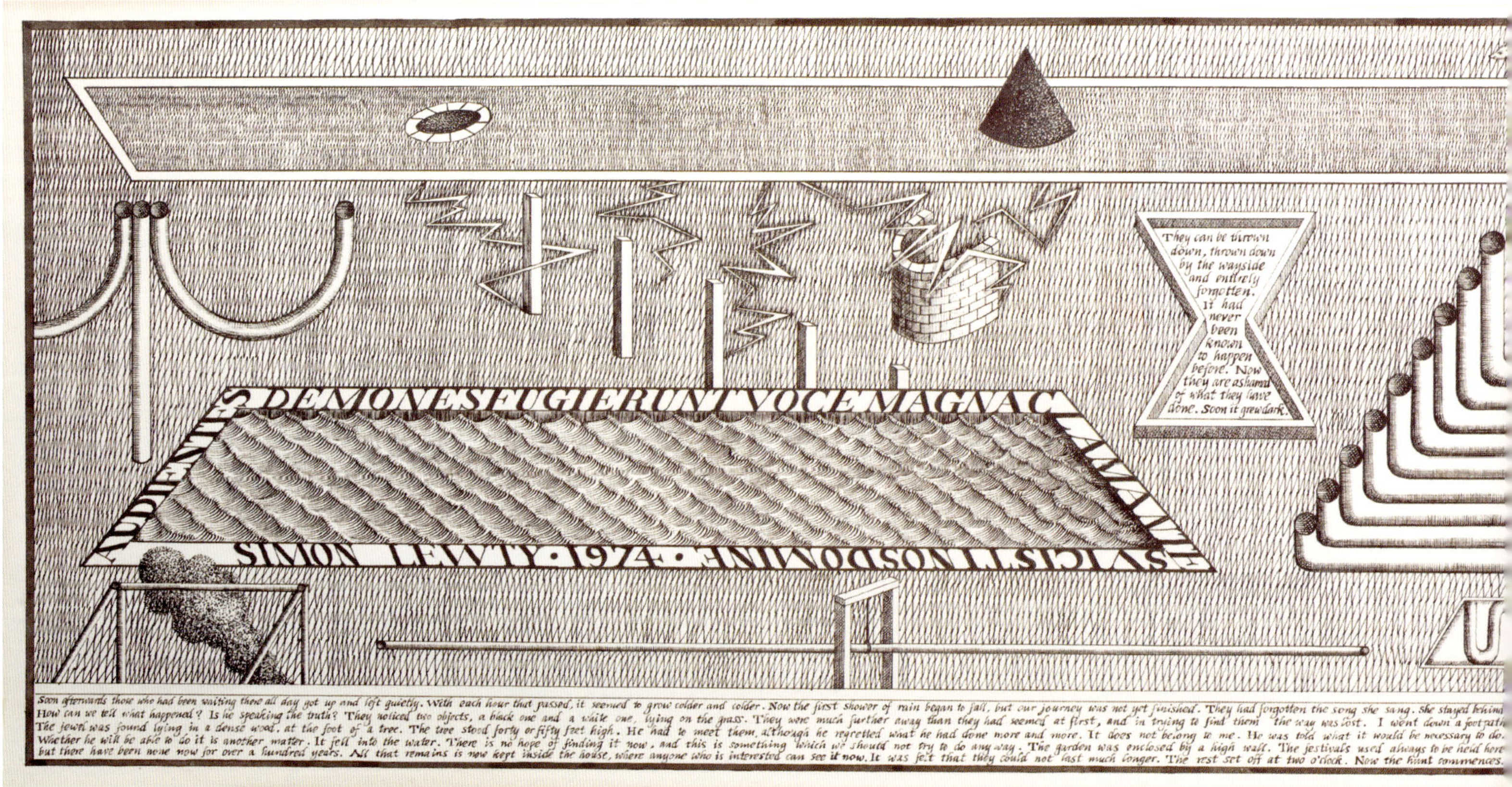
They can be thrown down, thrown down by the wayside and entirely forgotten. It had never been known to happen before. Now they are ashamed of what they have done. Soon it grew dark.
AUDIENTES DEMONES FUGIERUNT VOCE MAGNA CLAMANTES VICISTI NOS DOMINE
SIMON LEWTY · 1974 ·
Soon afterwards those who had been waiting there all day got up and left quietly. With each hour that passed, it seemed to grow colder and colder. Now the first shower of rain began to fall, but our journey was not yet finished. They had forgotten the song she sang. She stayed behind
How can we tell what happened? Is he speaking the truth? They noticed two objects, a black one and a white one, lying on the grass. They were much further away than they had seemed at first, and in trying to find them the way was lost. I went down a footpath
The jewel was found lying in a dense wood, at the foot of a tree. The tree stood forty or fifty feet high. He had to meet them, although he regretted what he had done more and more. It does not belong to me. He was told what it would be necessary to do.
Whether he will be able to do it is another matter. It fell into the water. There is no hope of finding it now, and this is something which we should not try to do anyway. The garden was enclosed by a high wall. The festivals used always to be held here
but there have been none now for over a hundred years. All that remains is now kept inside the house, where anyone who is interested can see it now. It was felt that they could not last much longer. The rest set off at two o'clock. Now the hunt commences.

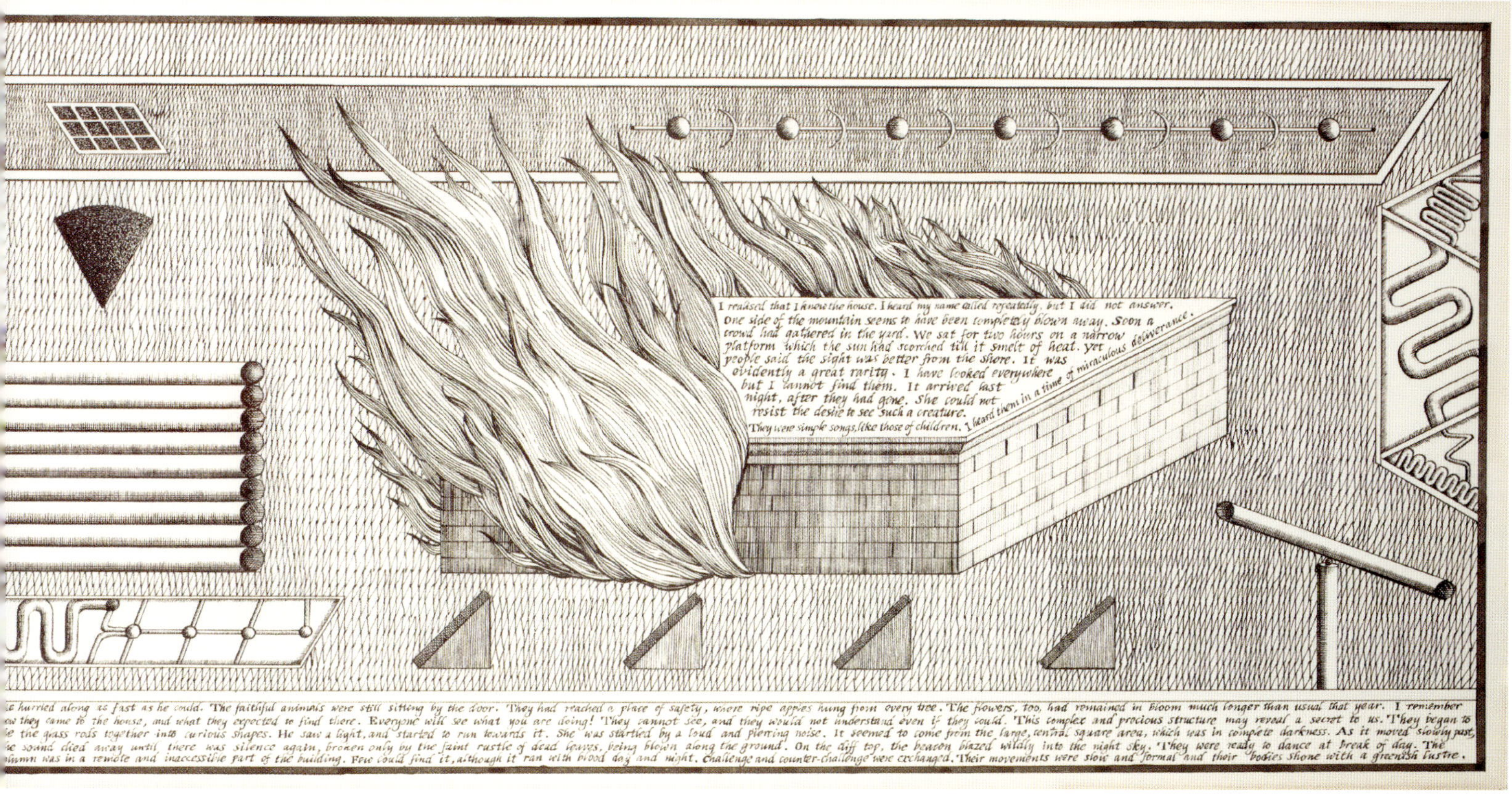
I realised that I knew the house. I heard my name called repeatedly, but I did not answer.
One side of the mountain seems to have been completely blown away. Soon a
crowd had gathered in the yard. We sat for two hours on a narrow
platform which the sun had scorched till it smelt of heat. yet
people said the sight was better from the shore. It was
evidently a great rarity. I have looked everywhere
but I cannot find them. It arrived last
night, after they had gone. She could not
resist the desire to see such a creature.
They were simple songs, like those of children.
I heard them in a time of miraculous deliverance.
hurried along as fast as he could. The faithful animals were still sitting by the door. They had reached a place of safety, where ripe apples hung from every tree. The flowers, too, had remained in bloom much longer than usual that year. I remember
they came to the house, and what they expected to find there. Everyone will see what you are doing! They cannot see, and they would not understand even if they could. This complex and precious structure may reveal a secret to us. They began to
the glass rods together into curious shapes. He saw a light, and started to run towards it. She was startled by a loud and piercing noise. It seemed to come from the large, central square area, which was in complete darkness. As it moved slowly past,
sound died away until there was silence again, broken only by the faint rustle of dead leaves, being blown along the ground. On the cliff top, the beacon blazed wildly into the night sky. They were ready to dance at break of day. The
was in a remote and inaccessible part of the building. Few could find it, although it ran with blood day and night. Challenge and counter-challenge were exchanged. Their movements were slow and formal and their bodies shone with a greenish lustre.

most likely to hear are those from the small business run by the owner of the property in the lower part of the building; once again, companionable evidence of a purposeful activity that does not encroach on his own. Recently rediscovering pages from early drafts of one of her novels given to him long ago as scribble paper, Lewty has made work incorporating sections of Marjorie's text (plates 46 and 48), the visual value of the typescript, the aging of the paper and his own markings taking their place naturally within his habit of incorporating found scraps of writing picked up in the street or lifted (often photocopied) from annotated books, sometimes his own, sometimes found in charity shops. If the inclusion of Marjorie's papers marries seamlessly with his established practice, it nevertheless also weights the work with an especial anchor and reinforces the undercurrent of a dialogue between the artist and other—always displaced—voices for which he provides another chance of being 'heard'.

Like any child, Lewty's early history bore the imprint of characters he would either never know or would encounter only whilst he was too young to decipher their significance for him. ("You must rear him", was his maternal great-grandmother's startling instruction to Marjorie on learning of his health at birth, a reference to her own children, not all of whom survived and amongst whom choices had to be made as to whom should be favoured when nourishment was limited; a family Bible from Lewty's father's side of the family lists the children who died in infancy.) When Lewty was born, in 1941 in Sutton Coldfield, a lot of embodied history lived in close proximity in the house as, in addition to her husband and first child, Marjorie was caring for Lewty's maternal great-grandmother, his grandmother and for his elderly great-uncle, Arthur Cox, a watercolourist and painter in oils and a former draftsman on a Liverpool newspaper. Given the method of indirect engagement that Lewty has come to perfect, it is perhaps significant that he *hasn't* got his own recall of Cox (who died in 1942) but learnt about him from the dual sources of family memories and the body of work which Cox left behind in the form of paintings and, crucially, two 1845 hand-written books of poems, stories and other texts interspersed with pen and ink drawings. The books are a legacy of the Pens, Ink & Paper Club of which one of Cox's forebears had been a member, and Lewty, aged about nine when he first encountered the Victorian books, remembers being fascinated. In his grandmother, Mabel Lobb's, rooms, an environment with her own furniture and very distinct atmosphere from the rest of the home and to which access was differently modulated, Lewty discovered Cox's box of watercolours and learnt of his great-uncle's passion for Turner. Now the owner of the *Pens, Ink & Paper* Club books (pp. 155–156), Lewty still delights in them, and his recording explores their possible influence on him as well as his feelings for two miniature early nineteenth century portrait panels of ancestors on his father's side and a plate, perhaps made for Wedgewood, decorated by a paternal uncle who worked as a painter of ceramics.

An important feature of NLS' recordings is their ability to re-create the period of each interviewee's formative years. It is otherwise often difficult for a generation even only slightly younger to grasp how quickly the world changes. Already, there are young adults who are surprised to be told that there hasn't always been a tunnel under the Channel linking England to France, and, for researchers brought up in an age where television and the internet are taken for granted, accounts such as Lewty's are an important reminder of how local a child's world could be in Britain in the years following the Second World War and of the consequent potent impact on the imagination that books, nearby objects and the surrounding environment could have with their intimations of the wider society. (Passing details like the mention of a domestic fad for sun-ray lamps can summon up a whole decade to those who shared those years and introduce new notions to those who did not.) Crucial to Lewty's nascent perceptions of the universe, was the wartime purchase his mother made from a door to door salesman of *The New Book of Knowledge*, a set of volumes that threw together entries on history, philosophy, politics, natural sciences, arithmetic equations and a mix of other unrelated information beside line drawings and pictures whose varied subjects were given a unity of scale by their relationship to the typeface (plate 56).[1] The series was a vital companion to Lewty when he was ill for a long period aged between six and seven, an experience which left him out of sync with his contemporaries with whom he was never to be much in tune again. Asked by a teacher what he wished to be when he grew up, Lewty answered, "Either Poet Laureate or Astronomer Royal".

Lewty's intense relationship with books has never waned. By the time he was ten he had a set of oil paints and, in conjunction with his early experiments with the paintbrush, was devouring illustrated books on art whenever he could lay his hands on them. After the family moved to Leamington Spa in 1950 (his dentist father was to establish the in-house practise for ICI), the municipal Library played a pivotal role in developing Lewty's awareness (particularly by providing access to *The Faber Gallery* series published in the 1950s) in tandem with visits to the town's art gallery and to the larger collections in Birmingham's Museum & Art Gallery and the Barber Institute. His interest in Samuel Palmer, Paul Nash, William Blake, Paul Klee and Giorgio de Chirico began before he was a teenager, largely triggered through reproductions in books and reading about the ideas underlying their work. There were no art classes at Warwick School after the age of 11, where Lewty was a fish out of water and deeply unhappy even though his talent for music theory and the clarinet led his tutor to hope he might make a career in music. Declaring himself to have been "resistant to anything but self-education", Lewty left school at 16, dodging the suggestion of others that he study languages at university, and was accepted at Leamington Spa art school (which was subsequently transmuted into Mid-Warwickshire School of Art), partly thanks to a body of paintings he'd made between 1952 and 1957, mainly still lives and landscapes, work surprising not only for its proficiency but also for the scope of its ambition and the reflected sophistication of the child's awareness of what other artists had been trying to achieve in the reproductions he had pored over with such care. Some of his early images remain part of Lewty's collection and gave rise to a section of his recording pinpointing the circumstances in which they were made and discussing his assessment of them at the time and in retrospect.

Fans of the mature Lewty's handwritten text works may be surprised to learn that the calligraphy classes on the Intermediate Diploma in Art & Design course on which he was enrolled were not among his favourites. Studied alongside anatomy, perspective, plant drawing, life drawing, 'figure comp', lithography, fabric design, pottery, sculpture and painting (but not in oils until late in the three year course), calligraphy and lettering were skills Lewty never expected to use and he cheerfully joined in with his classmates'

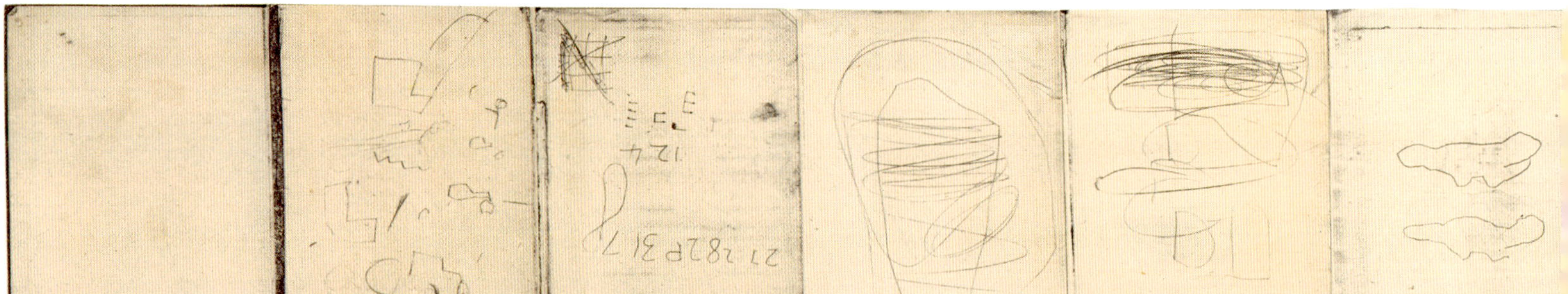

21 282P 31 7
124
As shells rise in ploughland, the glinting scales of mica rise in light, the wet light of parkland at the edge of the city, where burnt gorse fragments lie scattered at his feet. TO TOUCH IN SUCH A STILLNESS,
TOUCH OTHERS, TO TOUCH THE SILENT TREE.
"The book opens, and the long, impalpable story begins...
A PROMISE MADE, A SECRET KEPT.
THEIR ONLY ECHO A STIRRING IN FIELDS AND ROADS, THEIR ONLY PROMISE A LIFE.
FLUX OF LIGHT: GREY KING AND STAR QUEEN IN DAWN AND SUNSET GLOW, IN WASTE DAY AND RADIANT NIGHT.
THRUST, THE ANGUISH OF PURSUIT, THE WONDERING PEARL IN THE WAY.
In his bed the thought came upon him. He came up the road in sunshine and in frost.
OF CHANGE.
OF SEDIMENTATION.
THE YOUNG CHILD'S MYSTERY of altered lanes and streets.
IN SPRING the steam rushed out in a white cloud, and disappeared over the wall. IN SUMMER
IN AUTUMN the sun shone over the paths and the waters disappeared into the ground. IN WINTER they came to a wooden shed which was used as a store.
THAT THE CREATURE WAS ALIVE.
I would have told more, but the garden can now only be seen occasionally, UNDER SUN AND RAIN.
The moon shone brightly. The fields were covered in frost.
A stuffed crocodile hung from the ceiling of the hall.
THE MILK WAS POURED INTO A LARGE SAUCEPAN
PUT TO BOIL ON A GAS COOKER. HE HAD TO WALK UP AND DOWN THE ROAD. A THISTLE GREW IN A CRACK IN THE PAVING STONES OUTSIDE THE STATION ENTRA

56. *Sequence From Childhood*, 2002.

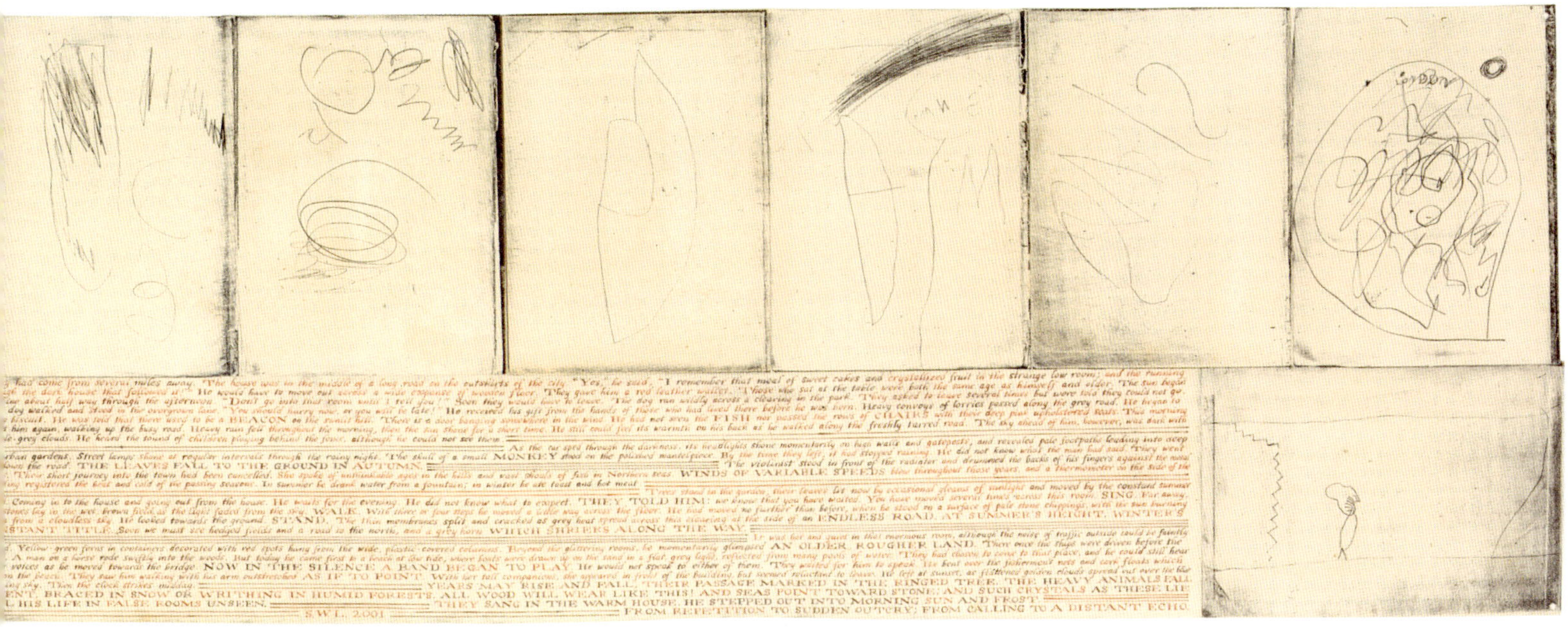

Lower left detail of 56. *Sequence From Childhood*, 2002.

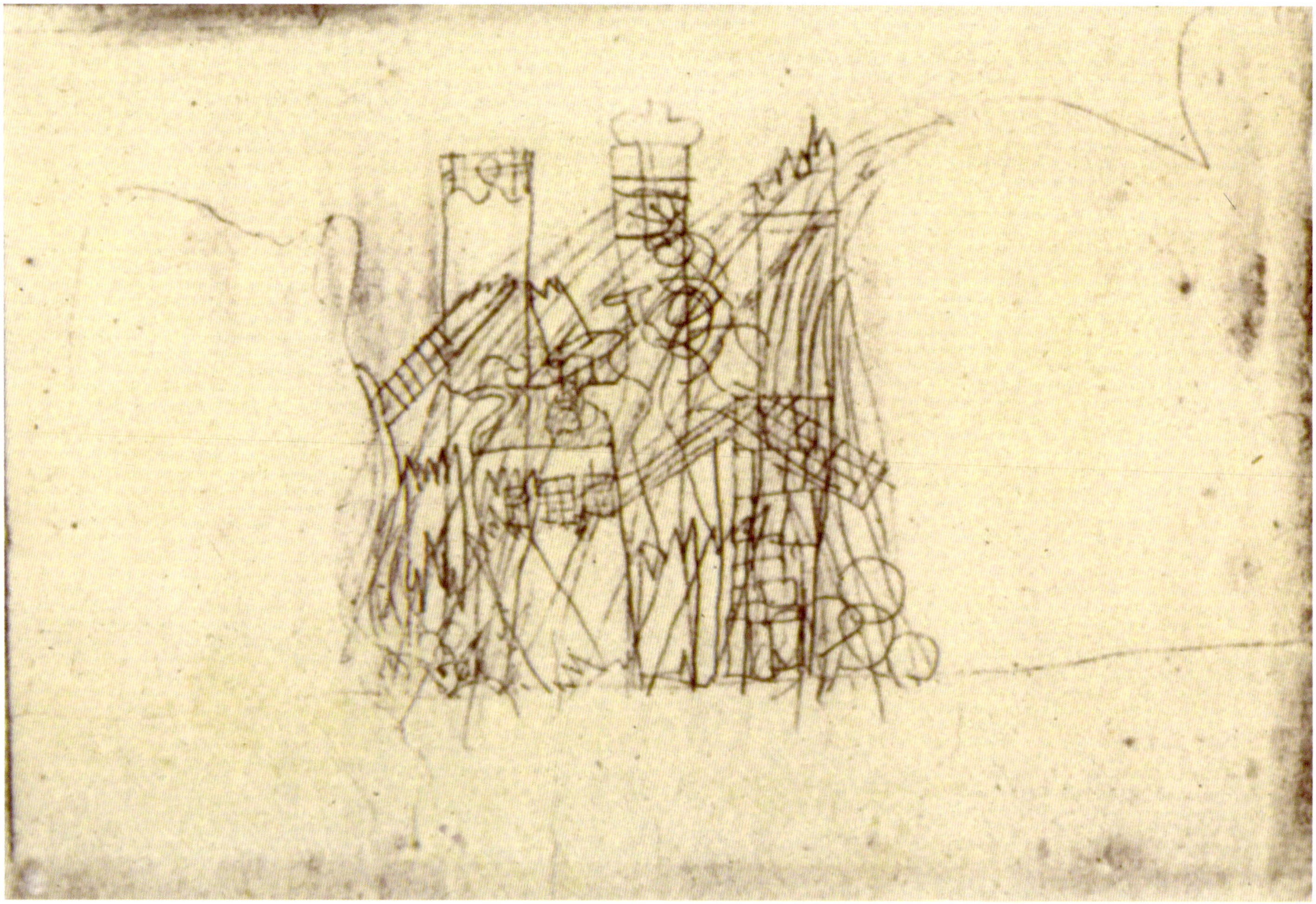

furtive rebellion in writing obscene words in ornate lettering when fulfilling the drudgery of exercises in historic script with a nib pen. In fact, the style which Lewty deploys in his current work has less to do with his formal training than with his natural handwriting although in the past he has used a version of italics derived from his student days. Among the richest passages of his recording are the parts in which he relishes the pleasures he now takes in forming particular letters, explores the nuances of the shapes of words written in French (for his 2006 *Mythe* (plate 49), *Echo* (plate 50), *Cephalus & Procris*), explains his use of sudden capitals mid-sentence or luxuriates in the contrasting textures of HB lead pencils and Derwent crayons. During the course of the recording he purchased an old Adler typewriter, a model whose keys had been manufactured to imitate handwritten script (plate 66), and spoke acutely on the piquant contradictions within the consequent impersonal-personal typeface the machine engenders, of his fascination with the uniformity and neutrality of typed words compared to his handwritten texts, and of his experience of typing on tissue paper ("like writing a whisper"). The recording also captures the clack of Lewty at work on the keyboard, an appropriately strange concert as well as an indicator of his typing speed. Not many months after he acquired the Adler, a subsequent

Lower right detail of 56. *Sequence From Childhood,* 2002.

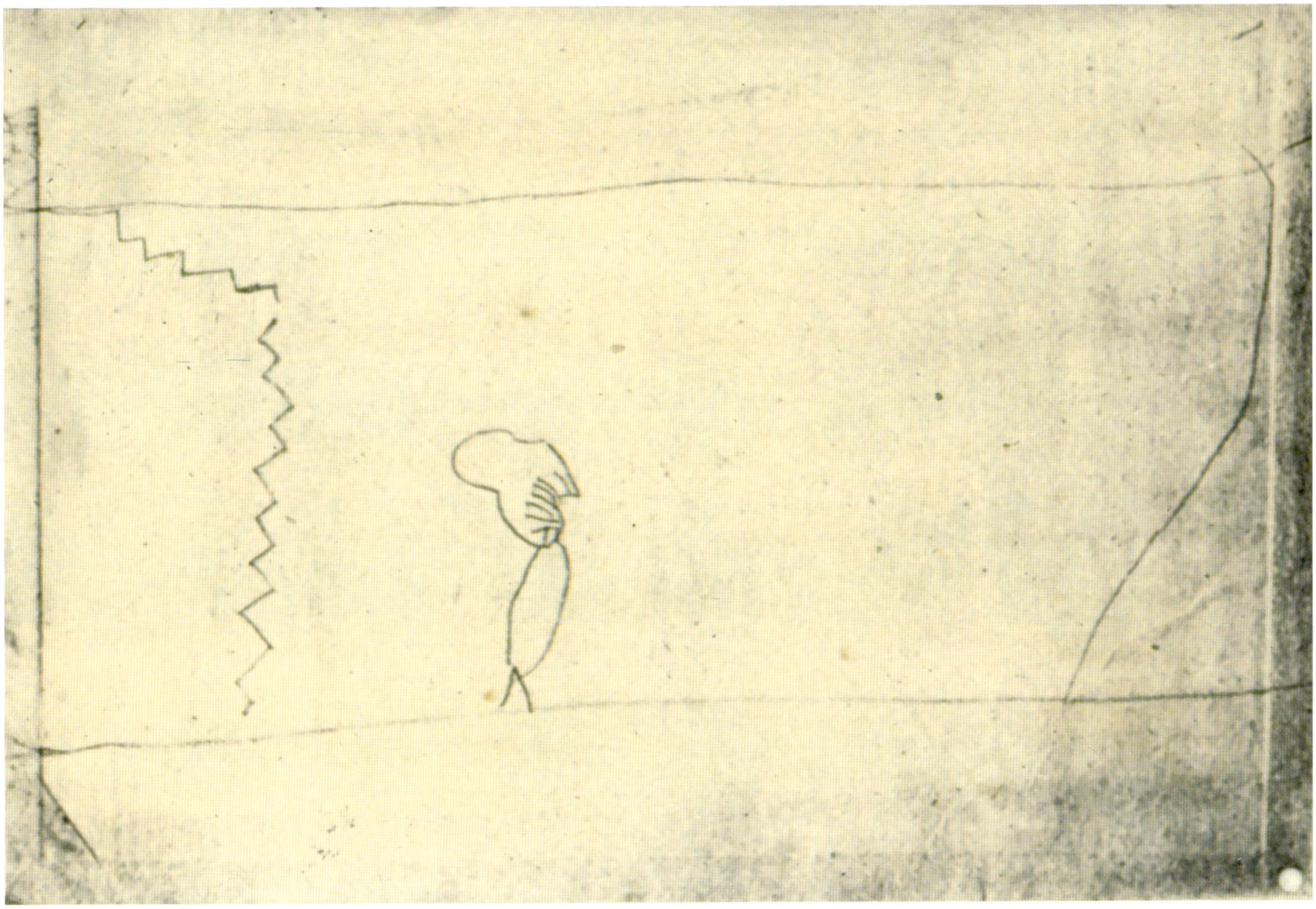

recording session documented the artist's description of his first use of Secretary script and his reasons for choosing this sixteenth century 'hand', whilst the fruit of this new labour (a work approximately 122 x 122 cm, entitled *Passing Days and Nights of Oblivion Will Drain Reason Before the Strength of the Flower*) had its first airing in a 2008 selected group show, Dialogue, at Art First (plate 67).

As well as the classes Lewty attended along with his fellow art students at Leamington School of Art, he taught himself Art and Art History to 'A' level standard (there was no-one otherwise to supervise him) and successfully passed these exams. At the stage of his course when students were to specialise, Leamington offered other options but not Lewty's choice, Fine Art, as a result of which he applied to and was accepted at Hornsey School of Art and moved to London during term times. These two years, and a further 12 months which Lewty spent in London in 1964–1965 after a spell teaching in Leamington, are the only parts of his life which the artist describes as lonely, yet they were also fertile, not only in terms of his own achievements but also because of his exploration of Cork Street and other commercial galleries and hours spent in the National Gallery, the Tate and the British

Museum, building on the occasional forays he had made on student trips from Warwickshire and laying the foundations for the many return visits he has made ever since. Delineating his Hornsey years as his 'Sickert phase', Lewty lived at least two lives, producing the prescribed work at the art school, where he learnt more of how to use oil paint and, in private in his lodgings, experimenting with pure abstraction. His teachers included Jesse Cast—a product of Tonks' era at the Slade—David Tindle, John Hoyland and Heinz Koppel, the latter being his tutor and a man particularly out of sympathy with the developments in Lewty's work which most excited his student. Happily, Koppel's response was balanced by the encouragement Lewty received from the Head of Fine Art, Maurice de Sausmarez.

An advantage of the NLS oral histories is that they can delve into the content of an artist's bookshelf and, as well as exploring current reading, can trigger discussion of long ago published catalogues and books and trace those titles which have had lasting impact. Jung was amongst the authors who captivated Lewty as a student at Hornsey (not least for the diagrams amongst the prose) and he also read Thoreau and Emerson at this period, and in recent years was to return to Emerson on the subject of the circle and the spiral. My conversation with Lewty threw up the importance to him of the catalogue for the Tate's 1964 *Painting and Sculpture of a Decade 1954–1964*, the exhibition being the first occasion on which he encountered the paintings of many of the American Abstract Expressionists in reality as opposed to reproduction, and saw them in the context of European modern masters and younger British artists. This Gulbenkian-funded exhibition had two curators, Alan Bowness and Laurence Gowing, the former being a fellow contributor to *Artists' Lives*; one of the most valuable aspects of the British Library oral history archive is the opportunity it provides (via the computer search tool of the summaries of all the recordings) to make cross-references between individual recordings and to gain multiple perspectives on the same exhibitions, incidents, topics and people. The arrival of the American abstract painters in Britain in the 1950s produced a particularly interesting dislocation, when past 'certainties' were dislodged and, in many senses, created a rare equality amongst art tutors and art students in their shared confrontation with a new pictorial language. Although Lewty is too young to have seen the 1950s London shows, his testimony is amongst those providing an insight into the influence of this shift as it continued its steady seep into the following decade, and his words therefore take their place within the collective history of the period.

Lewty's own immediate decades following his return to Leamington are amongst the most hidden in terms of outward signs of the changes in his work, a period on the surface accounted for by his teaching commitments and with few public signs to indicate the flow of experiment that his studio hours produced. In this sense the recording has an important role to play in asking the artist to reconstruct thinking processes, false starts, moments of breakthrough and something of the texture of the long, out of sight period of gestation before the sudden change in pace and reputation that followed hard upon his decision to sever his links with teaching and commit fully to life as a practicing artist. Indeed, we need Lewty's explanation in order to understand how two distinct periods—before and after his 1984 show at Birmingham's Ikon Gallery—link together as the previously little known artist (whose work had hardly been seen since an exhibition in 1968) became a John Moores Prizewinner in 1985 with a choice of two London art dealers (deciding on Berthoud rather than Edward Totah) and a three-person exhibition at the Serpentine shared with the photographer Fay Godwin and the sculptor, Richard Deacon. His buyers began to embrace distinguished collections such as the Ruth and Marvin Sackner Archive of Concrete and Visual Poetry, Miami Beach, and the Victoria and Albert Museum, and Lewty has never been without an energetic and supportive gallery since. (The economics of surviving as an artist are among the topics which the oral histories are well placed to elucidate; in Lewty's account the impact of the 1980s crisis at Lloyds of London on sales has an especial resonance in the financially troubled state in which we find ourselves today.) If catalogues and other published data provide the armature of these years, it is Lewty's spoken narration that fills in the muscle and flesh, a narrative that the future can interrogate and question, agree or disagree with, but nevertheless must acknowledge as the primary first-hand authority on the subject.

Ever since Vasari wrote *The Lives of the Artists* (and probably before), there has been great interest in the relationship between the life lived and the art made, and the twenty-first century is proving no different. What has since changed is the gift of technology that allows us, and each future generation, to hear the artist's version of events direct with our own ears and to assess this account alongside the distilled opinions and reactions of other commentators. Thanks to Lewty's patience, his honesty and his skills as a speaker, those seeking to understand more about him, his work and the sources behind it have an unparalleled document covering the many phases of his output and the landscapes—both evident and internal—that have fuelled and continue to feed his activities.

1. These volumes were also a repository for my earliest drawings and scribbles, made on the end papers. This 'archive' from childhood survived, embedded in the books, and in 2002 I used some of its imagery in *Sequence from Childhood* (plate 56). I don't think my early efforts are exceptional. Many children draw inside books. Years passed without my giving them any thought, until one day I rediscovered them and suddenly saw that they linked up with the present and I could use them. It was an unforgettable moment (SL).

57. *The Work of a Dismissed Servant*, 1990.

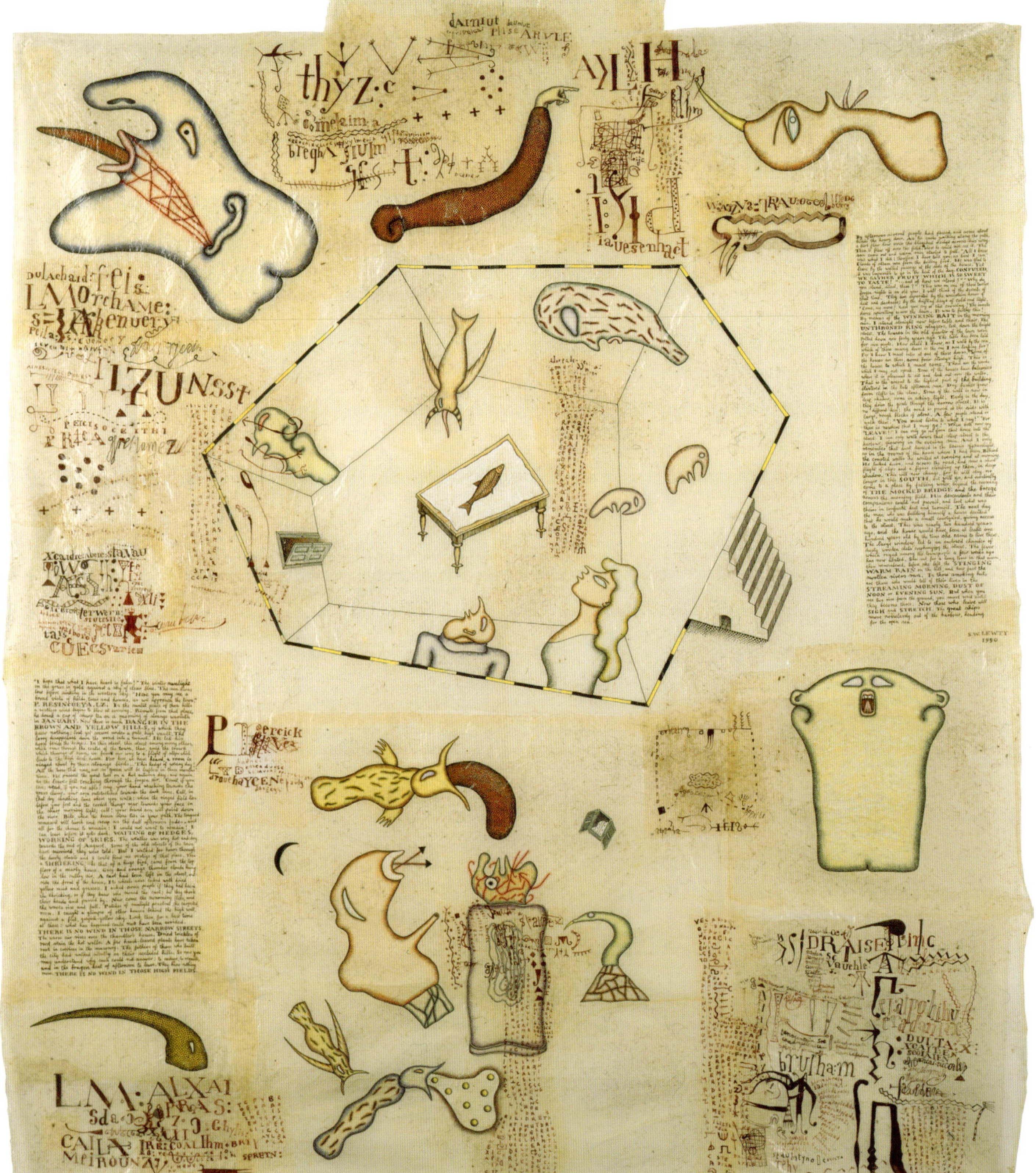

PITT RIVERS MUSEUM

CATHY COURTNEY/SIMON LEWTY
2009

The following is an edited extract from Simon Lewty's recording with Cathy Courtney for Artists' Lives, *an oral history project at the British Library.*

CC Could you tell me about your association with the Pitt Rivers Museum in Oxford?

SL The Pitt Rivers is a unique collection, the ethnographic branch of the University Museum. I was contacted by an artist called Chris Dorsett, who'd seen my work and wrote saying he was getting together an exhibition to be called The Upturned Ark, which would involve artists working as individuals—not as a group—being invited to go to the Pitt Rivers, to liaise with one of the curators there, and to be able to go out of hours to look through the reserve collections, to go through all those drawers and cupboards and things and to do a piece inspired by one's experience. It was a very open brief and the individuals involved all approached it in different ways.

I'd never been to the Pitt Rivers before, but as soon as I got this invitation I went straight along and I was just absolutely knocked sideways by this place. I was shown round by Hélène la Rue, one of the curators, and I realised this was the real thing, an untouched Victorian museum where the way the objects were presented was as important as what was being presented. And it had a history and a subtext and all sorts of connotations attached to it. It was an amazing treasure house of things.

CC What did you discover and what did you do?

SL My problem was what am I going to do because it was all just so absolutely seductively marvellous. I gravitated in the end to this section called "Magic Charms", a glass-fronted showcase and some standing ones and some horizontal ones with drawers underneath. It contained all sorts of quite weird things like sheeps' hearts stuck with pins and little objects which had been found concealed, like witchcraft charms, in the walls of houses. The one which I ended up with, and which I based my work on, was a thing I found in one of the drawers underneath the glass case. It was a ribbon screwed up into a ball, about eight inches diameter, a white ribbon with a black strip running right through the whole length, and it was stuck with pins at intervals. I think it was knotted. This was found in Malta sometime in the early twentieth century and donated to the Museum. It was a witch charm, a sort of evil-wishing charm, found inside a mattress in a house which was being demolished in Valletta in Malta. The handwritten label attached to this—all the Pitt Rivers labels were handwritten—gave all the circumstances of its finding and the date of it and said, "Thought to be the work of a dismissed servant." In other words, the servant who'd got the push had at some point managed to come back and secrete this thing inside the mattress, if you please, of their erstwhile master/mistress and the idea was it was sympathetic magic. If you can imagine, this cord was like your intestine or your gut, you know, it was tying you up in knots and sticking pins into you. And it was such a strange thing and I thought "Well, that's it, I've got to do something with this." I was absolutely entranced by this written label as well, and by this phrase: 'The work of a dismissed servant,' and it was the phrase that I carried away with me as much as anything else. And this kept on going around in my head, because I knew that what I would do would actually be one of my pictures, it would basically be a Simon Lewty. I entitled the picture, *The Work of a Dismissed Servant.* It was about five foot by four foot, quite big, and was installed in the Pitt Rivers for the duration of the exhibition. They removed some of the objects from one of the standing glass-fronted display cases and I installed this picture inside the cupboard. It wasn't quite all there yet because the question which I asked myself was, "Have I got the courage to put the magic cord in the installation with my picture?" I thought, "I don't really want to tangle with this, you know, for fear of [laughs] consequences." But I thought such a lot about it and I thought "Well, I've got to, I've just absolutely got to do this. I really have got to do it." The picture had the cord depicted in it, but I realised all along I'd had this idea that I wanted to actually put the cord physically in, sitting on the floor of the cabinet underneath my picture. So I did. Well, nothing happened and I'm still here, so you know, fingers crossed, it was okay.

CC How strongly did you feel that there was something alarming in it?

SL Well, I never know the answer to this, because I think there is this residue of superstition. I mean we call it superstition, what is left standing over from long abandoned belief systems—it wouldn't be superstition if it was fully conscious and fully rational. And so maybe there are traces of that. I just wouldn't want to commit myself one way or the other. I wouldn't call myself superstitious; if I'd been truly superstitious I wouldn't have had anything to do with it. I can think of some people who really are superstitious who wouldn't have touched the damn thing. People have had bad experiences, whether through their own psyches or through something we don't know anything about. I can understand that, but I'm not like that.

CC What about any sense of evil? Do you think evil is a reasonable word?

SL Well it struck me that there was a strong sense of evil, but it was an evil which wasn't being directed at me. When I was doing the picture I started to think about the dismissed servant and, without wanting to illustrate it in any shape or form, I started thinking what it would feel like to be someone out of a job in Malta in about nineteen hundred and something, which was a fairly exotic kind of frame of mind to put myself in. The sort of thing which a writer, I think, might have wanted to do, might have said, "I'm going to write the story about this servant, I've got to identify myself with this." I remember I even got hold of some old photographs of—I've never been to Malta—some photographs of Valletta, which were taken at the turn of the century, a fairly weird sort of place, a port with, you know, ramparts and castles and things. But I thought that would have been familiar to the dismissed servant. So in a way it was almost like a bit of method acting in a rather unsystematic way, I was curious to just feel that somehow.

CC Where did you get hold of the photos?

SL They were in my good old Book of Knowledge, my childhood encyclopaedia. The book came out in the 1930s so the photographs were taken, you know, any time prior to that, so it was probably in period.

CC And have you been back to the museum?

SL Oh yes, I have, several times. It's a wonderful place.

The 'magic cord' taken in situ in the Pitt Rivers Museum, Oxford, 1990.

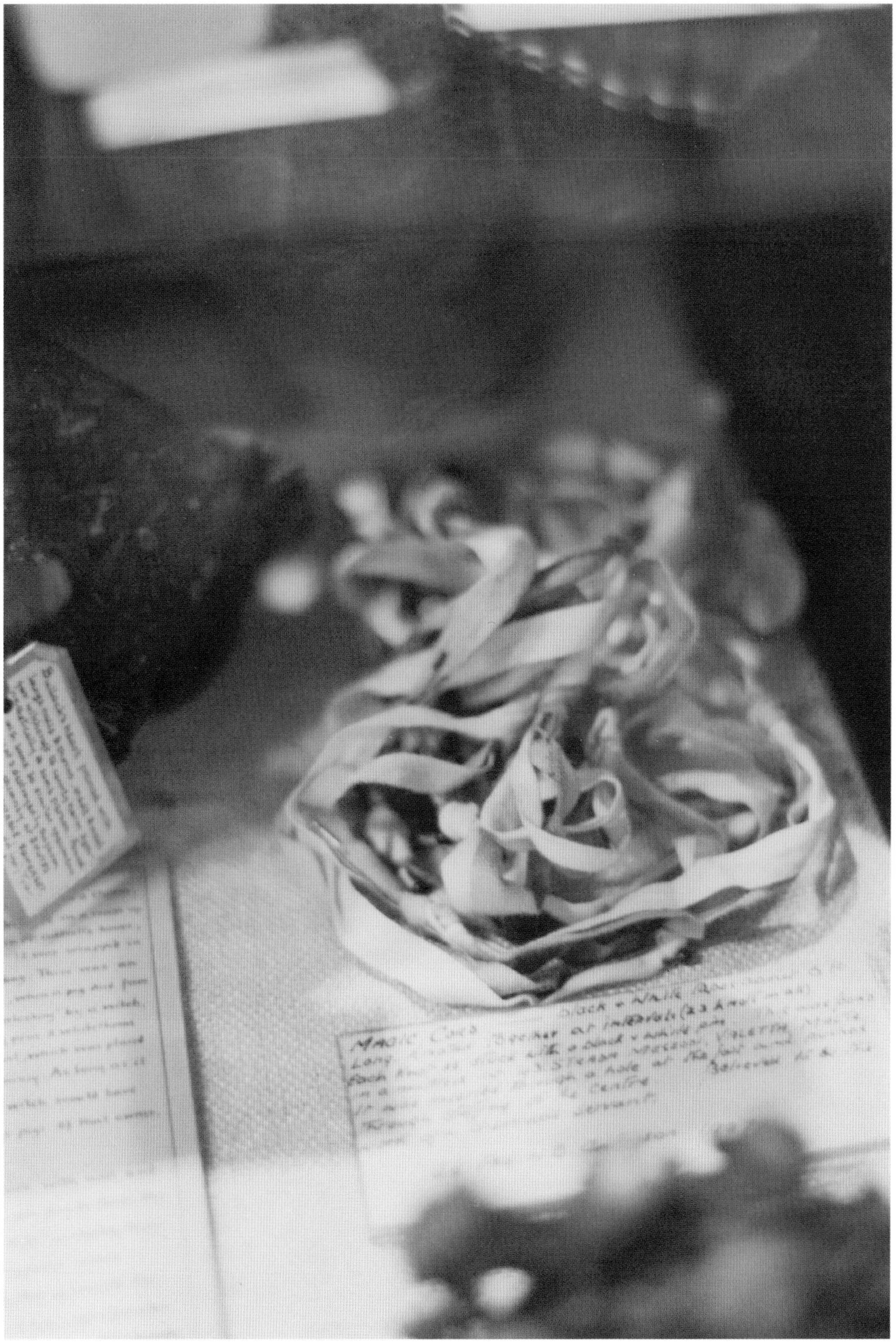

58. *Beach 1, 6.11.05*, 2005.

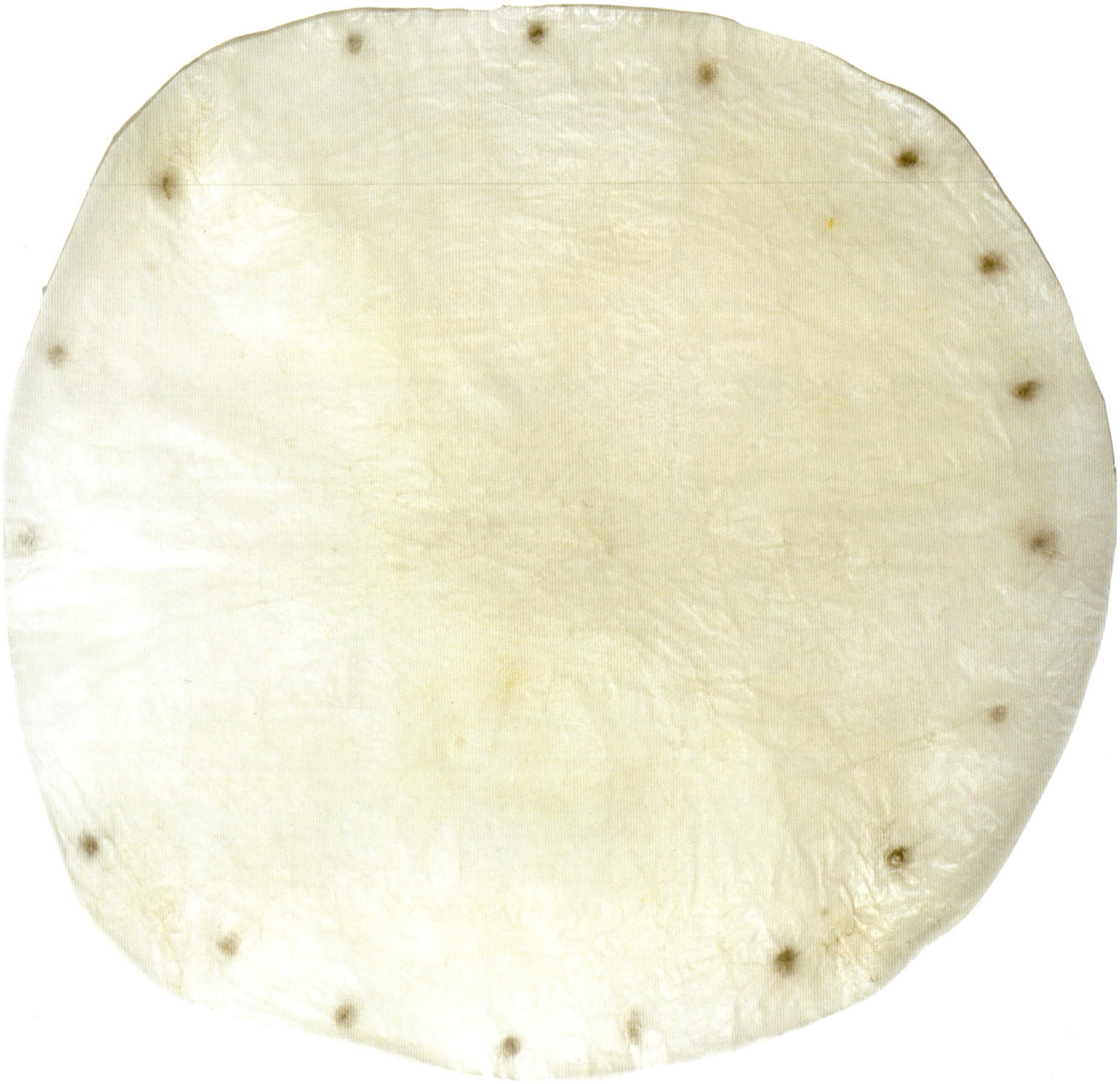

59. *Beach 2, 7.11.05*, 2005.

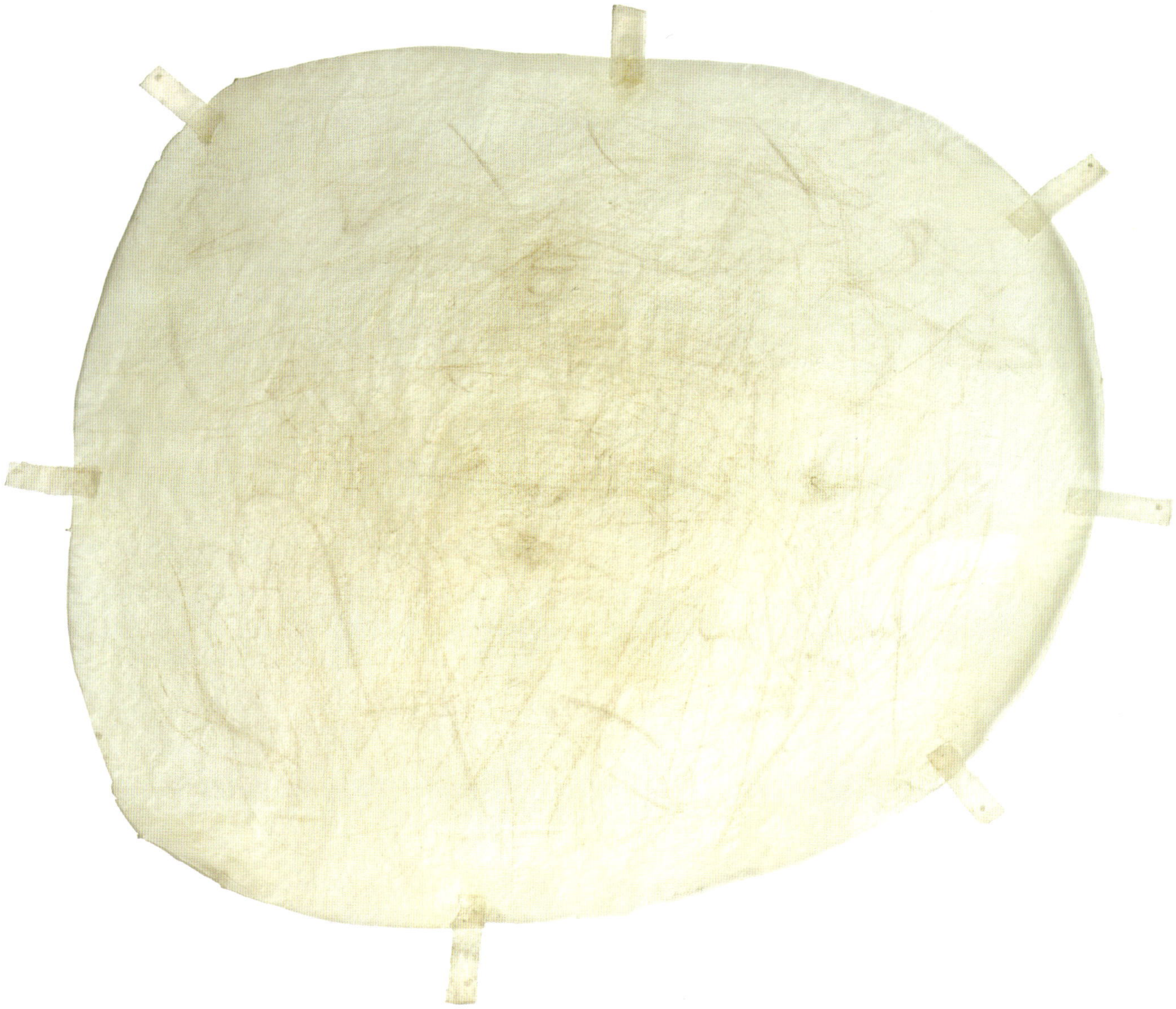

60. *First Snow of Winter*, 1981.

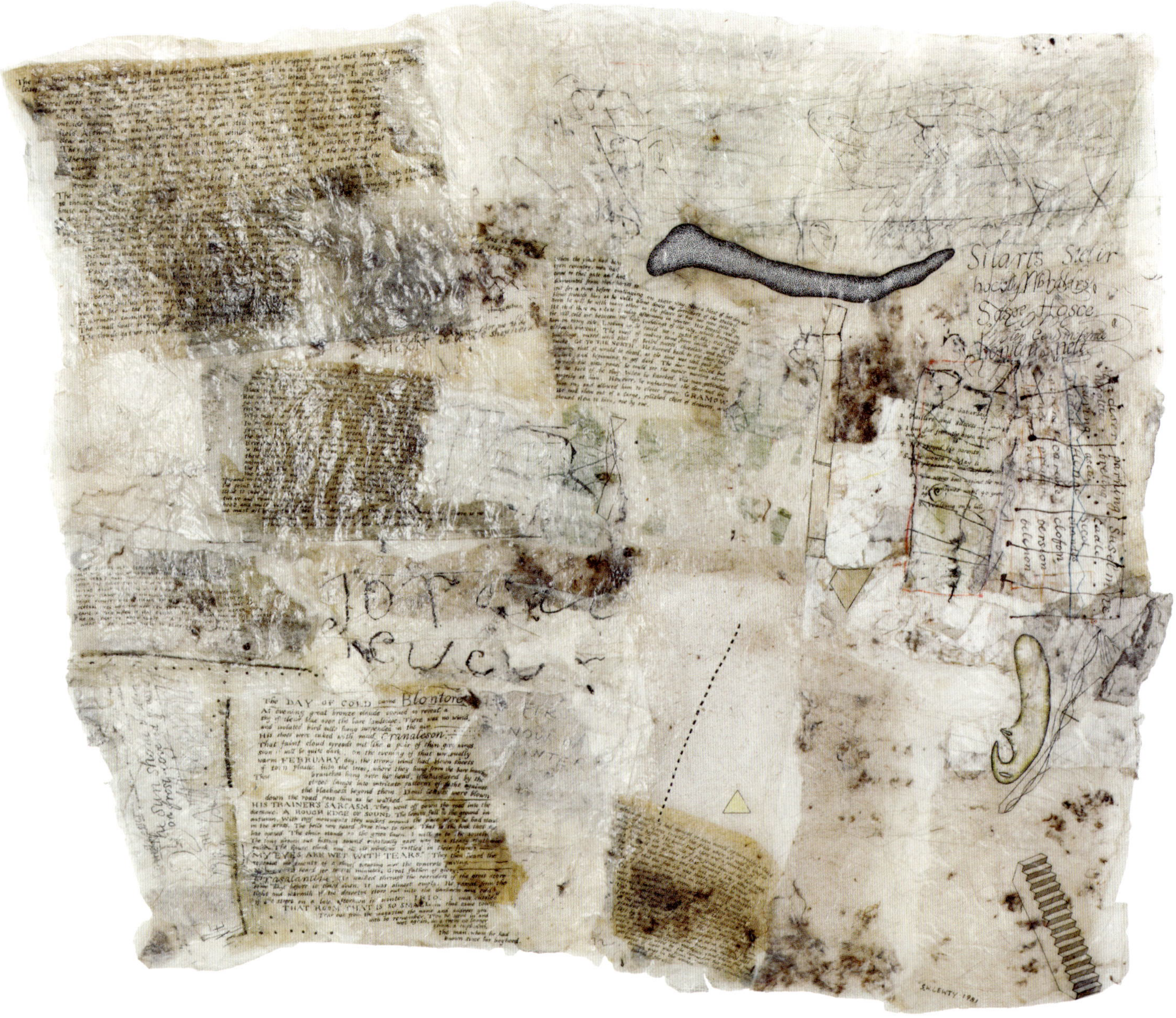

THE SELF AS A STRANGER

SIMON LEWTY
2007

Opportunities are often things you haven't noticed the first time around.
Catherine Deneuve.

INTRUSIONS

A large sheet of paper covers the end wall of the snowbound studio—white outside the window and white inside the room. Pencilled words partially cover the surface—hundreds of words. My eye moves over them, and into the blank spaces between them, the emptiness of the text that shapes them and is shaped by them. The whole surface seems to be moving, a flux, in which there are few constants, apart from the faint horizontal lines of the text which repeat, without repeating.... But I sense there is a connection, a rhyme almost, between this field of writing and what is happening outside the window.

Snow has been falling for several hours, gradually covering every surface. Swirling flakes, dark against the pale grey sky, white against the black of trees and the window blanks. Silently the wind blows a fan of white powder from the roof of the house opposite. Sometimes a single flake, moving in a different direction from the others, hovers round the window, like a curling feather on a journey of its own. The only sounds in the studio are the faint noises of the heating system and occasionally a muted phone call in the office below. The first snow of winter, like the approach of thunder in summer has always for me been a time of waiting and listening and heightened response.

Now the words on the wall seem to rise and fall, as though breathing. As I look more closely, phrases begin to emerge. Mimicking the rhythms and patterns of speech, they wander and drift. They appeal, they suggest, they insist, they hesitate, they contradict each other and themselves, they exclaim, they cajole, they question, they point, they rejoice, they sigh. They hint at many stories, but tell none.

up to me — I know, but — I don't really want to be a part of it
ring — why you think — I think — anyone might still be confused — th
— if I hadn't been — someone like that — maybe — I think — those questions
— what that would — mean? There is — a lack — when you look — at it — lik
thing you think of — every day — encouraged — towards a climax — but — of
o — people believe — it happens — had to allow — a great deal — no — I under
to be — something else — became — myth. It might help — to protect — there
Based on what they have — all they have — to say — I think — I can on
ink — what we're trying to do — looking at the benefits — you'll admit — questi
by all means try — but don't rely on them — too — many of them — but I think
e — but I do have — reservations — it is — no — because — everything — every sing
hey're — I think — we — are going to — as before — a time — the air. Decades —
in any way — but — I — did appreciate — that — it wasn't about — me — that's
course — everybody does — that's why I dont — I — try not to — oh of course I ap
forget that — because I — let me — tell you — I wrote a letter — and then
hen — you — yourself — it was — actually of course — in all seriousness — again
n — you — are left to realize — people — every — person — that it is all going
— for you — I certainly relate to those — themes — as painful as they co
that kind of — experience — I have to — what you want — to do — what you do
I think everybody — has experienced — without necessarily being — part of it
you thought — the way you behaved at times — it would lead me to believe
hat you make it — that includes — aside from — I think — whatever people
g forward. Every day — you — get — today is — in changing day — morning
lways — some — what kind of — effect — would you be talking about? For — a
to be — shown — there is one — that when — you do — would you see — tha
t really — doesn't have much meaning — so why do we see it — in that con
ng — I do believe that — there — probably are a lot of — misconceptions — o
it is — I think — it varies — to keep this — I do actually — that's the th
do you think — nearby — is this — a good idea? — I didn't know — what was co
so far — lacking — support — therefore — I am saying — I am sure — it refle
ke — we are still relying on — rumours. To count on — something — it ma
a perspective — which stands — the test of time — difficult circumstances — a
hese questions — I think the point about it is — society tends to be —
sceptible — they have their own — story — but in many ways it's also
to reciprocate — at least — to draw on — definitely — there — for a purp
end — perhaps — they are also — trying to find — there is that — a great
you can cross — doesn't have so much — to say — but essential — a world
nt — are you going — to tell them? there could be a problem — we recogniz
case of — how I lived — not as simple — as that — it's so hard — trust co
eally — believe — they don't know — I simply couldn't — tell them — an
hat sense — of playing — confidence in — refusing to play — some kind of —

opposite Detail of 61. *A Voice, a Recognition,* 2007.

Three hours later. The snow has stopped, and now the early afternoon sun is shining unexpectedly. A diamond-shaped patch of light is cast by one of the three skylights in the ceiling, and lies diagonally across the paper. Actually it is not lying still, but moving slowly across the text, as the sun moves across the sky. My writing hand moves too, at a faster rate over the paper, passing through the zone of light and out again into what seems like a chasm of shadow. It's difficult for the eye to adjust to the changing intensity of light, but such is the beauty of this winter sun-fall amid the snow, that far from attempting to shut it out, I want to welcome it and accept it as an invisible part of my picture. Perhaps whatever touches a surface changes that surface, even though the change can't be seen.

Then the sun passes behind clouds and this short day seems almost over. The huge text spreads out in front of me, a unified greyish white, and the eye reads:

> ' - begin - for failing - yet it begins here - before - echoed - for over ten years ... - I didn't realize I couldn't imagine - that it wouldn't - so I knew - and stopped. Drift - the intelligence of the beginning...'

Another piece of paper, another wall, another room, another season. This time the window looks out over the sea, an immense, glittering space of light, reflecting into the room and across the surface of the paper. I am working to the sound of the sea through the open window. The waves break upon the shore below, their endless surge and reflux one of the most ancient sound-lines. I am using a translucent tissue, almost weightless, and the writing is in coloured pencil. Its soft, waxy tip marks the surface in quite a different way to a lead pencil, and I'm having to go much more slowly and deliberately, otherwise the thin paper would tear. As I work, I can feel the pencil responding to the slight unevenness of the wall underneath, and passing it on to the micro-structures of the text. The warm sun and the sea and the rhythmic repetition of the lines induce a feeling of calm. The writing spreads over the surface in a violet flush. This work began partly as a 'found' text, with bits of overheard speech from many different sources. And if I look at my notebooks I'm reminded of how some of them came to me.

Two people, a woman and a man, are having a conversation on a train a few seats back from mine. It's a long, hot journey, and the conversation goes on and on. To while away the time, unseen by them, I begin to write down some of their exchanges in my notebook. Their voices rise and fall, occasionally pause—an exclamation, a laugh, both speaking at the same time. Who are they? What are they talking about?—impossible to tell, especially as their voices tend to drop away, and rise again to emphasise an 'and' or a 'but' or an 'absolutely'. So this was what I heard, the connective tissue of their talk, its silences and residues rather than its subject matter. When I read back my notes, they seemed like poetry. So voices other than mine could enter my work, not as direct transcriptions but more as traces of a passage. They have found their own place in relation to the other, different, 'voices' in my work.

The surface of writing is of both body and mind, and the one is never lost or subsumed in the other. I realise that I've always had the desire to make such a surface, and maybe my art originates in that desire. The process begins with another surface, usually paper, something supposedly blank and unwritten-on. Yet for me, this surface is not entirely 'other', and indeed not truly 'blank' —but more like a skin. The paper already has a character of its own. The desire is to secrete something upon it, or within it, to transform it and to be transformed by it. Perhaps such a writing is a tissue, rather than a narrative, a covering, rather than an exploration, a process of filling, rather than a state of fulfilment. If these words are like residues on the surface, at the same time they are the surface. Just as a tattoo becomes part of the skin it is inscribed on. And like a skin, this written surface does not deny its depths. It can be wounded, and it can absorb and heal. It can resonate like a stretched membrane to the echo of a deeper, more ancient surface. It has a memory of its own, as well as being a repository of memories. This is how it seems to me when I am working. A vibrant thing, yet receptive to many of the contingencies of the outside world which it filters and absorbs. Sometimes these intrusions from outside are quite concrete.

61. *A Voice, a Recognition*, 2007.

Over the last few years I have made a group of small pieces using found drawings and writing. Some are photocopies of scribbles and images which I discovered on the flyleaves and margins and inner pages of second-hand books. They ranged from the meticulous to the wild. I imagine most of them were done by children, but it's not possible to be certain of this. Some of them looked quite old. To come across the traces of another person, hidden inside a discarded book, can be very exciting. Other drawn-on pieces of paper were picked up in the street—sometimes literally from the gutter—soaked with rain and bearing the marks of car tyres that had run over them (plates 62 and 63). Pinned to the wall, these stained and abject fragments have been my companions in the studio over the months. They are so complete in themselves that sometimes I feel all I want to do is to present them by the simple process of transferring them to another surface, sometimes slightly enlarging the image. Or I might combine them with a written text. They are a complement to the larger, more ambitious works. I love their silliness and spontaneity, their smallness and secrecy. True graphic 'others', they have presided over my daily work, their pathos or cheerful spirit a silent reminder of unknown lives.

I have also made a small group of works in memory of my mother, the author Marjorie Lewty, which incorporate sheets of her discarded typescripts, a very few of which have survived thanks to having once been recycled to use as scrap paper on the back. My own scribbles and jottings can faintly be seen in reverse, making the pages into true palimpsests, surface and depth in one. I made them in Dorset, at a time when I wanted to work but was limited by the few scraps of material I had with me at the time. So they came out of necessity and were totally unplanned, like most of the best things in my life (plates 46 and 48).

Sometimes it's not doing the work itself that is difficult, so much as allowing yourself to do it and understanding what you've done. That understanding may be instantaneous or it may take years, but for me it is always linked to a sort of self-recognition. To see something of yourself in what is not you—another person, a place, an object, an idea, may be a joyful encounter, a disturbing shock, or a deeply strange unveiling. But it is always a re-cognition—through what you have made—of something perhaps already known, but not fully apprehended.

left 62. *Figure 1*, 2007.

right 63. *Figure with Tyremarks*, 2007.

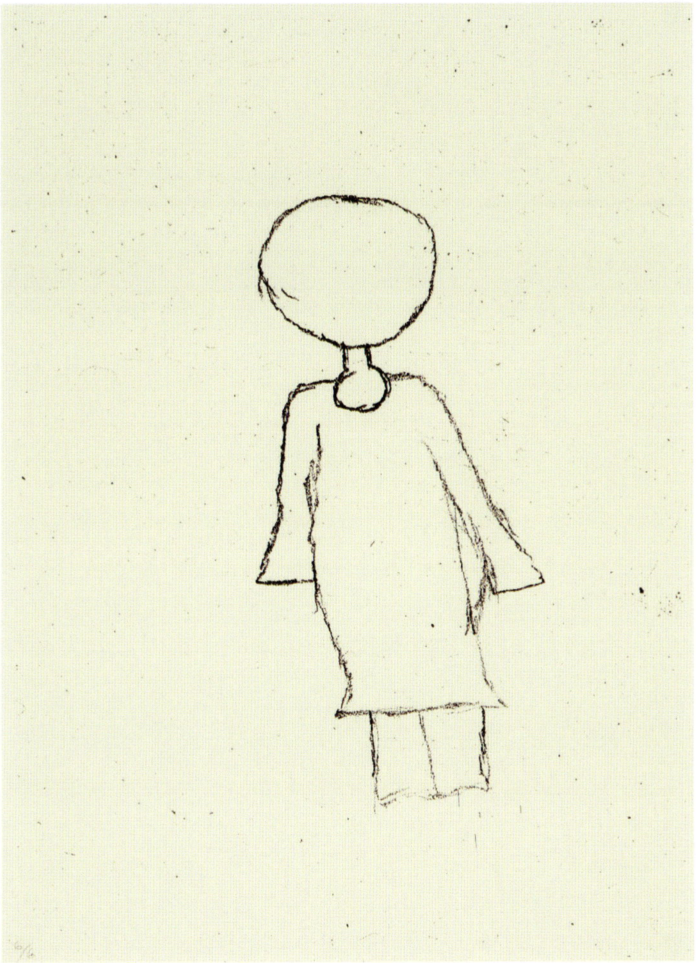

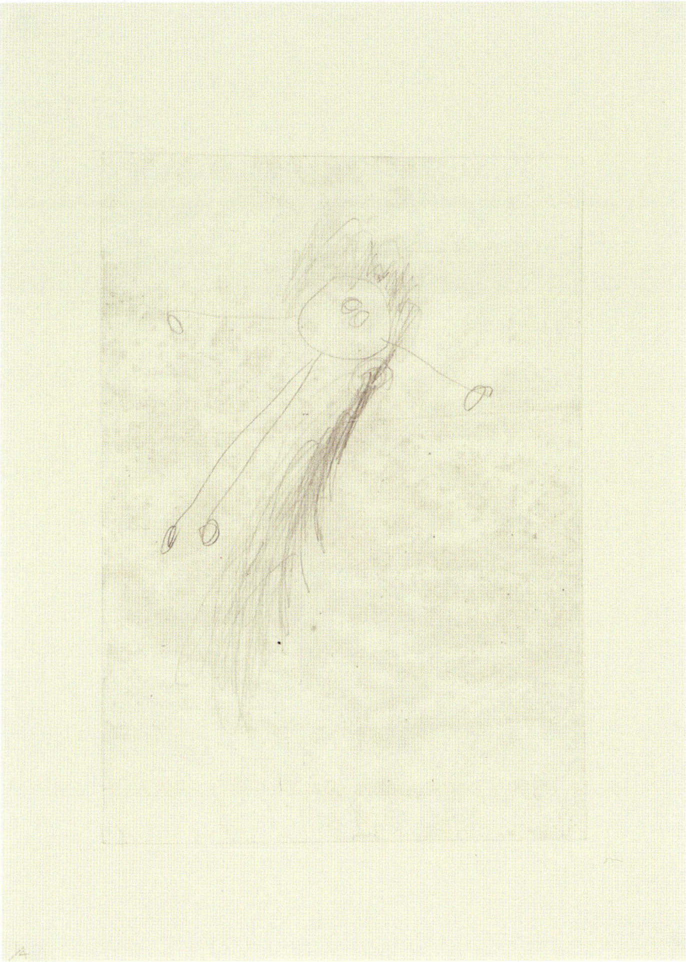

below and opposite 64. *Gift*, 2007.

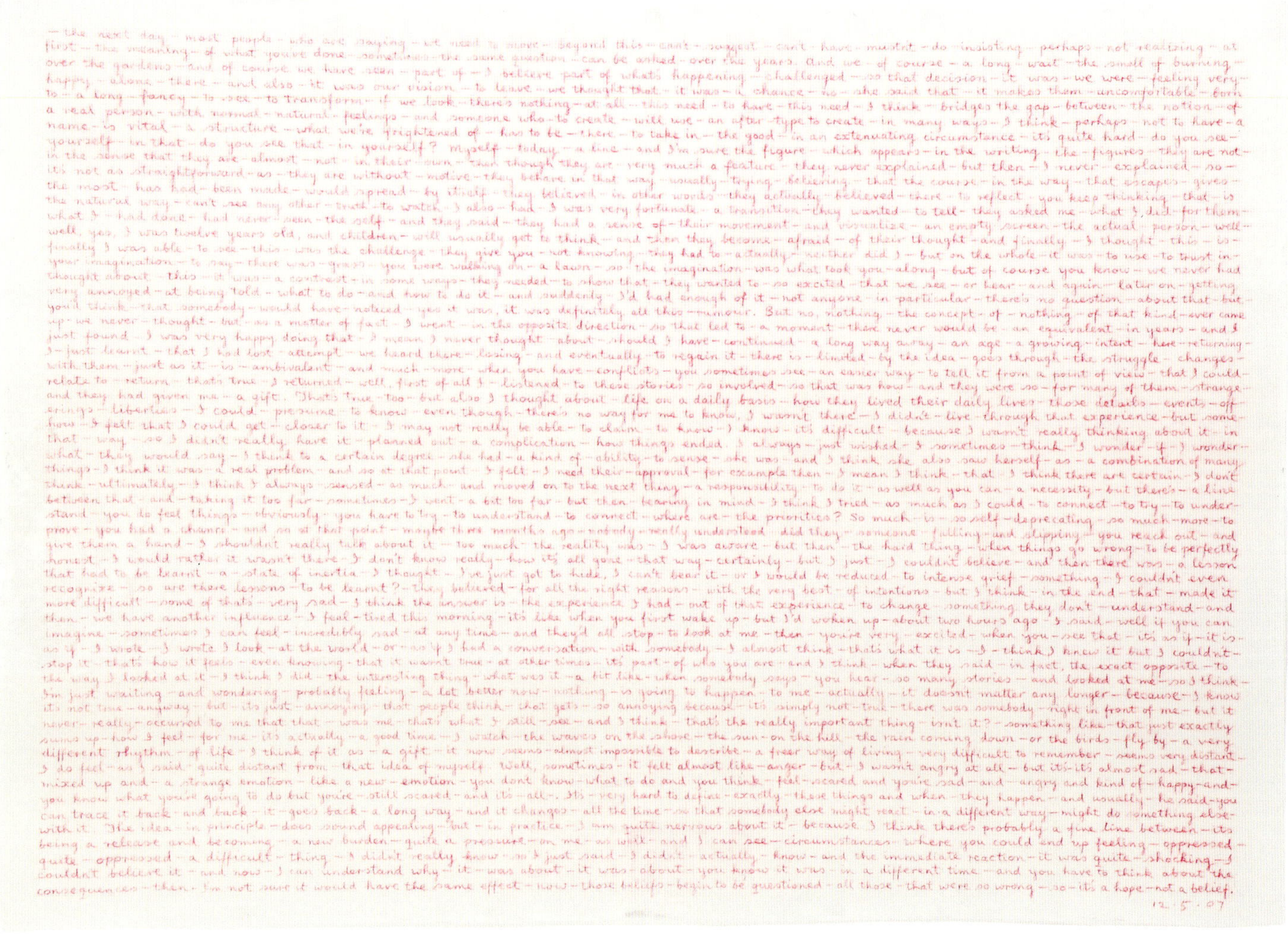

I'm just writing and
it's not true – anyway –
never – really – occurred
sums up – how I feel –
different rhythm – of
I do feel – as I said –
mixed up and – a str
you know what you're
can trace it back – an
with it. The idea – in
being a release and
quite – oppressed – a
couldn't believe it –
consequences – then –

that's altogether unusual — no — well, its not — it — is — unusual — it often
not their — fault — or mine — we just — dont want — to see — it — somet
and that's the — difficulty — I'm just trying — to — it put me — in a very d
t the sea — and the sky — until — I no longer knew — which was the dr
treat — a limitation — these words — may be — different — the essence — is t
— as being more — it was a secret — a permission — a song —. There wer
ways — even through — opposites — central — to their identity — yet strang
on — new ideas — from the same — idea. It was — a little while after — did
— a strangely moved surface — moved — and now still — because there
hings. You might notice — begin — to notice — it's an uncomfortable — you
dy's not saying — when we decide — when we make that unspoken decision
to — and I think that's pretty remarkable — yes, I had — well of course you
derstand — or not the sort of thing I'd — ever — talked about — before — whic
y — actually — moving — towards — something — they hope — that it is — a good
ts — just disappear — you don't — notice them — anymore — there is nothing — you
nessage — came across — so — I — rather — took it — to mean — I took it to — mysel
what we do know — whether — and when — early or late — may take — years and
— the risk — of something — going wrong — the important thing — the ot
— within the idea — to accept — a mistake — a morning — unheard — you
chance — gives consolation — return — a question — a change of mind — a lot
t they have always done — it doesn't — make it any easier — but — it help
on — a dream — but sometimes the dream — can fail — or seem to fail
in the road below — of an aeroplane in the sky above — tribute — ther
— the confidence — to wait — they can help — to explain — to persuade — them
— that isn't — to anyone's advantage — all those things — are true — I think — i
this need — trying — there is no risk — like this — risk — there is no su
had — completely — lost — the way — she had found — the way — another — w
— since — I think most people — would tell you — there have been times — when
eems — astonishing — they tell — their stories — we learn — so much — th
I don't think — they are — I think this is just one within a series —
thing — considered — to point up — silence. That can sometimes be — t
out — whether that's — a good idea — if you look — at it — and you see —
antastic story — or something — it's quite impossible — to work out — this — p
uch — to sustain — it doesn't move — it just — waits — for no particular rea
personalities are part of — what they do — and so what does it take for —
— to see through — it — the secret — the tears — so they are — known — I —
eat excitement — if you — know — what it was like — if you know — it's
idn't know where to turn — I had no idea — and — so I — took matters into
o' — nobody seems to listen — to what I'm saying — they're not even — t
— to explain — the difference between the two — and the attitudes — of th
ut — they are struggling — I think — there needs to be — there is — a chall
re wasn't — all that much — that could be done — at that time — to —

opposite and below 65. *A Cry Within a Mind*, 2007.

Detail from 66. *Places, Voices*, 2007.

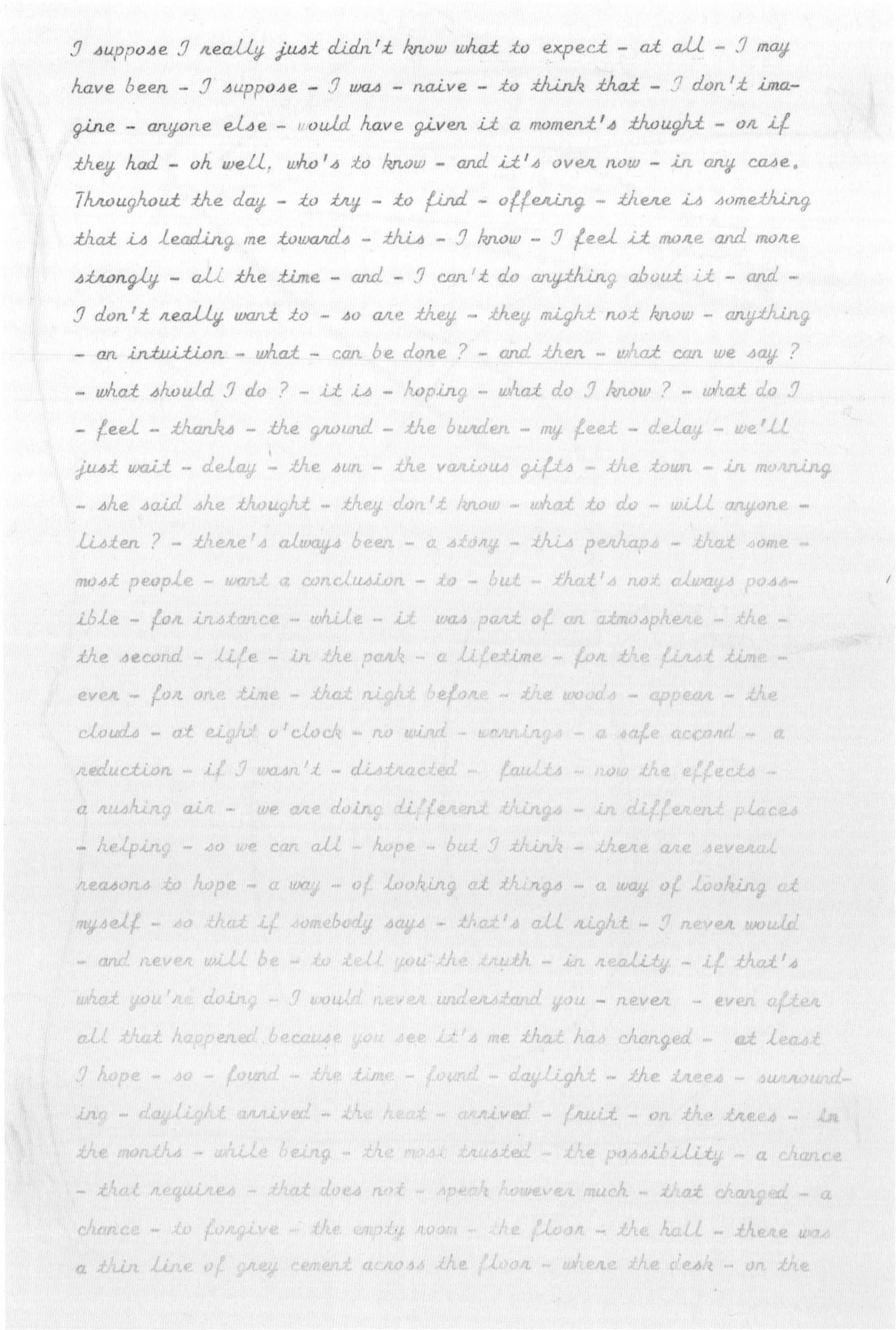
I suppose I really just didn't know what to expect - at all - I may
have been - I suppose - I was - naive - to think that - I don't ima-
gine - anyone else - would have given it a moment's thought - or if
they had - oh well, who's to know - and it's over now - in any case.
Throughout the day - to try - to find - offering - there is something
that is leading me towards - this - I know - I feel it more and more
strongly - all the time - and - I can't do anything about it - and -
I don't really want to - so are they - they might not know - anything
- an intuition - what - can be done ? - and then - what can we say ?
- what should I do ? - it is - hoping - what do I know ? - what do I
- feel - thanks - the ground - the burden - my feet - delay - we'll
just wait - delay - the sun - the various gifts - the town - in morning
- she said she thought - they don't know - what to do - will anyone -
listen ? - there's always been - a story - this perhaps - that some -
most people - want a conclusion - to - but - that's not always poss-
ible - for instance - while - it was part of an atmosphere - the -
the second - life - in the park - a lifetime - for the first time -
ever - for one time - that night before - the woods - appear - the
clouds - at eight o'clock - no wind - warnings - a safe accord - a
reduction - if I wasn't - distracted - faults - now the effects -
a rushing air - we are doing different things - in different places
- helping - so we can all - hope - but I think - there are several
reasons to hope - a way - of looking at things - a way of looking at
myself - so that if somebody says - that's all right - I never would
- and never will be - to tell you the truth - in reality - if that's
what you're doing - I would never understand you - never - even after
all that happened because you see it's me that has changed - at least
I hope - so - found - the time - found - daylight - the trees - surround-
ing - daylight arrived - the heat - arrived - fruit - on the trees - in
the months - while being - the most trusted - the possibility - a chance
- that requires - that does not - speak however much - that changed - a
chance - to forgive - the empty room - the floor - the hall - there was
a thin line of grey cement across the floor - where the desk - on the

66. *Places, Voices*, 2007.

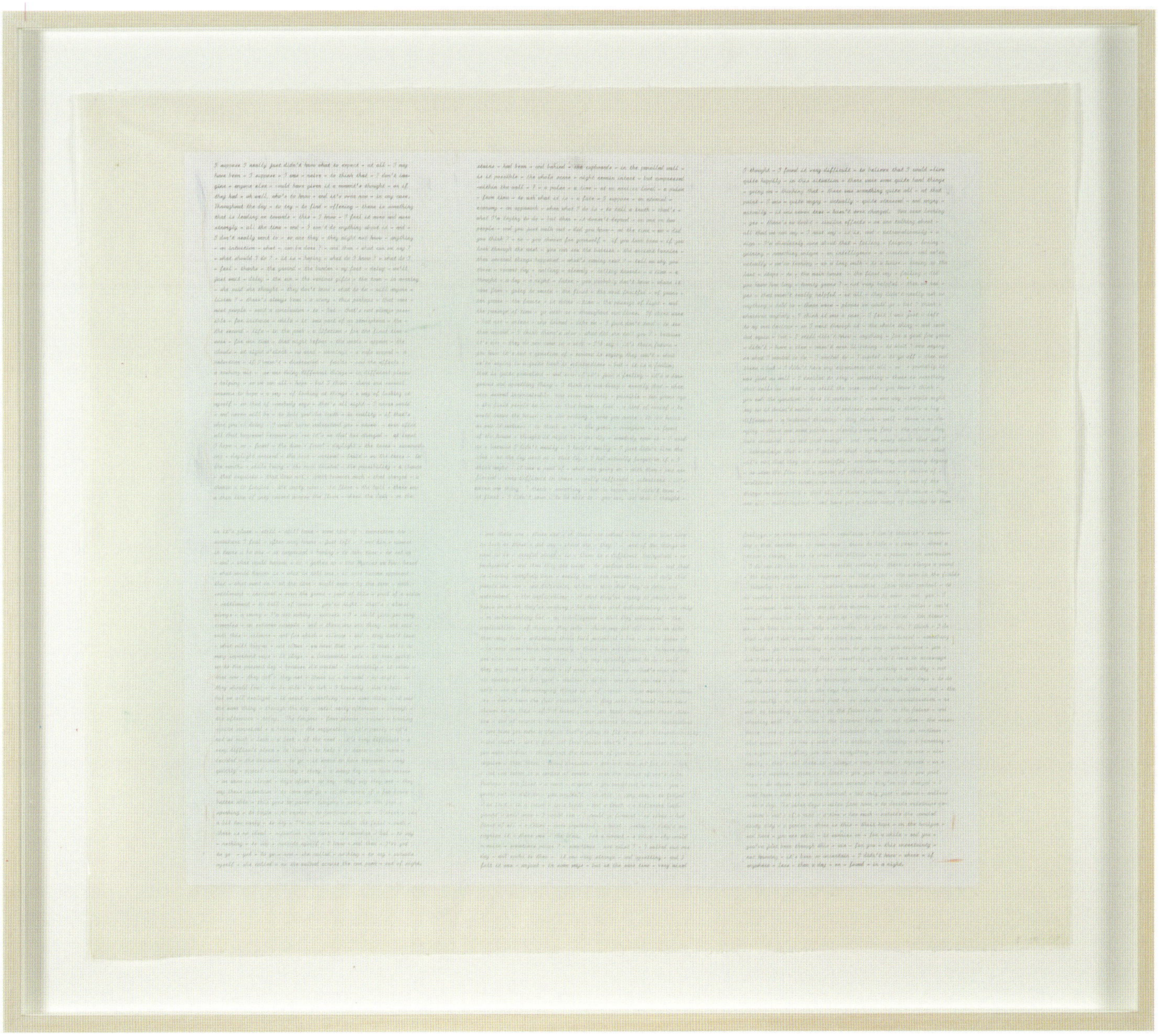

THE SELF AS A STRANGER

What I've written above relates to a specific time and mood, and a body of work that has already passed. And an even greater time—more than half a century—lies between the earliest picture in this book and the work I am doing now. Yet as I look from *The Writing on the Wall* (plate 8), which I made at the age of 16, with its panels of automatic scrawls on a strangely-lit de Chirico-esque facade, to the unfinished pictures that face me now in my studio—handwritten variants of italic and typewriting and the semi-legible 'Secretary' script of another age—I am struck by how similar they look! Although I know that my child-self and my adult-self are different in so many ways, I also know that both are 'I'. What then is the link? Who is this person who is both 'I' and 'not I'? These questions may be rhetorical, yet I sense that I have long been motivated by the need to find such connections through my art. To feel my way intuitively in a nexus of images and patterns of association, and listen for 'rhymes' between what was then and there and what is here and now. And to express what I find with clarity.

These 'rhymes' are linked to personal associations which, because they are subjective and often irrational, might mean little to anyone else. But they all come from life, and we all have them; so the personal may point to something more universal. Some were laid down years ago and their networks criss-cross back and forth over a lifetime. For instance, if I have an association between a memory of warm rain falling on a Birmingham street of my childhood and the idea of drawing with a pen and Indian ink, that association can be felt just as strongly to this day, when I dip my pen into the bottle. And there are many others connected with people and places and things and events strung out over the years, which are beyond the scope of this essay because although something of them may be told, as stories are told, their reality simply cannot be put into words. But they are immensely powerful. They are probably the most important source of my art.

I have called these connections "rhymes"; and I used to refer to them as "secrets"—which may have given a wrong idea, because the whole point of art is to communicate—but it does suggest that there are certain things whose integrity and interiority (inaccessibility even) should be respected. Perhaps the best word for them might be 'echoes': a resonance of something whose source has been lost. They are the traces of lived moments, and the artist, through recalling them in words and images, hopes to share something of them with the viewer, although the ways of that sharing may be unpredictable. Even though they may not reveal themselves immediately or directly, these echoes, like the sea, are forever murmuring their messages to the mind. The untold may be the source of an endless re-telling.

below and overleaf 67. *Passing Days and Nights of Oblivion Will Drain Reason Before the Strength of the Flower*, 2008.

- agree with - and my point was - it's - it's not th
lidn't agree with it - just - this feeling - of every tim
le - I think - the whole thing - has to - just has t
think - I suppressed it all - or - perhaps I just wro
the girl by the table - listening to the caged bird -
- when - many of us - find it very difficult - to adm
- then - because of what preceded it - and followed
n and on - and of course - they are just - forever -
empting -. Over the years - I do have to say - there
en - I didn't - I just don't know - I mean - I wou
n't know - how can you do - that - ? - all the way th
ARE VERY OLD" - she speaks - to the ti
t seem to have so much - to say - but is speaking
at that time - but - a constant revelation - I n
dreamed - it was true - and I found myself adj
of mine - no words - could describe it - if I nee
ies - it - is a great change - but - it doesn't chan
- I couldn't see - the pattern - something much
years - "NOTHING THERE - there's no
is - it's unbelievable - what an impact this is havi
rence - in future - to see - a threat - a way - ret
d of a story. I had a sense it would be difficult -
ut quite a lot of myself into it - for it - to come al
- as they are - then I would have something w
ee the point - of that - so - there is something -
nmediate concern - but - I started thinking - t
as trying to do anything like that - at all - no -

de on the roads that ringed the
the thronging crowds. This
d lines suspended high about h
ones strewed the ground, black
the complexity of low hills. B
rimbled stone. They looked o
sanche, shaft fire the trees
of a tiny fly through a fu
clearing; of two way from the
bright wind; of a frenzy
is this? O, it is a wave of
still. All of dancing, C
n enclosure surrounded by a low
d in a deep indentation shaped like

REVERIES AND TRANSFORMATIONS

SUSAN MICHIE/SIMON LEWTY
2009

These extracts have been edited from a dialogue between Simon Lewty and Susan Michie, which took place in the early months of 2009, using emails and 'Skype'. Some of the conversations went on for days, but it was not a seamless dialogue. Topics of conversation would change, as one thing led to another, and the flow of daily life went on, from teabreaks to days spent away from home and the computer screen. The breaks in the text indicate some of these stops and starts, and so make visible something of the structure of the dialogue as it unfolded. 'Skype', unlike email, takes place in real time, and has a faster rhythm and greater urgency—a kind of written speech. An icon of a small, yellow pencil moving on the screen shows each writer that the other is replying.

SM No doubt we'll find our rhythm once we start a proper dialogue. I can see you're writing away. I'm off to watch *EastEnders* but will leave the computer on and answer at 8-30.

SL Your pencil has started again. I've just realised that *EastEnders* is the first cultural reference we've made. The sight of that yellow pencil moving away so busily does remind me of Derrida and his ideas of *écriture*—in the beginning was the pencil...

SM *EastEnders* over. There's a v. good plot to do with two sisters falling out and all the misunderstandings that happen and how life seems to conspire to make matters worse. Compulsive stuff! Not having read Derrida I'm afraid I can't pick up on the reference... in the beginning was the pencil.... Really? Is he referring to the fact that culture begins with the pencil? Do fill me in...

SL Oh dear you're putting me on the spot now with Derrida! I've only read a smattering. I was thinking of his idea that writing is already there, in a sense, before speech, as a trace. But he's using the word in a special sense of what writing could mean. It's a fascinating thought—but I always feel I can be intrigued by philosophical ideas without really 'understanding' them. Anyway the moving pencils just made me think of it.

SM Found a wonderful quote by Oscar Wilde: "Education is an admirable thing, but it is well to remember from time to time that nothing that is worth knowing can be taught."

SL Marvellous! Thinking more about writing, which I've been doing a lot today. Sometimes when I'm writing slowly and carefully as in calligraphy, I become aware of each word, even each letter sometimes as it is forming under

Marks, details from Simon Lewty drawing (top) and Susan Michie drawing (bottom).

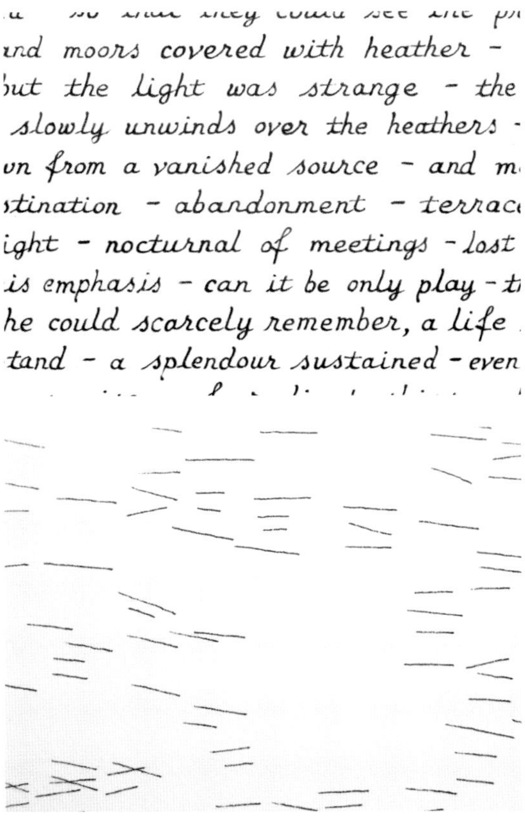

the pen—it's quite strange—as if almost forgotten traces of other, earlier languages, lie embedded in the words. Also each word becoming a thing in itself, quite apart from what it might mean, and finally, as the words run together, of the whole 'drift' of the text, of what is unfolding on the page. I nearly said the 'sense' of the text—but here again words get tricky when trying to describe it as I am now. It could even be a kind of non-sense... but certainly it is sense in the same way as you might talk about a 'sense of place' or of time. But I still think when I'm doing it, it feels more like being carried along on a drift...

SM I found another quote... George Bernard Shaw complained that 'fish' could just as sensibly be spelled "ghoti" (gh as in tough, o as in women, ti as in nation). But back to your writing—what earlier language are you referring to? Also, you often refer to my drawings as having a 'drift'.

SL Oh I think it's got to be that archaic 'child' language... where all the linguistic elements are in a kind of flux. More to say on this I know, but I'm thinking of drift now, in relation to your drawings.... Both in time and space. I think this could lead on... I'd love to unpick, if poss. what happens between your first setting up of the marks you are going to use and then (as you said yesterday) the actual process of doing them, when it is repetitive work, and you can listen to the radio....

SM I need a little time to think about what you've written so I'll have a cup of tea.

SM Actually, I don't know what you mean. When I try to get to the essence of what you're saying I can't find it. It feels like what you're writing (here) is covering up or masking something but this is just a question of language. Your language is maybe 'exploratory' and I'm looking for 'essence' which may, in this dialogue, create quite an interesting tension if you don't mind me tackling it like this, which I know you don't... 'drift'... such a lovely word. I remember when I was living in Devon that the farmers did something in the autumn called 'drifting' when they rounded up all the wild ponies for market where they were sold for meat and many people would turn up to buy the odd one for £10 or so to save them from the bullet. Re the drawings... I think you start with the word, which has a meaning, whether it's relevant to anything or not and I start with the mark and as you describe, the word loses its meaning as your process continues... is this right?

SL The difference between my exploratory approach and your essence seeking approach is really valuable. What you say is always vivid and unpredictable, such as the story about the Devon farmers and the ponies.

SM I've been ruminating and these are some thoughts...

Simon uses writing/text as a way into making an image. Words are on the surface (a skater's blade cutting into the ice). His starting point is the word. His words are a link to childhood thoughts, feeling, memories, images. Skyping with Simon has revealed 2 things to me: 1) words are his mark and 2) he uses words to obscure meaning. Meaning is achieved through the image not the words. Beneath the surface is where the raw material remains, out of necessity, hidden. There is a void between mark and meaning and this is where his art resides.

SL Well, you certainly bear out the theory that the best person to write about an artists work is another artist! Your perception of my work is so clear and acute, and it contains the seeds of many ideas we can develop. Everything you say is substantially correct, and I want to go through your thoughts and try to develop and amplify them a bit if I can.

Your image of the skater is not only a beautiful one, but it's conceptually quite precise—calligraphic writing especially is slower and more controlled than our usual scribbling—nearer to engraving. And the words are indeed on the physical surface. There is also something that for me is like a mental surface, a panel of meaning, which conceals a depth where the childhood thoughts and images etc. must lie. This is where ideas of origin, symbol, and archetype may come in—which I'm looking forward to exploring further as we go on.

Your first point: yes—words are indeed my mark.... Your second point—"he uses words to obscure meaning"—the more I think about it, the truer it seems to me. But not in the sense of obscurantism, being wilfully obscure just to create an effect, a sort of false aura of profundity—heaven forbid! But I have been accused of just that in the past—"too clever by half". Oh dear.

As to what that meaning is—and why I need to obscure it—why it is, as you say, hidden out of necessity, this would take us into a huge area, which again I need to think about before trying to go further now.

"Meaning is achieved through the image not through the words." This focuses on the whole question of how to 'read' the work, whether in a literal sense, actually reading the words—which for some people is not a problem at all, and for others seems to be quite insuperable—or of 'reading' as another word for a particular kind of looking.

Then there is the issue of what I would simply call 'misreading' whether deliberate, even malicious, or simply unintentional. For instance, I used to be often confronted by people who assumed my work was a kind of Monty Python parody—something I had never remotely intended—and of course it's almost impossible to get beyond that with some individuals once it's lodged itself in their minds.

I think your most telling insight is into that "void between mark and meaning... where his art resides". I want to explore, I want to explore! This seems to link the physical reality of the work and its material surface with the idea of an inner surface of meaning. And that link is made through an image—a particular image in a particular work.

SM Thought I'd begin with a quote I found about Jung's last dream: "In his last revelatory dream prior to his death, Jung saw a huge round stone engraved with the words 'And this shall be a sign unto you of Wholeness and Oneness'."

SL An amazing thought. Do you think he realised it was going to be his last dream?

SM Probably... what else is there to dream after that?

SL Quite. While we are on Jung, I've always been very taken with that idea that the unconscious is part of nature... seems to link in directly with our responses to things in nature, such as stones... & link them to the mind.

SM Having a bit of a blip "& link them directly to the mind" what do you mean?

SL Well possibly dreams provide the link?

SM Or is it that the object is the link... for instance... unconscious>stone>conscious... in other words certain potent objects stimulate a link.

SL I like that idea very much. It keeps the whole physical world of matter in the forefront which is very important I think—in art as in alchemy.

SM Maybe it's unconscious>stone>conscious>dream>unconscious so it's a sort of circle/cycle?

SL The 'progression' has expanded and expanded. What started out as a straight line now becomes circular. The image of the serpent eating its own tail. Much to think about....

SM Had very busy night of dreams last night... nothing significant just lots of people in a gallery... some familiar some strange... probably a result of the Tarot cards.

SL When you say nothing significant... but perhaps it is significant? Do you think the Tarot characters and images are like the people in ones life? All those people who drift through who one will never know....

SM I can't quite see that. The Tarot characters are so loaded with meanings that one 'knows' without necessarily understanding and the people who drift through our lives without becoming characters in our lives are just unknowns aren't they?

SL I've always thought it's very strange how certain people do become characters —almost like the characters in a play—one's own play.

SM Yes, that's an idea that's occurred to me quite a lot recently. The appearances and disappearances of people in one's life and then the ones that are permanent and after so many years the cast has become quite staggeringly huge!

SL Absolutely. I find the same. It's an amazing thought. Can we get back to dreams for a minute? I have a question I'd like to ask you—actually, I've a feeling I partly know the answer, but there may be more to say in any case. The question is: have you ever done a picture based directly on a dream? Something that had it's origin in a dream/image or dream/utterance?

SM Never!

SL Thought I'd have a bit longer to think about things... but no. As you know I've been finding recently that old dreams have been resurfacing in my work, and strangely rubbing up against things which relate to much more recent concerns.

SM I didn't know that... do go on.

SL What happened was when I started to look through old notebooks in connection with the project we were thinking about and came across some dream notebooks going back to the 1970s—with dates and times of dreams all written in. And I suddenly thought can I use them—directly—like taking a fragment of dream 'material' out of its time frame and setting it in a new relationship to 'now' especially to my semi-automatic texts from the last couple of years. It's what I'm working on at the moment. The surface seems very smooth and seamless but when you read the words there are some astonishing jumps and chasms and voids—as well as occasionally some surprising linkups....

SM Very Simon Lewty to juxtapose past and present like that.

SL Talk about 'marks' a bit—the first point you made in your summary. The word as mark. I find that interesting. I'm almost having a slightly different feeling as I am writing these. Words. Can you expand on this "word as mark" thing?

SM Well it's a very subtle thing... because of course when you write words people will inevitably look for a coherent meaning which is there—in bits and pieces—maybe not adding up to a complete whole, but for me the words are not just about meanings, in fact I experience your drawings as precisely that, images, the words are visual marks and the meaning is a secondary thing.

SL If the text was in a foreign language that you didn't understand at all—do you think your response to the words as marks would be greater—or might the experience of the whole picture be less interesting?

SM That's a very good point—it wouldn't make any difference to me at all—that makes my point really, I see your work entirely as a visual thing, like music, it's beyond the written word.

SL Last time you said that for you my words were not just about meanings, that you experienced them as visual marks, and the drawings as a whole as images, and the (literary) meaning was a secondary thing. And later you put it even more strongly when you spoke of going "beyond the written word", and experiencing my drawings as "entirely a visual thing". I find this response on the one hand strangely reassuring (because it's very much how I myself experience the work when I'm actually making it, and it's important to me that it should be visual) but on the other hand what you say is challenging, because the actual meaning of the words, what I call their "burden" of meaning, doesn't seem to want to be cast off so lightly. What happens to those meanings? Where do they go? Might I just as well be making gestural marks? That's my big question to you this time.... I'm pretty sure you're not thinking of something like Zen calligraphy and brush drawing. Because what you said was that it was the *words* that

Pens Ink and Paper 1845, two pages from the book.

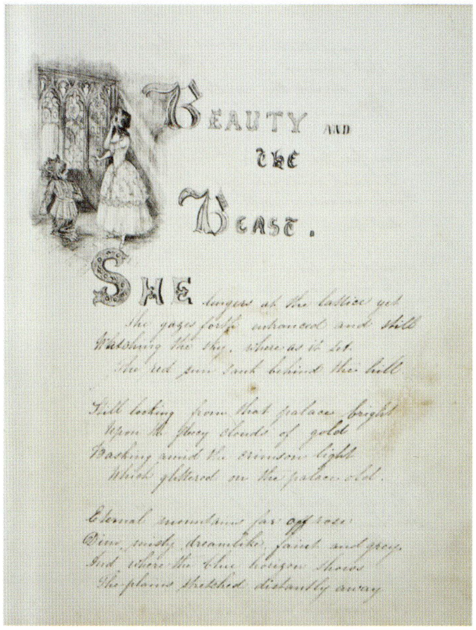
Beauty and the Beast.

She lingers at the lattice yet
She gazes forth entranced and still
Watching the sky where as to set
The red sun sank behind the hill

Still looking from that palace bright
Upon the fleecy clouds of gold
Basking amid the crimson light
Which glittered on the palace old.

Eternal mountains far off rose
Dim, misty, dreamlike, faint and grey.
And where the blue horizon shows
The plains stretched distantly away

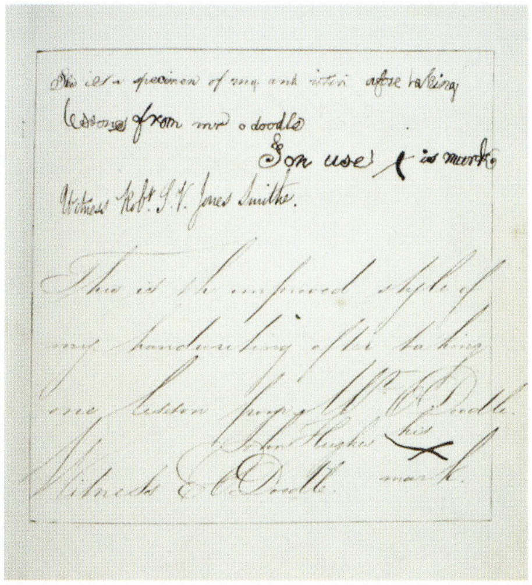
This is a specimen of my writing after taking lessons from Mr Doodle
[illegible] his mark
Witness [illegible] Jones Smith.

This is the improved style of my handwriting after taking one lesson from Mr [illegible] Doodle
John Hughes his mark
Witness E. C. Doodle.

were my marks. So there's a residue of content in there somewhere that is terribly important and simply won't go away; significant meaning that won't be transcended, or sublimated as in Zen. I know this is a gross over simplification of Zen, but for the sake of argument we'll let it stand. And that meaning has something to do with the word, in the Western sense. But how are those words to be used? What *kind* of meaning can they embody? Perhaps you'll be able to throw some light on this, from your work in poetry as well as in visual art.

Something else came up when we were talking today, about those earlier artists, like Mark Tobey and Julius Bissier, who were fascinated by Chinese and Japanese calligraphy, and the thought behind it, at a time when all of this was still fairly unfamiliar in the West. I think they both resisted the temptation to go the whole way down that oriental path. Although it gave them such important and precious insights, they wanted to keep a certain distance from it in their work, to find their own way. The 'signs' in their paintings had to be bearers of universal and personal meanings. Also they were certainly not just aesthetic objects, or pseudo-mystical in an undemanding way. Those pictures need to be 'read'. For me too it's that extra significance of words that generates the tension that I need. I can't really explain what it is, if I could I'd be able to 'explain' my pictures. It's a creative tension.

SM The question of meaning is, of course, vital to your drawings. The whole point, as I see it, is that you have to use text with meaning otherwise you might just as well copy large chunks of the newspaper or any chosen bits of literature, poetry or even extracts from the bible! So your elegant prose is what gives your work such depth and appeal. Even if we, the audience, don't read the words from top to bottom, we know at a glance that there is meaning hidden in those lines of text if we want to find it. I see this all linking up with *Pens, Ink and Paper* but you've taken it to another level of sophistication because you're a professional artist.

The whole issue of Chinese and Japanese calligraphy that we touched on yesterday is the same thing. Those marks are so seductive. You take a big soft brush and dip it into a pot of black ink and with a flick of the wrist a sumptuous splodge goes down on paper... but what does it mean? That's why we mustn't do it! We could churn out dozens of delicious ink drawings but we're not Chinese or Japanese and so we would be mimicking something without any understanding of the language and it would be an utterly pointless practice.

So back to your writing. Your work is writing as image but it can't be just any old writing. It has to be your writing that describes memories, thoughts, dreams, observations, etc., and then the viewer looks at the writing and it holds its own as an image but we can also dip into the writing as writing and find fragments of Simon Lewty. So when you say "For me too it's that extra significance of words that generates the tension that I need" you've defined your method.

When I said that I experience your drawings as entirely visual, I meant that, but from an entirely subjective point of view. I'm sure there will be people who relate almost entirely to the written word and on both counts there is much to enjoy.

Pens Ink and Paper 1845, title page of the book.

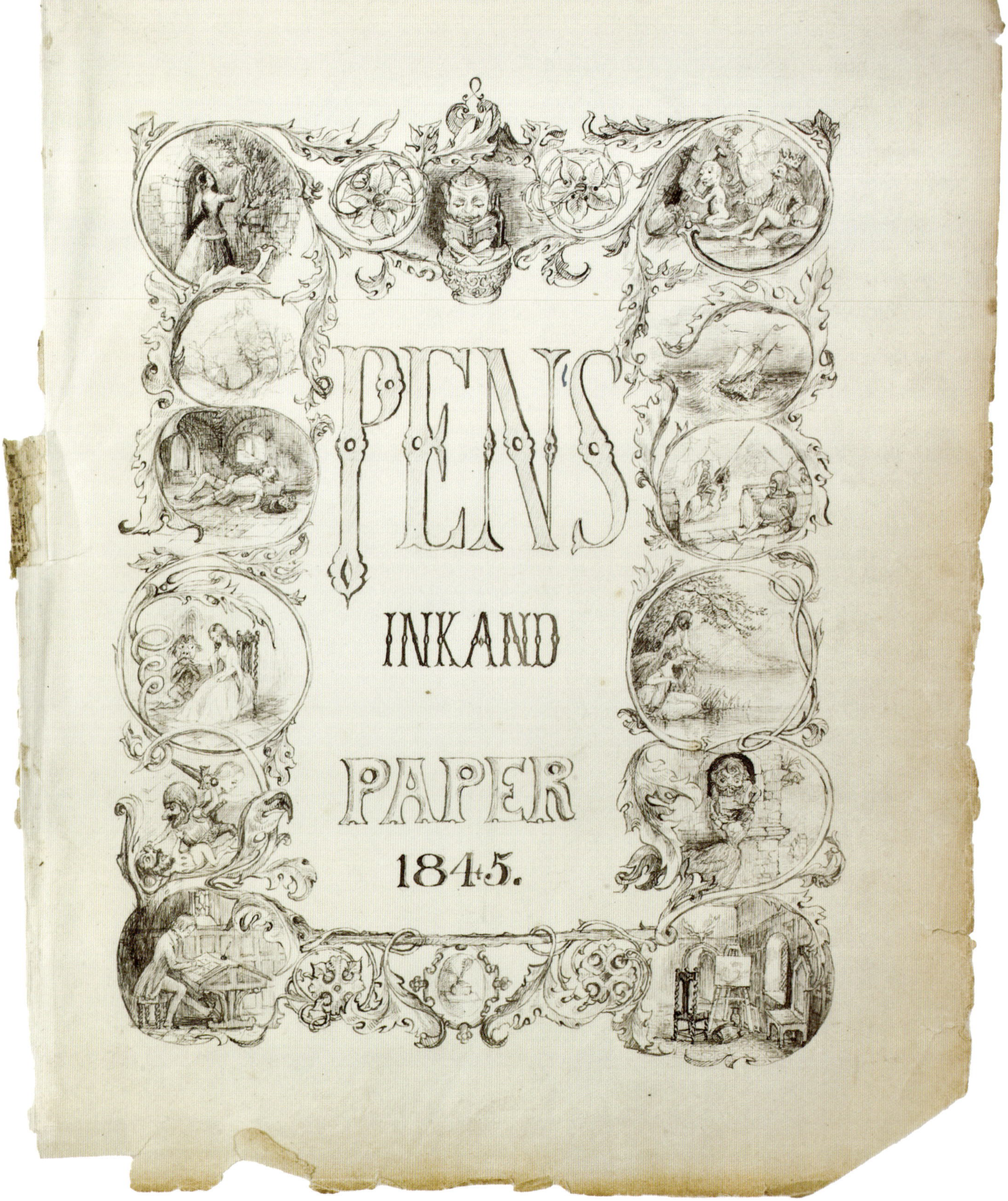

SL I wanted to ask you about the language poets and their approach to language. It was a revelation for you to discover their work?

SM It was. It was the most liberating experience to discover that there were people out there in the world (and the room I was in) who did not accept, would not follow the given literary traditions.

SL I can sense that in what you say. And when we were talking the other day you seemed to be pointing to some similarities between those poets and my own approach to language, which I think of as 'non convergent' in relation to those same traditions.

SM Well, when I read your book I was v. interested in how you came about constructing the text. It reminded me of some of the post modernist/ L=A=N=G=U=A=G=E poetry that I had read when I was studying.

SL I feel I've got to bite on it now and try to say how I did go about constructing the text. Which I'd like to do but may take a bit of saying... I assume the book you mention is *Cradles of the New*?[1]

Well it was made in the same way that I've always used text in my pictures, and still do. I started off with just getting down as quickly as I could a tangled knot of text which was part remembered dreams part childhood memory, and part a kind of semi-automatic writing. Hang on I've got a copy here on the shelf... then I worked on it spinning it out, allowing anything that wanted to come in to do so. It was as though a strange 2-way process was at work. On the one hand I was releasing meaning from the words I was using and on the other it was as though meaning was going to the words....

TIME was of the utmost importance—not that I had any desire to write about time as such, but as though I sensed that time was the framework within which everything had to develop. I started off in an almost deliberately archaic way, with an epigraph from William Morris of all people and set a scene of 'tale-telling' in a sort of timeless narrative way like stories round the fireside of ones childhood. Then I think I intuitively blew it all wide apart with a complete paradox—writing about 'a late time which was yet so early'—as though William Morris had met up with Einstein and relativity! Maybe it was the logic of the dream—and that set the scene for everything that was to follow.

SM Why was TIME so important?

SL I've always been fascinated by time... for x number of reasons. But what starts *Cradles* off was seeing the gravestone, in a churchyard in the Cotswolds of an old man, a shepherd, who had died in 1906 aged about 100, an incredible age for those days... he would have been born in the reign of George III, I think, lived through the whole of the nineteenth century and died in the year that my mother was born. Looking at his inscribed tombstone was like looking down a vast tunnel with me at one end in the here and now, 1980 something and that inconceivable unknown at the other end. The two points meeting at that 'now moment' in the churchyard. It was an amazing experience. Well that's just chronological time I suppose, but that is strange enough to think about... then there's dream time too... it goes on....

SM Could you explain "a late time which was yet so early".

SL Poetic image, to be explained with great care, if it's possible... let me think... oh... yes it was as though I felt that that point—when the shepherd came into the world and became a part of historical, chronological time, along with the rest of us, both before him and after him, was 'late' in relation to the 'timeless' world of mythic time—but in relation to me in the 1980s it was 'early'. Sounds cumbersome, and even as I write it down I'm aware it sounds too literal and there's something else that utterly eludes me. An enigma. But does that make any sort of sense at all, as far as it goes? It's hard going but valuable to put me on the spot and to have to try to explain.

SM You've explained it perfectly. It's maybe pedantic of me to ask you to spell it all out like this but on the other hand it's incredibly interesting to unpick your method and it won't detract from the poetry at all.

SL Re-reading the opening page of *Cradles of the New*, I think that I can take it as representative of my writing as a whole. Although it's some years since I wrote *Cradles*, and there have been a few new developments, I think the way I approach writing is essentially the same now as it was then. In that first page there are several strands of material: 1) The image of the old shepherd and his life (of which I know nothing, apart from what is written on his tombstone). With all the time associations I mentioned yesterday. 2) The sculptures around the door of that little church. Biting, gaping, snarly, beaked heads (like the ones at Lincoln Cathedral—only on a smaller scale). There's also a marvellous primitive relief carving of Jonah *inside* the whale. It's an amazing eruption of paganism/animism into a place of Christian worship. One of my all-time favourite churches! The shepherd like others in the village must have been familiar with these images all his life. Just imagine living to over 100 in the place where you were born... and we're not talking about a remote Medieval person here but someone who lived into the twentieth century, right in the wings of our modern age. 3) There are also references to my dreams. I had a dream of a statue whose hand had been cut off... and another of having one's way forward blocked and having to escape by crawling under a net... quite uncomfortable, physical imagery. 4) A memory of a journey in an almost empty train a few years before. (Just occurred to me: three journeys—Jonah in the whale; escape under the net; train journey).

All this was in, or beneath, my mind at the time, so it was I suppose the raw material. I wrote it down in a flow, like automatic writing, not stopping to reflect. Then as I teased the threads apart or pulled them together in the writing a kind of rhythm emerged which seemed to create a structure and a space. Sometimes the meaning seemed to emerge *from* the words, and sometimes, in a way hard to describe, it seemed to go *to* them, as though attracted by a kind of magnetism. Things fitted together in an unforeseen way.

Finally, the visual stage, writing it all out by hand, unifying it and making it visible as a graphic sign, as an image made of words with its own new identity—which can often take me by surprise. Out of a tangle of archaic material something which seems quite new can emerge. Of course, trying to describe all this is being 'wise after the event'—because nothing is worked out in advance. It all seems incredibly chancy at the time. A sort of intuitive scanning process. But maybe one's unconscious mind makes more sense of these things than it gets credit for.

SM OK... so now I have to rethink everything because we're getting to the nitty gritty—text as meaning. I've been reacting, largely, to the visual and treating the text as secondary. Tut tut!

Am now going to think....

So what's happening is that Simon is explaining his writing process which to me, has similarities to the way that some of the L=A=N=G=U=A=G=E poets might go about constructing their poems. One of the aims was to challenge the conventional use of the English language inherited from the European literary tradition; a fundamental difference being Simon's work isn't politically motivated in any way.

How I understand it is that Simon makes a many stranded commentary and the absences in the writing create a quiet pace in which to contemplate the fragmentary glimpses of his experiences, whether dreams, journeys or observations.

He has intuitively invented a language in which he can tell things while at the same time keep secrets. The revealed and the hidden. The written and the withheld. The words make the images. The images are words.

I have always looked at Simon's work and see the words/sentences as marks. The arrangement of these marks on the surface being his art and now I realise that beneath the surface the words describe another kind of image. So there is looking at the image and there is reading the image. Both exist. One kind of image is seen, the other is imagined.

And now I see why he has let go of drawing his images as he did in his earlier work. There is no need to show the pictures because they are in the writing and the writing has become the only necessary thing to look at. The image is the secret we share with him.

SM (Referring to one of SL's suggested subjects for discussion). The male/female thought processes subject is fraught with dangers, for instance, if I say that it is more likely that a man will interrupt a woman during the course of a conversation than the other way round (there has been research on this topic that proves this—and if a woman does do the interrupting she is usually an academic or high-achiever in a man's profession) I'm going to be accused of bias. I'm really interested in the politics of conversation though. The reason I brought up the male/female thing during our Skyping was because I became aware of how different our thinking processes are and I just wondered if it was a factor. One thing I associate with male thinking is the desire to have references, to build a conversation on facts etc.. It's the foundation on which ideas are built. So, traditionally, men will talk about 'things' or 'places' or 'facts' and women will talk about 'what happened to who or the feeling behind a situation etc. speculation even. It now gets v. tricky and of course 'male' and 'female' aren't just men and women but the man in woman and the woman in man.

SL I'd like to take up the male/female in relation to art. I've always been fascinated by things to do with the process of artistic creativity itself. Klee was one of my very first gurus and I read his texts on art when I was probably too young to understand them properly—but just because I loved his pictures and was fascinated to know more. But the other thing I intuited about Klee at that time, and with de Chirico, is that in fact nothing can be explained...

Giorgio de Chirico, *Mystery and Melancholy of a Street,* 1914.
Oil on canvas, 87 x 71.5 cm (Private collection).

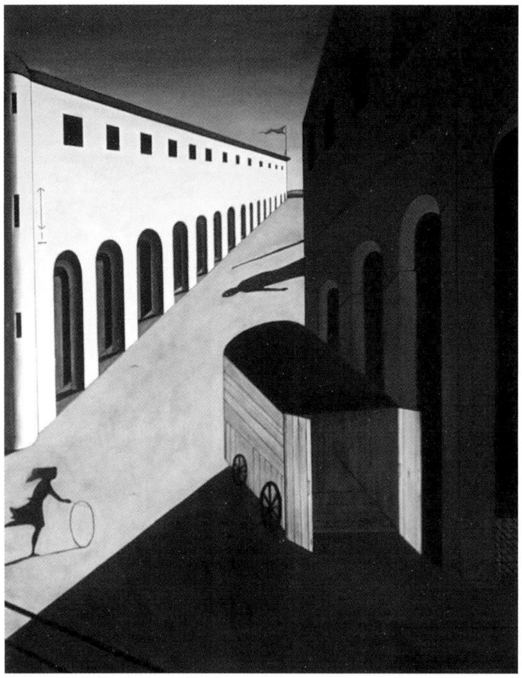

absolutely nothing. You can talk and write endlessly about ideas, as both these artists themselves did with great insight and poetic evocation, but the pictures themselves remain enigmas. The beauty of those enigmas is what resonated for me. It was like something I already knew in an intuitive way. That was where it all began, years ago, and it still draws me on. So if, as you say, 'male' thinking originates in the desire for facts, references, idea structures, etc., here was an area where none of this applied. If I had started out with the (male?) desire to find out 'what makes the wheels go round', I soon discovered that this was not the right way. What I sensed was more to do with listening for correspondences than reaching certainties. To respect those enigmas. Is this approach that of the 'woman in man' you mention? Anyway, there have always been these two things. But the ability to speak and write about art has absolutely nothing to do with making art—which is a mystery for me.

SM Reading through your response I hit on something really interesting. You say "But the other thing I intuited about Klee... the pictures themselves remain enigmas." That whole passage links up with what I was saying about your work and that it can be understood in two ways. For me, first the writing as visual marks and then the writing as prose. Both art but experienced so differently. The enigma begins when (we) try to articulate an image. If you are the kind of person who can accept an image as an image then no verbal explanation is necessary. The image only becomes an enigma if it has to be articulated; then language becomes wholly inadequate and the meaning starts to chase its tail. Even with narrative paintings, portraits or landscapes, they have to work visually and it's at that level that something works for me or not. This is where your work comes in as it works both ways: the visual enigma and the written enigma, each element bringing a bit of the other to the surface.

The reason I'm more interested in abstract art is that it's like music. It's understood without words. There are many words one could use to describe certain sensations related to the piece of work being heard or looked at and it's a marvellous thing when you can share that experience with other people.

SL Yes this is where Klee comes in and de Chirico too. Although they are so different I always think of them together, maybe because I discovered them at the same time. The strangeness of de Chirico's early work is one of the most amazing things in early twentieth century art. One contemporary critic spoke of them as being not paintings so much as a writing down of dreams. They seem to emanate from his experiences of seeing things of the material world as though for the first time, with an almost hallucinatory clarity, so that they appear as unutterably strange... and yet as the same time strangely familiar. This was the feeling I had when I first saw them in b/w reproductions, paintings with unforgettable titles like *The Enigma of an Autumn Afternoon* and *Mystery and Melancholy of a Street.* I felt that I was looking at something I already knew. Perhaps they are glimpses into an archetypal world, where things appear as signs. In de Chirico's case it seems to have been almost like a psychic gift, because later on he completely lost it—his later work is quite different and often embarrassingly bad.

SM We grew up at a time when Klee's work was very much in evidence. For instance, I think there were mass produced posters (was the company called Athena?) of works by Klee also Dali, Miro, Klimt et al. They were all out there with the exception of your great Bissier who seems to have slipped through the mass production net. Interesting what you say about Klee being an enabler. Of course, he was of the old school whose attitude was quite different to what is going on today with the mania for celebrity, winning prizes, making headlines, etc., but maybe there are many kinds of artists. There are the extroverts who are openly ambitious, want an audience and all the gongs—NOW! Picasso falls into that category. But what about Braque who hardly gets a look in and was, in my opinion, much more interesting. He was a thinker and Picasso was a performer. We just have to know ourselves and not think we're something we're not. We come from a generation who believe in certain values. Values, that if you declare them, sound rather quaint, like good manners or the v. English idea of not trying too hard to win, to achieve things by hard work and good practice but dubious activities have always gone on haven't they—wasn't it Michelangelo who kept the Sistine Chapel locked so that only his trusted assistants had access to what he was doing?

SL Your mention of Athena posters took me right back—yes indeed, I had some of their prints hanging in my bedroom when I was about 15 or 16. Klee, Miro, Dufy. There weren't all that many to choose from then. Now there are 1,000s. The top 10 is quite predictable: Van Gogh in the lead, Dali, Klimt, etc., so not much changes. I thought I'd search for Bissier and found there are 19 to choose from! (Pablo weighs in with 640.) Then of course there are the hundreds of kitsch imitations, which is a bit depressing. How dead they look....

SM Want to pick up on our earlier conversation in which we were discussing this tricky question of other people's ideas and why it is or isn't justifiable to use them.

The influence of great artists like Tapies or Twombly goes without saying. They opened doors for many artists and we can see their influence, whether consciously acknowledged or not, in a great many works of contemporary art. At some stage we are bound to owe a debt to certain artists but we move on and find our own language.

The v. tricky area is when, as artists who are working outside the 'great' definition, we find our work being plagiarised.

I said earlier, that for me, the knowledge that the marks I make have come from myself, my thoughts, my experience and not from someone else's thought is the thing that sustains me. It's not that I'm preoccupied with uniqueness. It's just that I need to feel that I've come to certain ideas from an independent thought process. I would feel that I'd been lazy if I hadn't found it for myself. It's for this reason I loathe all the signposts they put up around the countryside telling us which way to go and what wildlife we will see on a particular route. The wild places are being turned into theme parks. Disneyland in Dorset! It's a dumbing down of experience. No risks. No danger. No death. No life....

SL On plagiarism. You aren't my only friend and colleague who has suffered from this recently and having had a taste of the same thing myself, it's in my mind again.

As you know, literary plagiarism is rife in academic institutions, something which they've realised now. That poster you told me about in New Hall, Cambridge was revealing. In visual art the problem is more difficult to prove and is compounded by other things. Plagiarism is a murky grey area, unlike forgery which is a crime and you can go to prison for it. Art plagiarism may not be as literal as with written material, but the motivations and the outcomes are the same. It may be even more insidious, if it tries not only to ape the look of another artist's work, but to lay claim also to some of the motivations, 'mythology' and spirit of that work. Sometimes even the titles. Where there is big money involved there are usually lawyers on call and I wouldn't think someone putting sheep, etc., in formaldehyde would get very far, assuming the stuff was being shown and offered for sale to the public. One letter would be enough to scare them off. But, and this is my second point, in addition to being morally wrong, and perhaps in some cases legally actionable, the thing which my mind always keeps coming back to is—what on earth is the point of it?

SL Following my thoughts over recent days has led to so many things, all mixed up, but funnily connected I feel, although the connections are difficult to sort out. Perhaps I'm wrong. Anyway, it's too much for one email so I thought it would be better to divide it into smaller 'bites' and get your responses as we go.

Picasso first: I'm glad that you approve of what John Berger said—I rather thought you would! It's such a cautionary tale—how Picasso ended up the captive of his own great gifts, his cult, his myth. And it raises other issues. A lot of what B says stems from his Marxist perspective, but that interests me less than what he has to say about magic. B was struck by the insatiable curiosity of the public about the artist's life. People are fascinated by the idea that here is a human being just like you and me—and yet different, special. So everything to do with Picasso, his relationships with women, those endless photos of him on the beach, at bullfights, etc., with friends or in solitary self-communings in the studio, or playing the clown, it was all meticulously chronicled. Hundreds of books were compiled. Possibly it had more attention than his work, except something very major and public, like *Guernica*. Well, celebrities make good copy. And as you said, Damien Hirst and others have learned that. There is a potent fascination in the idea of the artist as magician. The shortcomings of the art itself can be glossed over. One sentence stuck in my mind. Berger quoted from one of Picasso's all-too-uncritical chroniclers: "For Picasso, of course, 'art' is a side-issue".

Interesting to compare with Joseph Beuys. Again someone who, in addition to his art, created from his life a very potent and glamorous myth. The artist as shaman, as a 'guru' with 'disciples'... even ritual clothes... I sense that the reasons behind what Beuys did were different and (although I'm not uncritical of Beuys) more *interesting* than Picasso's and it would be wrong to equate them. But they both sensed peoples' need for the magical, and both were essentially prophet/showmen in the ways they projected themselves. Behind all this there seems to lie a deep need which they tapped into. People with little or no magic in their lives need to believe, want to believe in the magic of art. Going back to that most ancient and primitive belief! This is the first stage, the Picasso/Beuys stage, where the artist is seen as someone 'special'.

The second stage is maybe what's happening now, where anybody can be special, become a celeb, wear trendy clothes, get drunk on camera, say outrageous things, make millions, etc.. And increasingly emerge as 'artists' too! Perhaps this is the post modern stage. Matt Collings wrote in this month's *Modern Painters* of how crappy the art scene is now—I felt like saying hmmm... but you endorsed it in the first place! Art as fashion.

Whatever it was, that 'something' that led me to become an artist and still makes me persevere year in and year out, in what by Picasso's standards or Beuys' or Hirst's, is an incredibly private journey and a very limited lifestyle, was not I think primarily fame or big money or celebrity. No, I think what drew me was a kind of magic, and I just knew I didn't want to do anything else. It was the magic in art, and making that magic that fascinated me, not the thought of being a magician. But the thought remains: is the artist special? Or (as somebody said) is everybody a special kind of artist?

I know Braque is an artist you greatly admire, and I wonder if you've come to that telling bit in Berger's book where he talks of the parting of the ways between Picasso and Braque after the First World War, and after the Cubist adventure. When Picasso joined the world of his wealthy patrons and Braque's work retreated more and more into inwardness. I remember you telling me about Braque's experiences of being wounded in the war... I'm sure this must have played a part. Anyway, their ways diverged more and more with the passing years, and I wonder if Braque looked at his old comrade and felt that Picasso had betrayed something quite precious. Was it that inwardness?

SM I'm at a bit of a disadvantage because I'm only about a third of the way through the book.

It's not that I approve of John Berger, as you say, I'm full of respect. I'm reading it slowly because there's so much to take in and having grown up with the Picasso hype and yet not having followed it particularly it's like having lumps of my life filled in!

One of the things that occurs to me is that there are introvert artists and extrovert ones (I've talked about this before, I know) like anyone else in the world. So clearly, Picasso, Joseph Beuys, Damien Hirst et. al. fall into the ex-artist category while Braque and Agnes Martin, for instance, fall into the int-artist one. So for the media-sated world we live in how much more copy they can extract from the ex-artists than the int-artists. Picasso, at the early onset of media insatiability was a gift. So, for an artist to be catapulted into the limelight there has to be a story. The ex-artists perform their stories and the int-artists sit quietly in their studios. Too much exposure would affect an int-artist badly and not enough would drive an ex-artist to distraction. The quote from the all-too-uncritical chronicler: "For Picasso, of course, 'art' is a side-issue" sort of underlines this.

Artist as magician is something I've been thinking about recently. Since we live in a godless society in the West, the artist has acquired a 'magical' status I believe. How the 'work of art' comes into existence can't really be explained. It is one of the few mysteries we still have and unlike science because science is looking for the answer whereas the making of art is an ongoing process without an end. Art sort of runs alongside society commenting, reflecting, etc.. So now, because we have no god and we're desperately looking for meaning, the artist has stepped in. Some artists know this. Beuys being the obvious one. Did Picasso know it or did he just naturally step into the magician's shoes I wonder? It seems to me that being a prodigy he was 'chosen' and had the personality to embrace it.

Our need for magic has created an enormous appetite for art. A piece of art on the wall means a piece of magic in your life. How was it made? Why was it made? Who was the person that made the magic thing?

Being an artist for me is not 'special' and this is where our experiences separate. I know for you, the magic of art was an extremely powerful pull and continues to be so. I had to de-mystify art before I could do it. My family, steeped in paint for three generations, had to be exorcised.[2] My struggle was to lose art before I could find it. Now I'm left with a practice that I do, fairly rigorously, because that's what it's come to. A mark on paper. By repeating my mark over and over again, day in and day out, I've managed to find my own art. But no, I don't think the artist is 'special'. I think we're lucky to be able to do it and some art is wonderful but I don't believe the artist is a shaman any more than a doctor who has insight or a teacher who has the patience to draw out the best in a pupil or a psychoanalyst who enables a person to let go of their demons. What the artist has is time to think....

SL It's so interesting to tease out these strands of thought and not quite know where they will lead. Your response to my Part 1 made absorbing reading, and reveals something of how your practice as an artist relates to these big 'abstract' issues we've been discussing, and which it's so important to discuss. This is always a complex relationship and one that goes on evolving, while returning obsessively to the same nexus of ideas and methods and marks like a recurring theme in a piece of music. You write with moving clarity on how you had "to de-mystify art in order to do it... to lose art in order to find it". Profound observations, drawn from your own hard-won experience.

Anyway, I want to follow this idea of inwardness for a bit longer. I suppose, being introspective by nature, what so interested me about Surrealism, right at the beginning, pre-art school, was that here was a whole movement directed specifically towards that inwardness. Of course, I didn't see it then in that sophisticated way—I just looked at Klee, de Chirico, Arp and all of them and thought THIS IS IT. A group of artists who set out to explore consciousness through art and thereby to 'change the world'. This was the 1920s and 30s when artists could say such things. Surrealism gave me (still at that time a pupil at an English public school) permission to go down that path of nonconformity. There was an element of private rebellion in it but I wasn't so interested in changing the world as in exploring the mind. I felt incredibly happy and encouraged to find out that inwardness was definitely an option, and could be pursued through art.

I didn't think of it as 'magic' then but I suppose it was a certain kind of magic, that comes from making something happen that surprises you. You are right to say that magic continues to exert a powerful pull on me. My abiding interest in dreams, automatism, and serendipity comes from this. As though it were possible to become responsive to the world in a different way, without losing ones reason. To sense the wind-ness of the wind in a field, the sea-ness of the sea's rhythm, the strange immateriality of the so solid concrete and glass and tarmac which surrounds one in a modern city. And to sense that mysterious ground of experience beneath these things and its echo in my mind. So difficult to describe... When we were children we would watch raindrops running down the window pane, and exult in thunderstorms, or be scared stiff... and value our dreams (or be scared stiff by them likewise) and a whole world of other 'childish' things. Actually, I still do all of these and maybe that comes closer to what I want to say. You grow up, you lose the child's vision, you have no choice, and it would be utterly disingenuous to pretend otherwise. (Paul Klee had some trenchant things to say about this, wounded by accusations of 'childishness' in his drawing....) You may even find yourself trying to write like I am now, to reflect in words on these impalpable, wordless things. But if you are a certain type of artist you are drawn almost inexorably to make your art out of them. Even if, as with me, it is an art perversely made out of words. They seem to visit you in a strange way, as though they had a message for you. I hope this doesn't sound too far fetched.

It's not shamanism. Is shamanism really valid or meaningful outside its tribal and nomadic context anyway? I wonder. By the time Beuys has left the Steppes and has filtered down to the West Midlands there's not much left. Art, now, has become a private thing, and no amount of 'audience participation' at Tate Modern can really alter that. Occasionally, as with the Doris Salcedo *Shibboleth*, the work is strong enough to communicate across many barriers.[3] You say what the artist has is time to think. Absolutely. And how valuable if that thought can be communicated in such an unforgettable way.

SM One thing that occurred to me was that at the same time Klee, de Chirico, Arp and the others were painting, psychoanalysis was entering the picture (literally!). The ideas of Freud and Jung were beginning to filter through and the artists were echoing that move into working with the unconscious and of course we, the public recognised, whether consciously or not, that these were thoughts that had meaning for us. So our generation were growing up with a whole new visual language that contained magic and truth as far as we were concerned and an escape from Victorian heaviness. By responding to those ideas and images we were of our time.

Magic is a slippery subject, as difficult as trying to explain the reasons for making art and that's the thing, the outcome of magic can't be explained any more than how a work of art comes about but both have an end product.

I was wondering if Joseph Beuys' work was only potent when he was alive which suggests that his art was himself (like a shaman). In my opinion his art seen in Tate Modern or wherever, looks tired and lifeless. I met up with Richard Demarco who was conducting an invited group of people round the big Beuys retrospective at TM Richard Demarco was his usual self, brimming with intense admiration for the man.[4] I'm afraid I was more or less appalled (apart from some interesting things in glass cabinets, but then I've always liked things in glass cabinets). But thinking back, Richard was trying to impress us with what Beuys stood for, the importance of his message, his connection with the natural world, etc., but I found those dusty bits and pieces on the floor didn't convey much of this.

I've always disliked going to the houses or studios of dead artists. You see their paint brushes, palettes, notebooks, etc., relics religiously preserved but without the vital energy of the person, that of course lives on in the work. But in Joseph Beuys' case the vital energy does not live on in the work. The relics of his work are just reminders of the tools he used to create his magic which vanished with his death. Really, his work should be ritually collected and destroyed because the art has gone but his myth will last. Keeping his art alive would have to be done with words... how neatly that brings me back to your work.... the magic of the written word and we're back to the beginning. Your words, your mark.

SL I'm genuinely unsure about Beuys. I think he's been over-rated, but I wouldn't write him off totally as a charlatan, as Peter Fuller did. Actually I'm not even really sure if he's an artist, because I think one has to rid one's mind of theories to make art. Intuition must take over. For B theory was his life-blood, he tried to be a sort of artist/scientist/prophet/political philosopher. All deeply serious and sincerely held positions. He spoke of science as being like a necessary strait-jacket through which his art had to pass in order to find liberation. But his ideas got stuck in dense sticky material like flies on a fly paper.

I have to say that only one really resonant idea (for me) has ever emerged from Beuys' work. And it may not even be entirely his own but that doesn't matter. And it is exactly that—an idea. I hope I'm not going to explain it incorrectly, but it comes from the space/time notion of transformation following captivity. So if space (matter) is confined, time (mind) can be released. An exchange of energies. As in Beuys' now well-known life/mythology he was saved from death when his plane crashed during the war, by nomads who wrapped him up and cared for him. A near-death and rebirth experience. I'm sure that's what all the wrapping up in felt and coating with fat and honey and living in a cage with a coyote etc. are about. Those 'systems' of compressors, filters, pumps and so on which he uses in his sculpture to evoke something between organic, wild nature, and a machinic world. A world of compression and release. The trouble is with Beuys that the thought gets devoured by the sheer material presence of his work. He seems to have had little feeling for the faculty of imagination.

But you don't have to see it that way. I had a more abstract, perhaps poetic take on that idea: I thought about (something which we have sometimes discussed) how, after death, a person's life can be seen as a totality... of how death completes life. This is a very important idea for me.

The journey through materiality releases something into time, and perhaps releases time itself (depends how you think of time). I don't need to do a part time degree course in physics, or read all the books. I can take the idea in all its immateriality and economy, perhaps only partly understand it or even misunderstand it—and it still resonates in my mind and can become creative.

I agree with your main idea, that Beuys' work was only potent when he was alive. Each subsequent exhibition now seems to prove it. Shamanism makes use of vital energy to achieve its ends, so when the shaman dies his power dies with him. Something which may not be the case with an artist, at least not the sort of artist whose work is making something—some thing, that is, rather than making him/her self. We may all need to make fetish objects from time to time; but I've come to think that my main activity as an artist is directed towards something different. If it involves 'magic' it's a different kind of magic. Perhaps it's wrong to call it "magic" even... but it's very potent. I think this may be where the mystical diverges from the magical. And perhaps art insists on keeping a respectful distance from both. This speculation sets off many thoughts for me... things which go to my work, things I haven't resolved. Hard to unpick.

SM You've obviously investigated Joseph Beuys quite deeply and come out the other side. You'd probably enjoy talking (or should I say listening) to Richard Demarco about his collaborations and journeys with Beuys. I've always thought that the stories about him being dragged from his plane and healed by nomads was just that, a 'story'. Like German folk tales that go back centuries. He's created one of his own which will no doubt be told down the centuries. It almost seems irrelevant whether his work is good or not. But what I get from you is that it's the ideas behind the work that interest you. You say you're not even really sure if he's an artist. Then I say, "what is an artist?" Aha! Is an artist a person who transforms an idea into something else? Is your interpretation of Beuys' work: "... but it comes from the space/time notion of transformation following captivity" the same thing?

On a personal note, I was so comforted after my mother died by your idea that "death completes life". It's such a natural cycle when you can see it like that and explains why we can never really understand the whole of life because death is the missing part and is the thing we cannot while alive, experience.

SL In a way, I'm the worst person to comment on Beuys, as I sense the main thrust of his work was political, rather than aesthetic. (Not that I'm a total paid-up aesthete either, as I think that's a seriously self-limiting position. The St Ives syndrome.) But it's like knowing if you're an introvert or an extrovert—there's no point in pretending to be something you aren't. Some artists I know and respect have said to me "But Simon, EVERYTHING is political!" Sorry. I do have a blind spot. And I know I'll have to 'do' the political in a minute....

You suggest (although you do it by a rhetorical question) that the artist is someone who transforms an idea into something else—which reminded me of the title of that seminal 1969 exhibition, *When Attitudes become Form*—the first major showing of American and European Conceptual Art in this country.[5] It's what's now called an 'iconic' exhibition. I remember seeing it, Beuys included, along with Land Art, Arte Povera, various kinds of Conceptual work, etc., and it made a deep, deep impression on me. It was so exciting. I knew it was very revolutionary, much of it, and some at least of the artists were openly politically committed.

I reflected for weeks and months on what I had seen that day, and I think it actually changed some of my attitudes. But I felt that the whole issue wasn't about the actual things on show, so much as the ideas to which they gave rise. For me, those piles of felt and earth and ashes and bundles of sticks and lumps of clay and plasticine were not there as ends in themselves (although some of them were incidentally very sensuous and beautiful things), but as metaphors for various immaterial states, perhaps even psychic states, for ideas in short. So while for the artists they might have originated in ideas, or sensations, somehow the process of embodying them in matter became one whereby the idea could be released at the other end totally transformed. Richard Long's walks are an excellent example. The 'innocence' and simplicity and self-sufficiency of his art form was, and is a wonderful justification of 'Art as Idea'—in his case grounded in real physical experiences. As in alchemy, where the transformation is in what happens inwardly to the alchemist during the course of his operations. And perhaps also like alchemy it's a circular process.

Whichever way round it is, I think transformation is the key word with Beuys. And for him the ultimate transformation—he said it himself—was of the social order. A kind of revolution. He saw creativity as the instrument of that, and his idea of creativity was very democratic—everyone a creator. He saw his role as an artist to provide a catalyst which would release the creativity in society as a whole. So art is certainly not an end in itself. Beuys wanted people to come out of his exhibitions as changed people. But in what way? That's the question. We may respond as individuals, but in ways unintended by Beuys. The artist cannot vouch for other people's responses to a work of art, even less the responses of a whole society. Paul Klee's reflective words in another context always echo in my mind: "... the people are not with us".

The way we responded to Doris Salcedo's work, knowing nothing of its heavy political underpinning, seems to bear that out. I'll always think of that day. And how I had to read all the literature. What was the 'right' response? Did you need to know all about DS's political position? Well, in the case of that piece, all that remains (apart from that faint scar on the floor at TM, like a healed wound) is indeed an idea, a memory of a time, a response, which lives on as an idea, if it lives at all. I actually find that scar quite potent, as sometimes remembered things and associations seem more potent than the original experience.

SM The whole issue of politics and art is a tricky one isn't it. I think politics is a subject like any other and one artist is motivated by politics where another might be inspired by light. An artist who makes art for political reasons might use light as part of his/her pictorial vocabulary e.g., a context in which light represents freedom. Another artist might use light in a purely poetic way but in a certain context this could be interpreted as political as that kind of poetic freedom isn't permitted.

Art should be a revolutionary act we're told, should break boundaries, shake the bourgeoisie, show people new ways of looking at society/the world, shatter the status quo, etc.. Some artists find themselves living or working in a situation where they have to make political choices and their art will inevitably reflect that choice. Did Doris Salcedo think of the 'crack' as a political idea first or an idea which became political I wonder. Reading her catalogue notes I was less convinced by the politics than the work, which I liked.

People's lives can be transformed by art but by the doing of it rather than the looking at it. An active life rather than a passive life. That is really a revolutionary concept re art. We should make art not just stand in galleries looking at art which we're told is great but might not be. We should decide for ourselves. If we all make art of our lives society will be a better place. The crashing of Beuys' plane, nearly dying and being saved by a tribe of nomadic people is a wonderful fable for this moment in time.

SL Your first paragraph when you talk about an artist using light left me desperately trying to think who it was (Rothko, or possibly Newman) who said something like "My art, rightly understood, is really about freedom." So interesting that... as Rothko had been quite radical in his early days, associated with left-wing intellectual circles in America in the 1930s and 40s before the US govt clamped down hard on such things for fear of communism. Do you think art can still shock ?

SM Yes, I do. I had two incidents when I was writing poetry that I found quite incomprehensible at the time. I'd been to Italy to stay with some friends. Someone they were very close to had just died. They had been to the mortuary the day I arrived and one of them, being a photographer, took a couple of shots of the body. It was a natural thing for her to do. I tried

Photographic sequence taken by Susan Michie's mobile phone of Doris Salcedo's *Crack/Shibboleth* in Tate Modern 2007–2008.

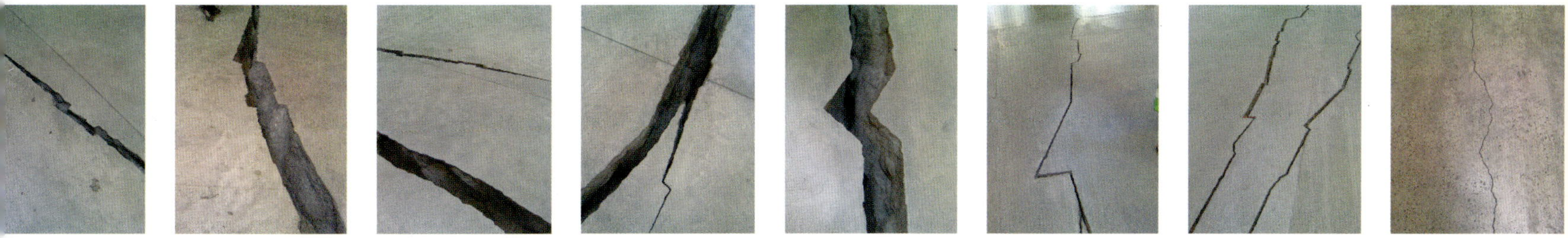

to write a poem about this incident and how, driving through the beautiful Tuscan landscape, the fields were full of dried up sunflowers. They were wilted and black. Acres of them. My poem was received with, yes, shock! Why would I want to write about such a morbid subject? The other was when I wrote a poem about a painting my father had done. I was describing his process and how he used the image of a Japanese woman in a kimono as the basic idea. The poem was about how an artist sees something and uses it, in this case a woman. During the painting he detaches himself from the woman as a human being and she becomes his subject. He owns her so to speak. An interesting idea I thought but nobody seemed to get it and I was accused of being cold.

SL So art can still shock!—and most interestingly, you link what you say to your own experience.

We are vulnerable the moment we show our work to other people, precisely because the artist *may* challenge conventional attitudes to life, death, beauty, ugliness, etc., so that people feel threatened. They rush to condemn, not just your work but you—a moral condemnation.

Yet there are happy moments when you do get a positive response. It doesn't matter if it sometimes seems superficial, because there are many levels, and perhaps what we call superficial may have more to it than we think. Who knows what is involved when a person responds to a surface?

Sometimes I sense that whatever it is that is most inward to me as an artist has spoken to something equally inward in another person, and been recognised, and this is the most valuable of all responses.

In the meantime, and for whatever reasons, we make our art. Perhaps it's rather like putting a message into a bottle and launching it on the open sea, not knowing if it will ever be found, or if a remote finder might share its message.

But maybe that's a subject for another time....

1. *Cradles of the New*, Prest Roots Press, 1994.
2. Susan Michie's father, Alastair Michie, and her grandmother, Anne Redpath, were both distinguished painters.
3. *Shibboleth*, Doris Salcedo, London, Tate Modern, 2007-2008.
4. *Joseph Beuys*, London, Tate Modern, 2005.
5. *When Attitudes Become Form—Works, Concepts, Processes, Situations, Information*, curated by Harald Szeemann, London, ICA, 1969.

opposite and overleaf 68. *To Unexplained Day*, 2002.

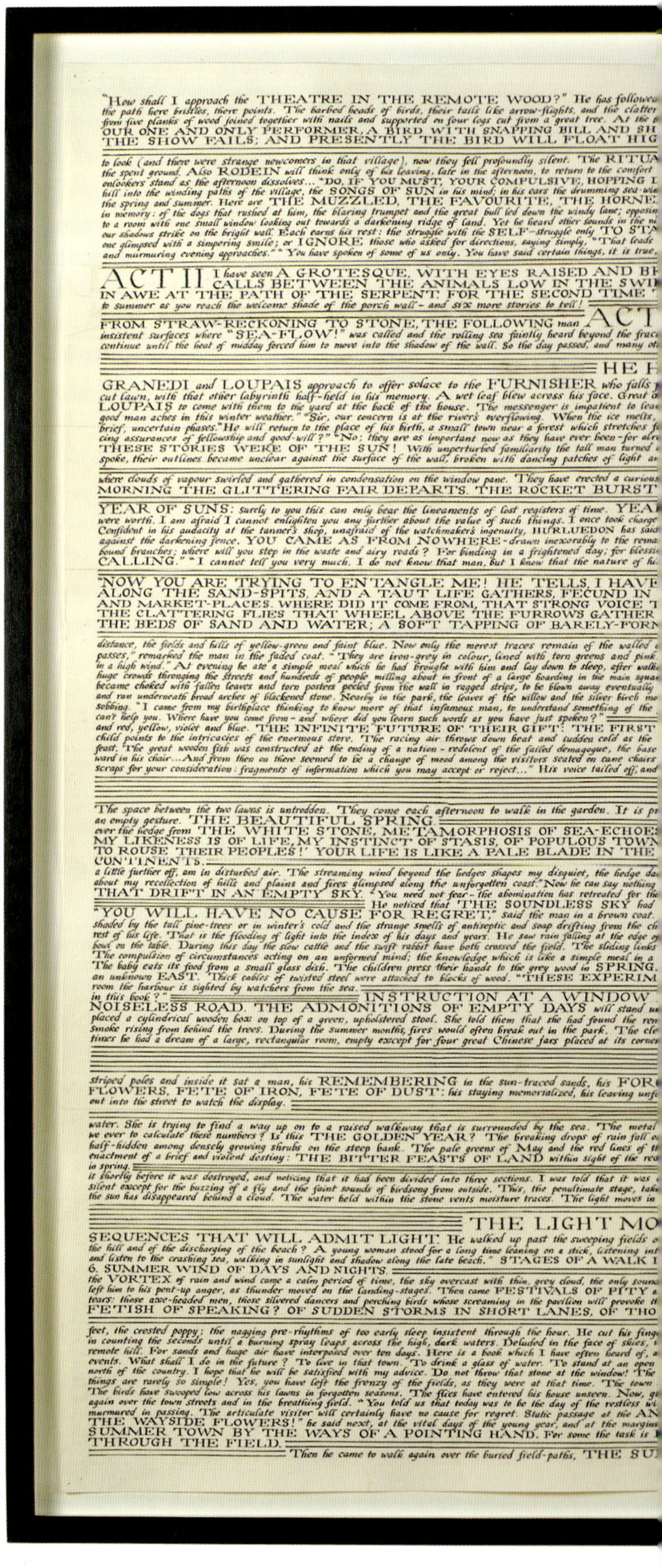

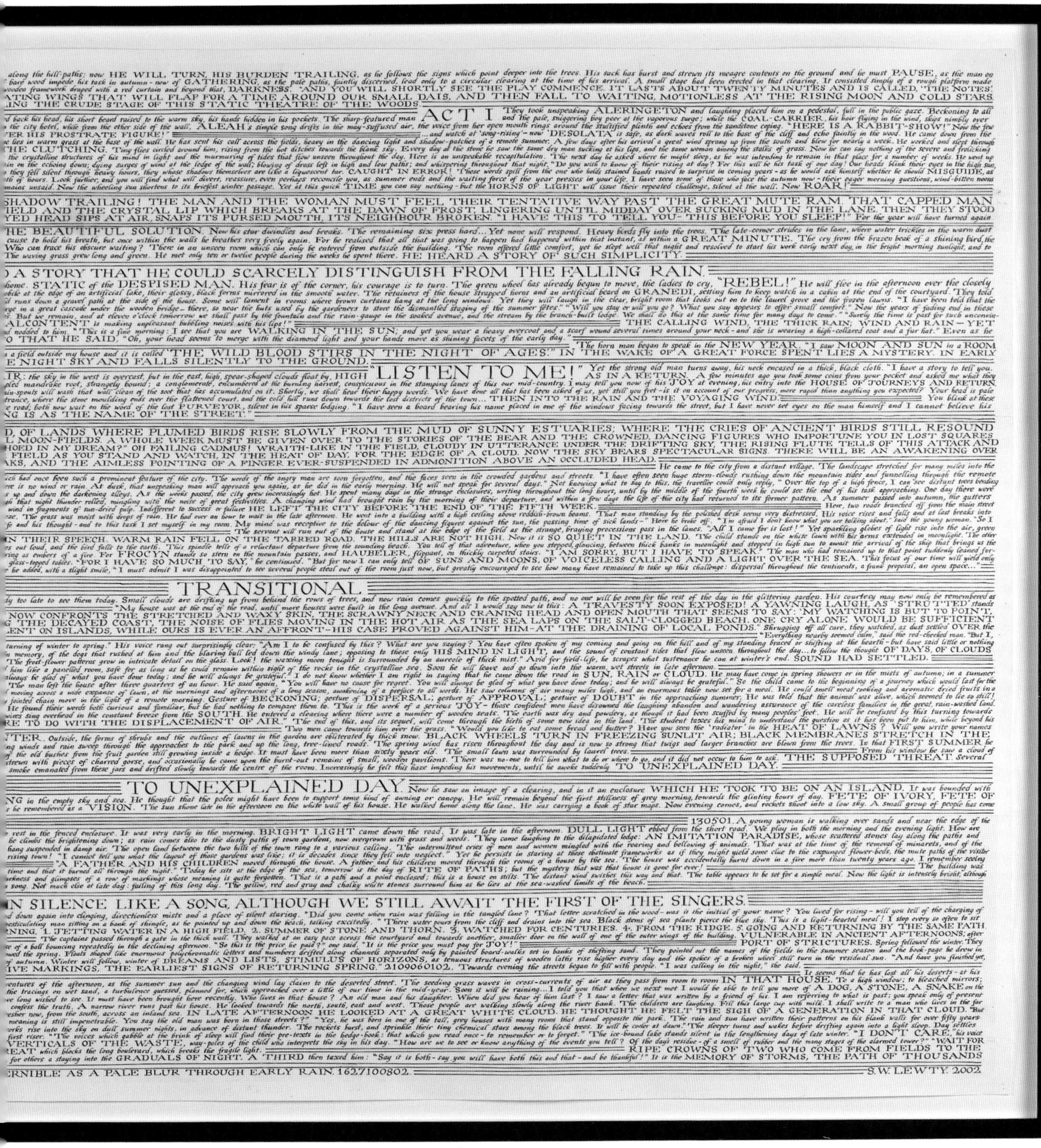
ACT I
SHADOW TRAILING! THE MAN AND THE WOMAN MUST FEEL THEIR TENTATIVE WAY PAST THE GREAT MUTE RAM. THAT CAPPED MAN
A STORY THAT HE COULD SCARCELY DISTINGUISH FROM THE FALLING RAIN.
"REBEL!"
THE WILD BLOOD STIRS IN THE NIGHT OF AGES.
LISTEN TO ME!
OF LANDS WHERE PLUMED BIRDS RISE SLOWLY FROM THE MUD OF SUNNY ESTUARIES; WHERE THE CRIES OF ANCIENT BIRDS STILL RESOUND
TRANSITIONAL.
TO UNEXPLAINED DAY.
IN SILENCE LIKE A SONG, ALTHOUGH WE STILL AWAIT THE FIRST OF THE SINGERS.
ERNIBLE AS A PALE BLUR THROUGH EARLY RAIN. 1627100802.
S.W. LEWTY. 2002.

there is no wind or rain. At dusk, that unspeaking man will approach y
times up and down the darkening alleys. As the weeks passed, the city gre
hrough that night thunder rolled, mingling with the noise of great festivit
ring wind in fragments of sun-dried pulp. Indifferent to success or failure H
breeze. The grass was moist with drops of rain. He had over an hour to wa
is life and his thought - and to this task I set myself in my room. My m

The s

Y IN THEIR SPEECH. WARM RAIN FELL ON TH

cries out loud, and the bird falls to the earth. This spindle tells of a re
stirring as embers of a fire. For FROCYN stands so stern on the
nall, glass-topped tables. "FOR I HAVE SO MUCH TO SAY," h
ause he added, with a slight smile, "I must admit I was disappointed to s

TRANS

ready too late to see them today. Small clouds are drifting up from

"My house was at the end of the road,

T NOW CONFRONTS THE STRETCHED AND WA
ONG THE DECAYED COAST, THE NOISE OF F
SILENT ON ISLANDS, WHILE OURS IS EVER A

the turning of winter to spring." His voice rang out surprisingly clear:
ar in memory, of the dogs that rushed at him and the blaring bull led
ng. The frost-flower patterns grow in intricate detail on the glass. Look!
ound him like a panelled room, safe for as long as he could remain with
ill always be glad of what you have done today; and he will always be g
hop. The man left the house after three quarters of an hour. He said
and moving across a wide expanse of lawn, at the mornings and afterno
isely jointed chain move in the light of a remote morning. Gesture of B
om. He found their words both curious and familiar, but he had nothing
ne wires sing overhead in the constant breeze from the SOUTH. He
ARE TO DO WITH THE DISPLACEMENT OF

INTER. Outside, the forms of shrubs and the outlines of lawns
lowing winds and rain sweep through the approaches to the park and
one of the old bushes from the fruit garden still growing inside a hedge.
ere strewn with pieces of charred gorse, and occasionally he came upon
tish smoke emanated from these jars and drifted slowly towards the cent

TO UNEXPL

TING in the empty sky and sea. He thought that the poles might
This he remembered as a VISION. The sun shone late in the aftern

again, as he did in the early morning. He will not speak for several da
ncreasingly hot. He spent many days in the strange enclosures, writing thi
A changing wind had brought rain by the morning of their departure
LEFT THE CITY BEFORE THE END OF THE FI
n the late afternoon. He went into a building with a high ceiling above redd
d was receptive to the dolour of the dancing figures against the sun, th
ant will run out of the house and stand at the edge of the field as the
TARRED ROAD. THE HILLS ARE NOT HIGH. Now it
tant departure from the sounding beach. You tell of that adventure, when
untain passes, and HAUBELER, flippant, on thickly carpeted stai
continued. "But for now I can only tell OF SUNS AND MOONS
several people steal out of the room just now, but greatly encouraged to s

ITIONAL

hind the rows of trees, and now rain comes quickly to the spotted p
til more houses were built in the long avenue. And all I would say now
KY SKIN, THE SCRAWNY NECK AND CRANING H
ES MOVING IN THE HOT AIR AS THE SEA I
AFFRONT–HIS CASE PROVED AGAINST HIM–

Am I to be confused by this? What are you saying? You have often
wn the windy lane; opposing to these only HIS MIND IN LIGH
waxing moon tonight is surrounded by an aureole of thick mist." A
sight of the rocks in the crystalline sea. Soon he will leave and go d
teful." I do not know whether I am right in saying that he came down
in, "You will have no cause for regret. You will always be glad of what
of a long season, awakening of a preface to all words. He saw columns of
CKONING; gesture of DISPERSAL; gesture of APPROVA
compare them to. This is the work of a serious JOY– those confid
tered a clearing where there were a number of wooden seats. The eart
R." The end of this, and its sequel, will come through the birth of
Two men came towards him over the grass. "Would you like to ea
the garden are obliterated by thick snow. BLACK WHEELS
the long, tree-lined roads. The spring wind has risen throughout th
must have been more than sixty years old. The small lawn was su
burnt-out remains of small, wooden pavilions. There was no-one to t
of the room. Increasingly he felt this haze impeding his movements, unt

AINED DAY. Now he saw an image of a clea
ve been to support some kind of awning or canopy. He will remain b
n on the white wall of his house. He walked home along the lane. He

69. *Secretary Exercise Card*, 2009.

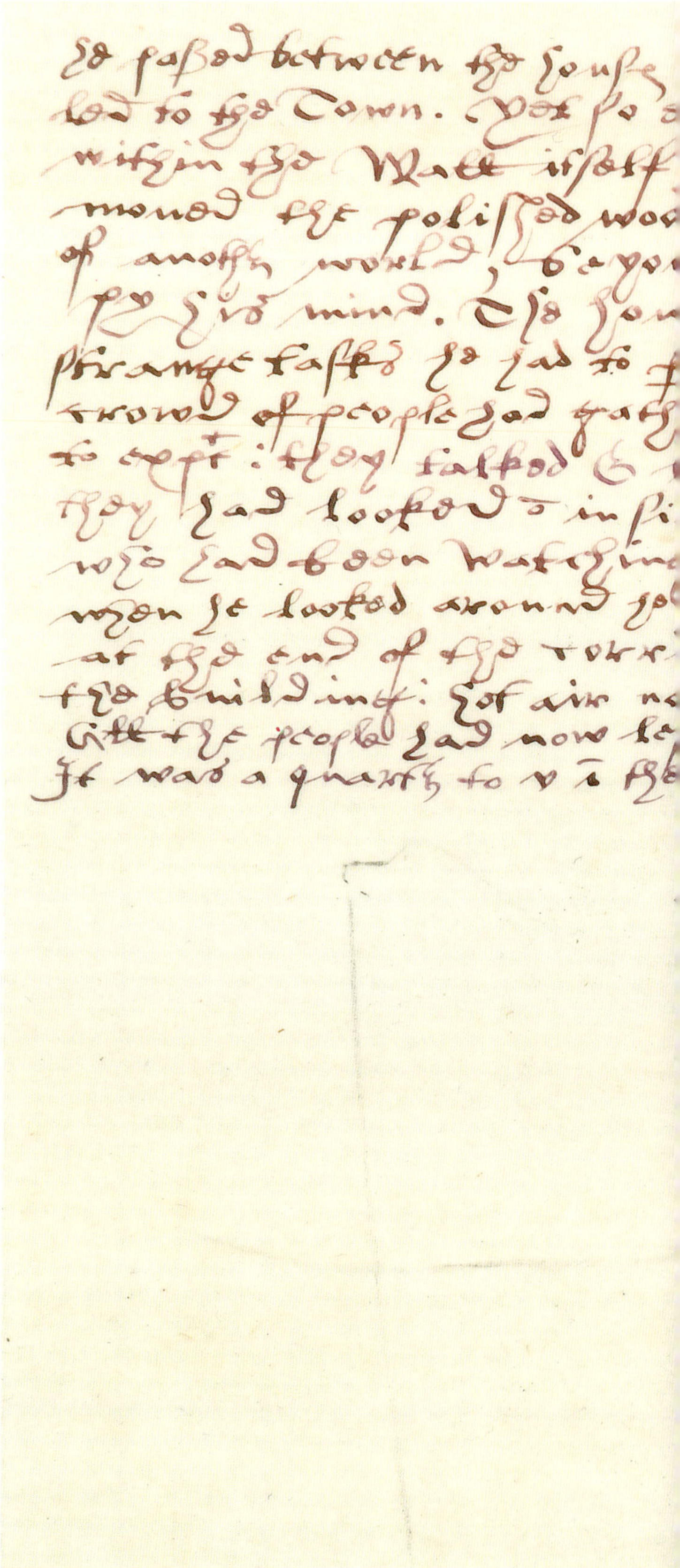

ging his song, early traffic passed: the Great Roads wo
y in the day, but yet remaining altho now suppressed
is recollection of that place: with headless laughter there we
n shelling from the walls: What of Johns? Thought
he hundred daily round of existence continued to roun
: the end is the hedge: When he had finished the
m he walked out of the room & down the corridor, a small
d at the top of the stairs. I am sure they did not know what
ngshed amongst the steps now as I walked past where earli
re: Now after half an hour had passed the merchant
began to wonder whether anything more was going to happen
realized that man had left: I saw him disappear around a corn
, he knew that he would then go down the stairs and out of
rushed through the hedging vents that lined the walls.
The sound of traffic could be heard from the street below.
ternoon: at that same time huge cloud of evening filled the field.

below 70. *Proximity of Dream 3*, 2009.

opposite 71. *List*, 2008.

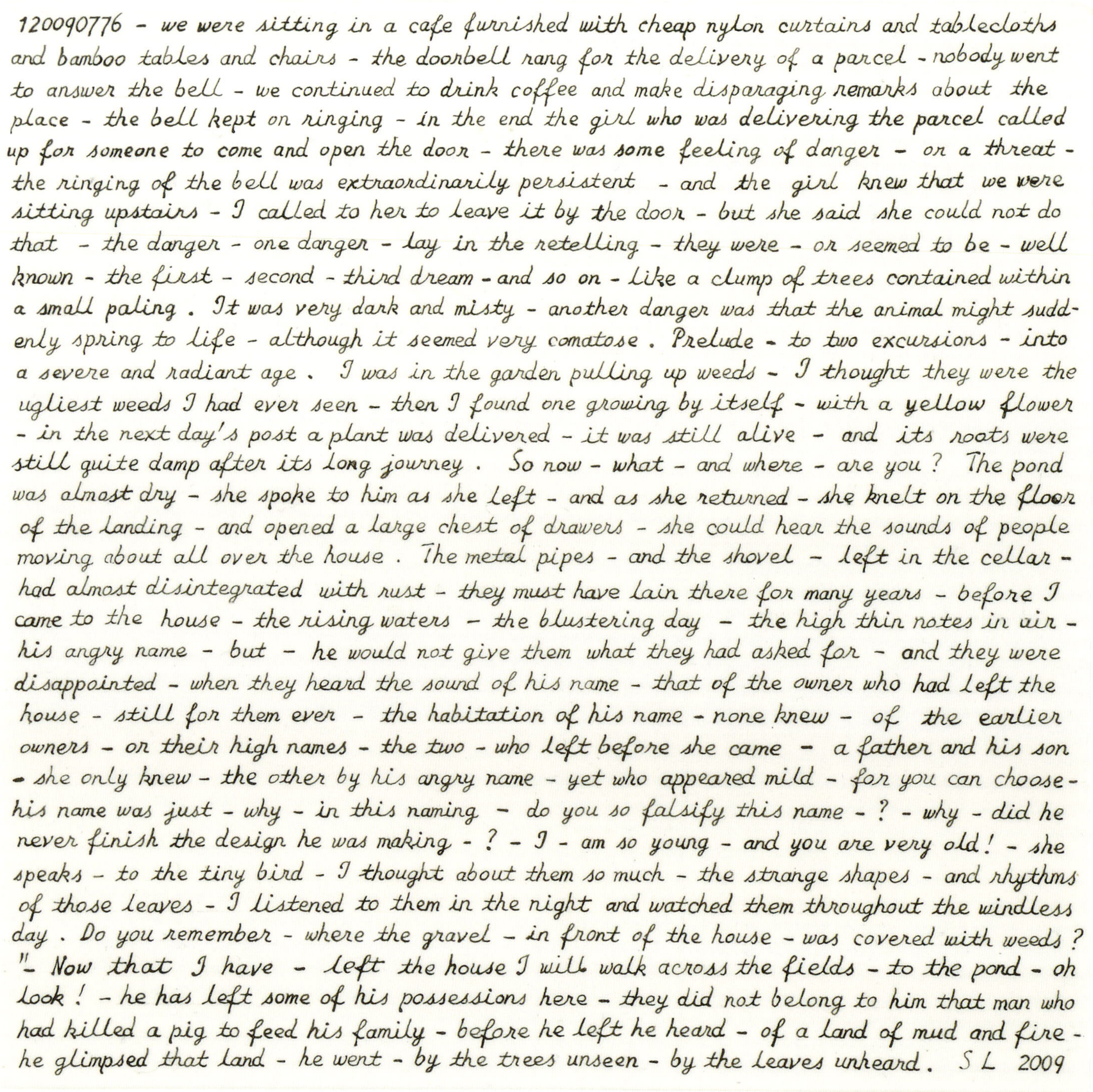

120090776 - we were sitting in a cafe furnished with cheap nylon curtains and tablecloths and bamboo tables and chairs - the doorbell rang for the delivery of a parcel - nobody went to answer the bell - we continued to drink coffee and make disparaging remarks about the place - the bell kept on ringing - in the end the girl who was delivering the parcel called up for someone to come and open the door - there was some feeling of danger - or a threat - the ringing of the bell was extraordinarily persistent - and the girl knew that we were sitting upstairs - I called to her to leave it by the door - but she said she could not do that - the danger - one danger - lay in the retelling - they were - or seemed to be - well known - the first - second - third dream - and so on - like a clump of trees contained within a small paling. It was very dark and misty - another danger was that the animal might suddenly spring to life - although it seemed very comatose. Prelude - to two excursions - into a severe and radiant age. I was in the garden pulling up weeds - I thought they were the ugliest weeds I had ever seen - then I found one growing by itself - with a yellow flower - in the next day's post a plant was delivered - it was still alive - and its roots were still quite damp after its long journey. So now - what - and where - are you? The pond was almost dry - she spoke to him as she left - and as she returned - she knelt on the floor of the landing - and opened a large chest of drawers - she could hear the sounds of people moving about all over the house. The metal pipes - and the shovel - left in the cellar - had almost disintegrated with rust - they must have lain there for many years - before I came to the house - the rising waters - the blustering day - the high thin notes in air - his angry name - but - he would not give them what they had asked for - and they were disappointed - when they heard the sound of his name - that of the owner who had left the house - still for them ever - the habitation of his name - none knew - of the earlier owners - or their high names - the two - who left before she came - a father and his son - she only knew - the other by his angry name - yet who appeared mild - for you can choose - his name was just - why - in this naming - do you so falsify this name - ? - why - did he never finish the design he was making - ? - I - am so young - and you are very old! - she speaks - to the tiny bird - I thought about them so much - the strange shapes - and rhythms of those leaves - I listened to them in the night and watched them throughout the windless day. Do you remember - where the gravel - in front of the house - was covered with weeds? "- Now that I have - left the house I will walk across the fields - to the pond - oh look! - he has left some of his possessions here - they did not belong to him that man who had killed a pig to feed his family - before he left he heard - of a land of mud and fire - he glimpsed that land - he went - by the trees unseen - by the leaves unheard. S L 2009

thrown
biscuit
deaf
enamel
fade
born
counting
tambourine
fold
easy
reach
bag
oven
bridge
gone
land
curtain
shell
belt
telephone
she
infinite
bridge
sponge
yellow
sash
rage
case
foreign
hoe
dig
ten
saw
moisture
outline
dish
sensation
egg
hen
cat
chalet
ten
toe
shower
quest
line
yeast
lent
bitter
rain
relief
oven
laugh
fix
beyond
map
bright
triangle
flour
month
hook
card
dome
window
hook
spot
dialogue
seal
score
water
harp
source
rain
beach
rose
tall
stairs
hand
must
pendant
tree
believe

1981

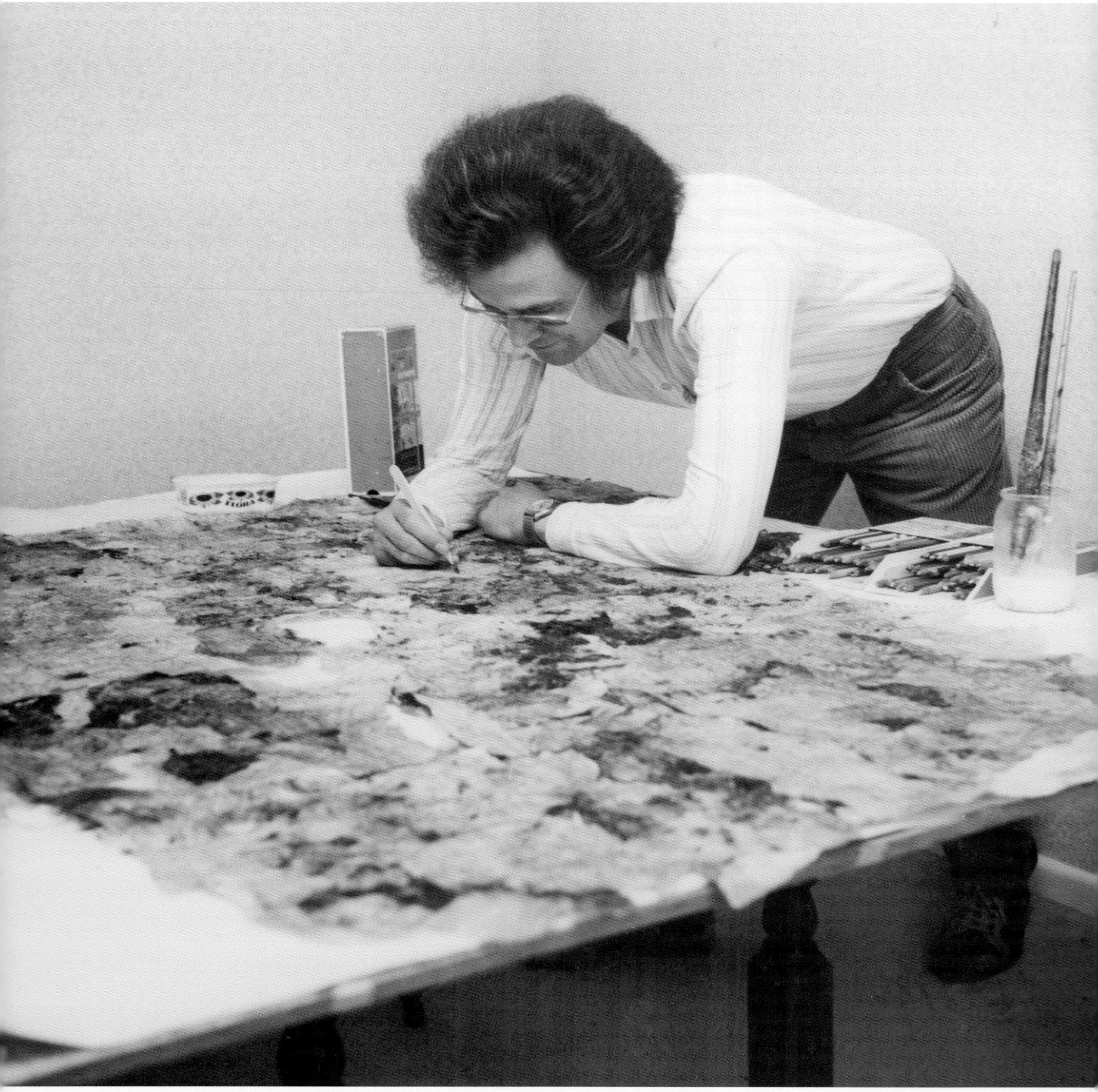

1982

1985

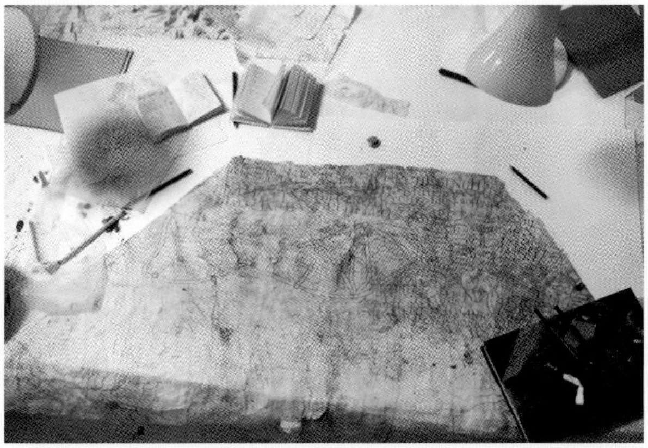

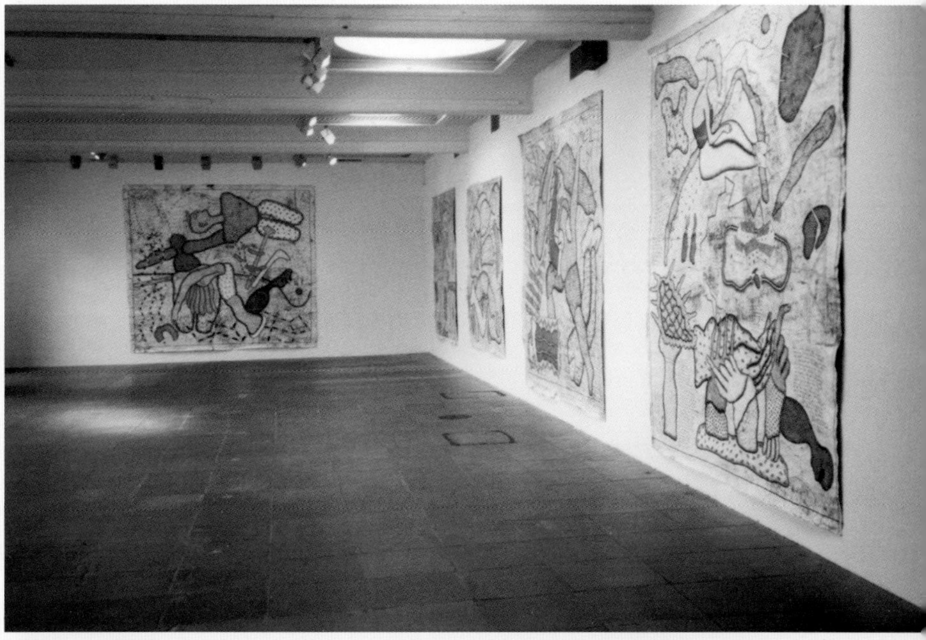

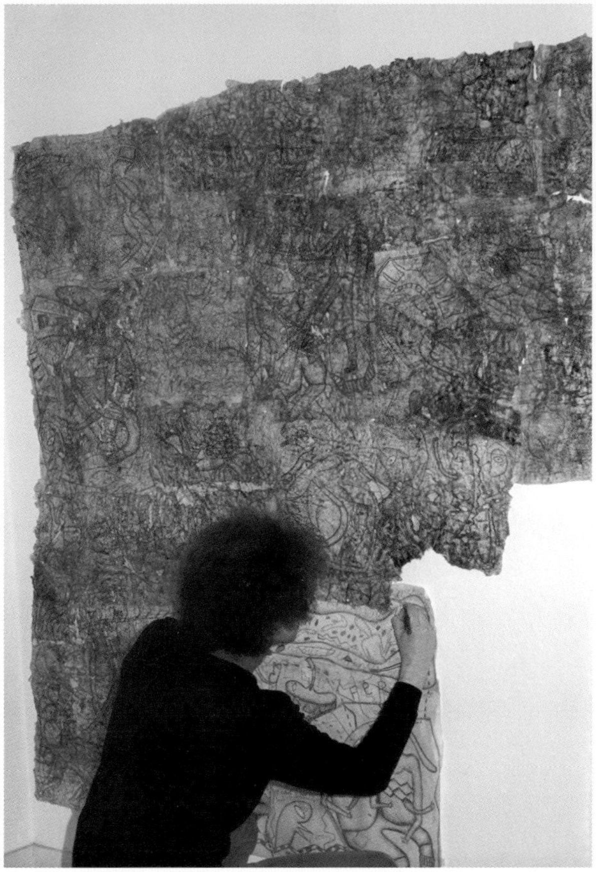

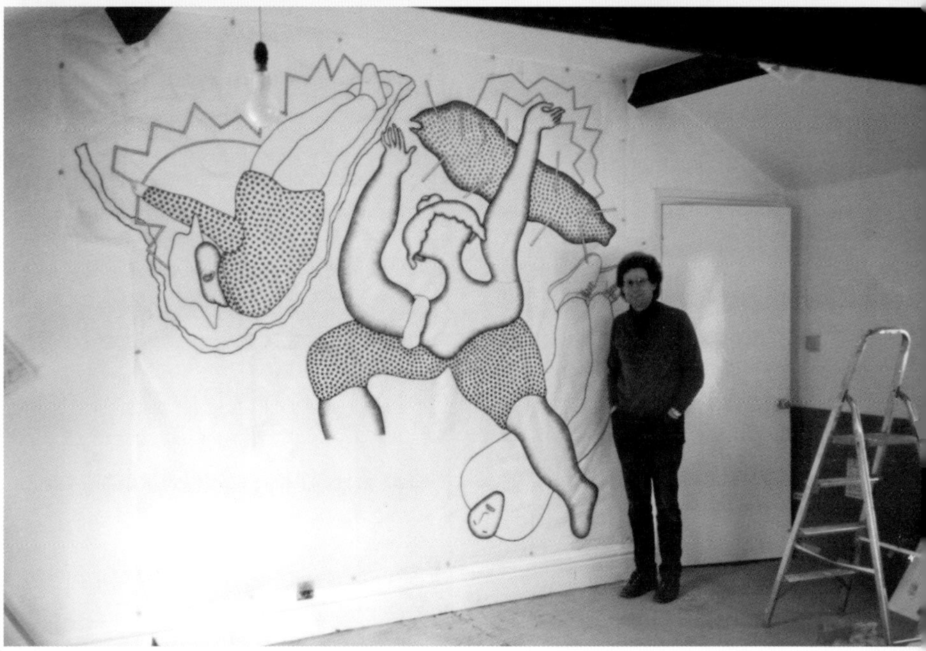

SWANAGE STUDIO

opposite Simon Lewty working on a drawing.

above *Drawn Piece*, studio shot.

SERPENTINE GALLERY

top Installation shot.

bottom Artist with Serpentine exhibition work in progress.

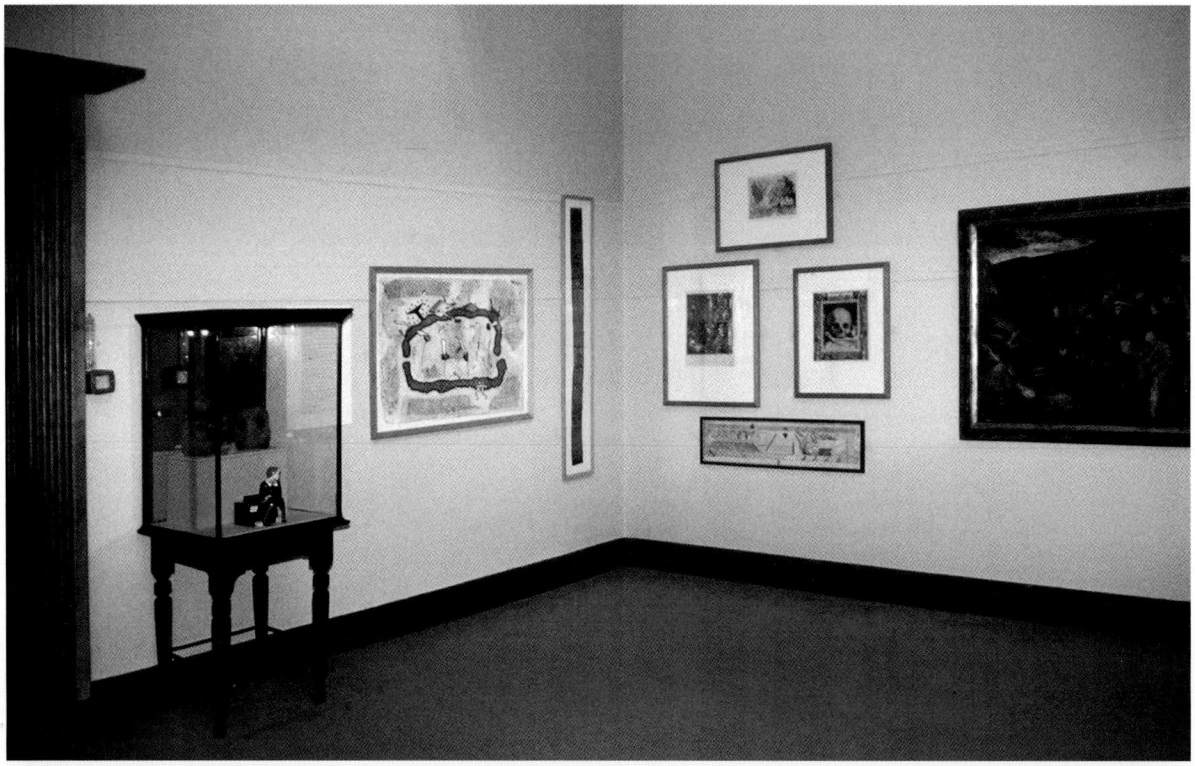

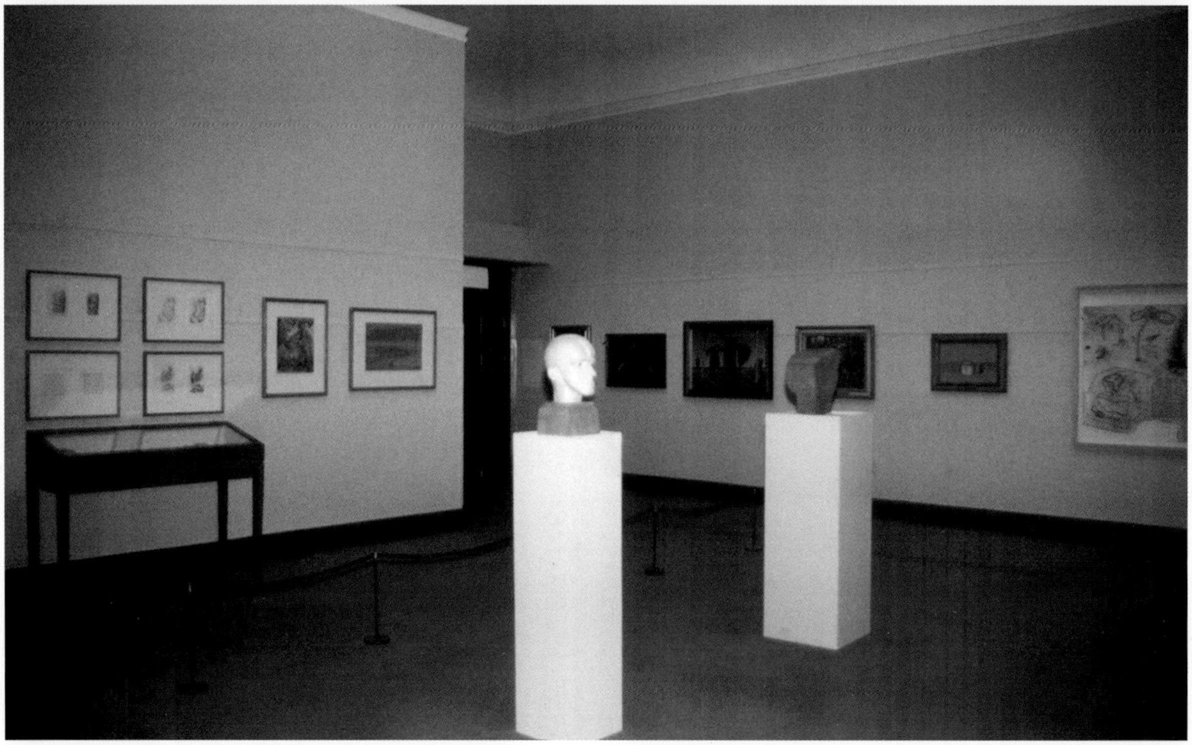

BIRMINGHAM MUSEUM AND ART GALLERY

Chosen Objects exhibition, installation shots.

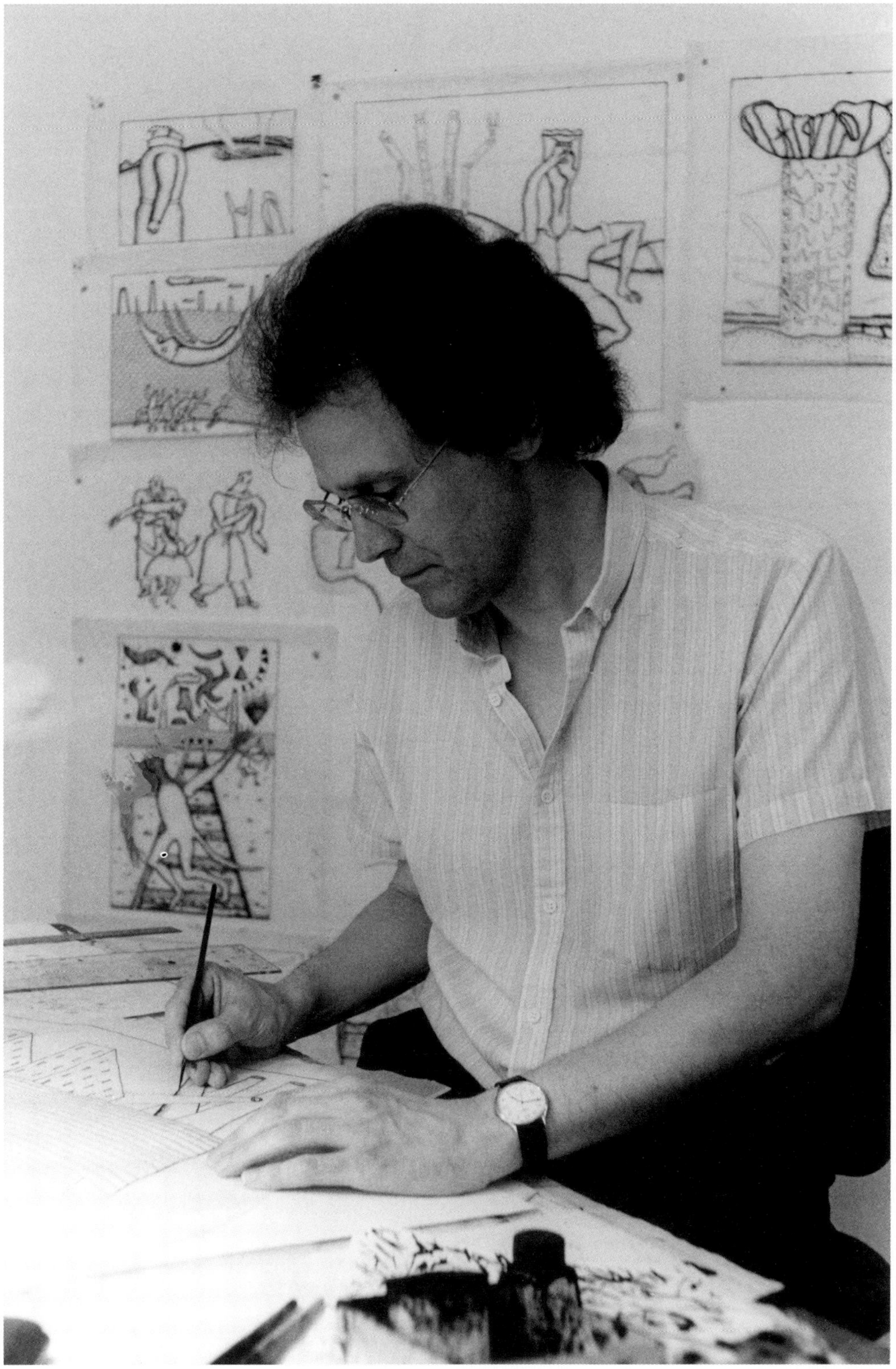

LEAMINGTON SPA STUDIO

Artist in studio.

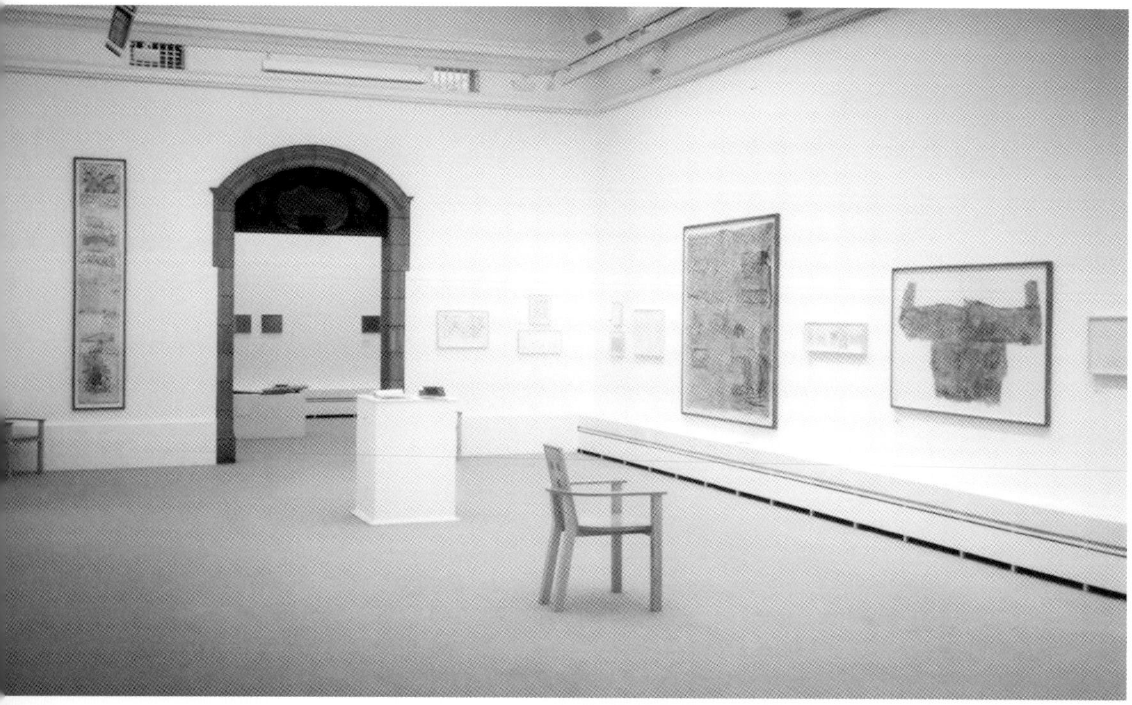

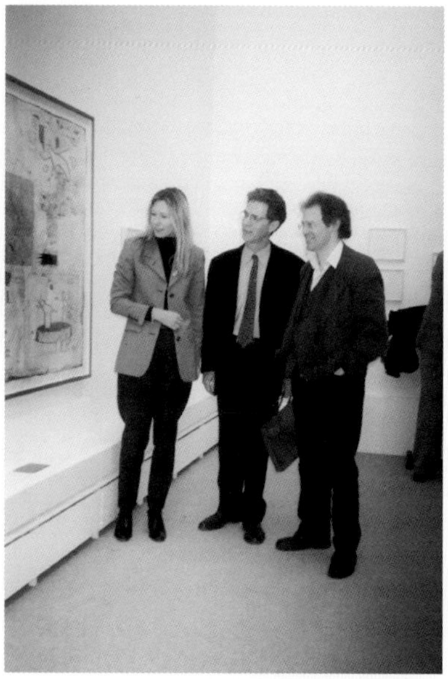

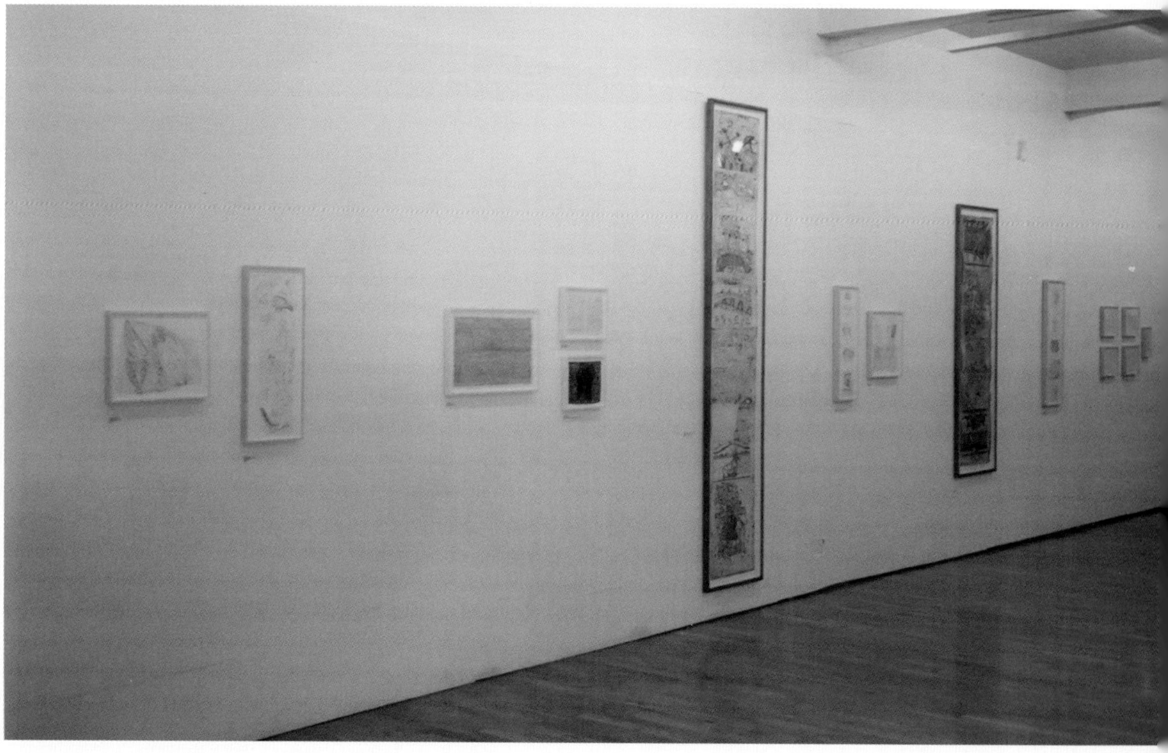

WORCESTER ART GALLERY

top left and bottom right Towards Drawing installation shots.

bottom left The artist with Paul Hills and Clare Cooper.

2000

2008

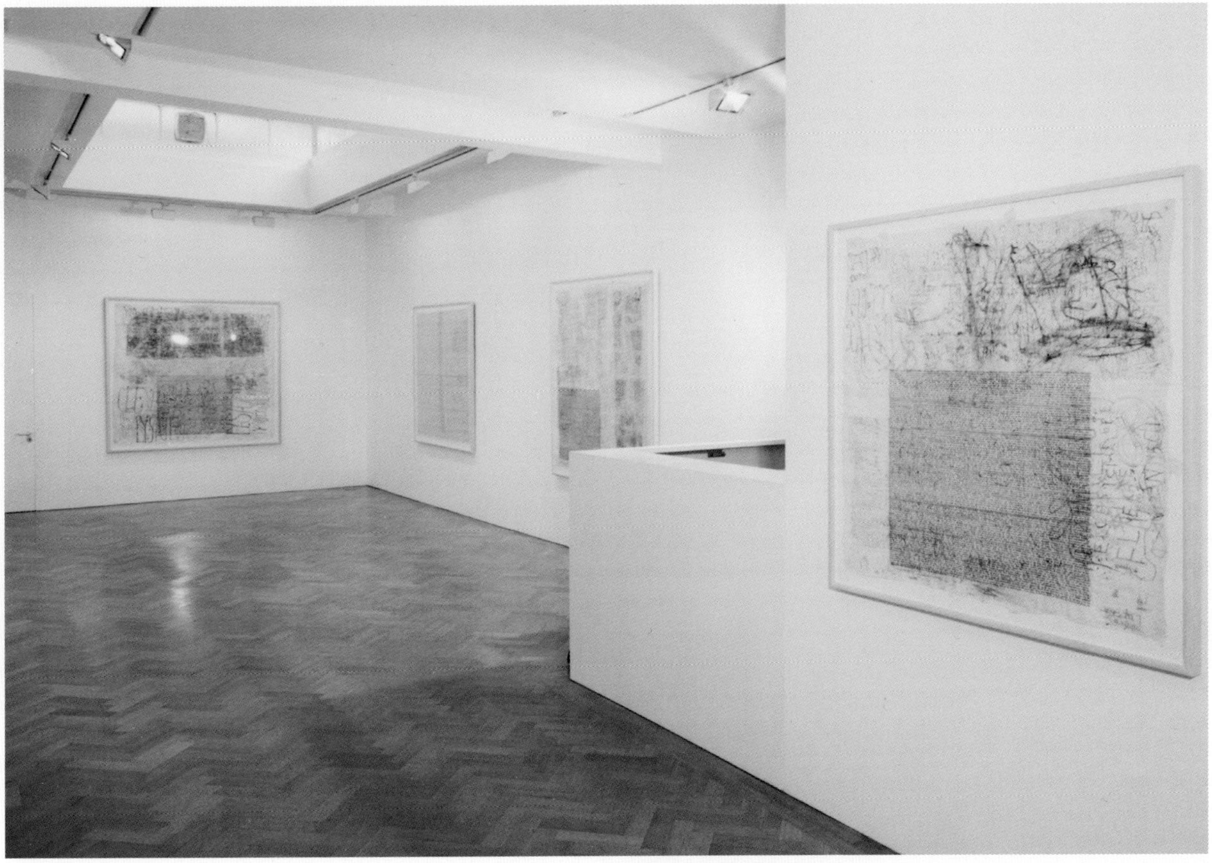

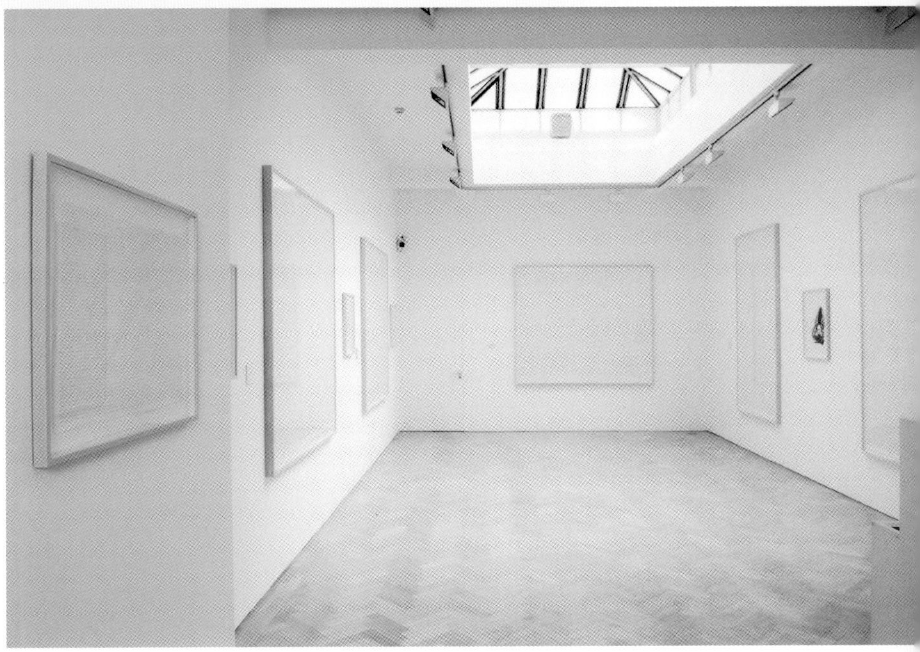

ART FIRST, LONDON

Episode installation shot.

ART FIRST, LONDON

The Self as a Stranger installation shot.

LIST OF PLATES

1. *Path*, 1991.
Ink, crayon, acrylic on paper, 192.4 x 28.6 cm, (Collection of Ann and David Maxwell, UK).

2. *Chalk Script Ballard Down*, 1994.
Colour crayon, acrylic on paper, 42 x 75 cm (Simon Lewty/Art First).

3. *Box Pew*, 1994.
Ink, crayon, acrylic on paper, 39 x 89 cm (Private Collection, UK).

4. *Pointing Man*, 1990.
Ink, crayon, acrylic on paper, 87.6 x 76.2 cm (Private Collection, UK).

5. *Well He Said*, 1985.
Ink, acrylic, crayon on paper, 284.5 x 261.5 cm (Private Collection, UK).

6. *The Passage Towards Stone*, 1983.
Acrylic, ink on paper, 156 x 156 cm (Art First).

7. Study for *The Passage Towards Stone*, 1983.
Pencil on tissue paper, 22 x 26 cm (Simon Lewty/Art First).

8. *The Writing on the Wall*, 1957.
Ink, watercolour on paper, 14 x 23 cm (Simon Lewty).

9. *Of Ancient Breathing*, 1991.
Ink, crayon, acrylic on paper, 244 high x 30.5 across cm (Sackner Archive of Visual and Concrete Poetry, Miami, USA).

10. *The Landing*, 1990.
Ink, crayon, acrylic on paper, 76 x 89 cm (Worcester Art Gallery, UK).

11. *Over Old Fields*, 1980.
Mixed media on board, 38.7 x 59 cm, framed size (Simon Lewty).

12. *As Soon as the Skies Darken*, 1979.
Mixed media on paper, 60 x 60 cm (Collection of Mary Riley, UK).

13. *Ochre Triangle*, 1968.
Paper collage on board, 42.5 x 42.5 cm (Simon Lewty).

14. *Text On Tissue Paper*, 1980.
Ink, PVA on tissue paper, 32 x 47.5 cm (Collection of Clare Cooper, UK).

15. *Automatic Drawing*, 1994.
Pencil on paper, 26 x 33 cm (Simon Lewty/Art First).

16. *Pages From a Notebook*, 1990.
Pencil on lined paper, 19.5 x 25 cm (Simon Lewty/Art First).

17. *Ritual of a Landscape*, 1975.
Pen, paper, ink on paper, 12 x 92.9 cm (Simon Lewty).

18. *Hymns to the Sun Misheard*, 1986.
Crayon, charcoal, acrylic on paper, 175.3 x 176.2 cm (Collection of Everard Peters, UK).

19. *And Told Them of a Story Half as Old as the Field*, 1986. Ink, crayon, acrylic on paper, 91 x 120 cm (Birmingham Museums and Art Gallery).

20. *Beyond the Field*, 1988.
Pencil, crayon, ink on paper, 45.4 x 109.5 cm (Sackner Archive of Concrete and Visual Poetry, Miami, USA).

21. *But Who Tried Without Success*, 1986.
Crayon, charcoal, acrylic on paper, 145 x 170 cm (Victoria & Albert Museum, London).

22. *Over the Bay as Across Fields*, 1986.
Charcoal, crayon, acrylic, 145 x 170 cm (Collection of Muriel Salem, UK).

23. *Garden Plan and Room*, 1986.
Pencil, acrylic and crayon on paper, 38.4 x 57.4 cm (Potteries Museum & Art Gallery: made for the National Garden Festival, Stoke-on-Trent, 1986).

24. *Out in the Open Air*, 1989.
Ink, crayon, acrylic on paper, 115.6 x 125.7 cm (shown in Chosen Objects Birmingham Museum and Art Gallery, UK) (Simon Lewty/Art First).

25. *Where Have You Come From?*, 1991.
Ink, crayon, acrylic on paper, 148.5 x 56 cm (Simon Lewty/Art First).

26. *Life Without Name*, 1989.
Ink, acrylic on paper, 120.7 x 129.5 cm (Collection of Michael Donnelly, USA).

27. *The Palimpsest Letter*, 1990.
Ink, acrylic, 132 x 151cm
(Collection of Clare Cooper, UK).

28. *Voices in the Close Country*, 1991.
Ink, crayon, acrylic on paper, 148.6 x 71.8 cm
(Simon Lewty/Art First).

29. *The Lured King*, 1989.
Ink, crayon, acrylic on paper, 115.3 x 120 cm
(Simon Lewty/Art First).

30. *In the Lost Town*, 1992.
Ink, crayon, acrylic on paper, 116.8 x 45.7 cm,
(Harris Museum, Preston).

31. *The Secret Way*, 1992.
Ink, crayon, acrylic on paper, 46.5 x 33.5 cm
(Collection of Charles and Tessa King-Farlow, UK).

32. *The Question*, 1994.
Ink, acrylic on paper, 51 x 74 cm
(Collection of Joe and Moira Gallagher, UK).

33. *He Departed Like A Stranger From His Own Habitation*, 1994. Pencil, crayon on paper,
86.4 x 144.8 cm (Private Collection UK).

34 *The Guide*, 1994.
Ink, crayon, acrylic on paper, 169.5 x 46 cm
(Collection of Ross and Vicky Cattell, UK).

35. *Inner Sea*, 1995.
Pencil, crayon on paper, 104 x 140 cm
(Leeds City Art Gallery, UK).

36. *Rebuke Of Light*, 1999.
Ink, acrylic on paper, 197 x 70 cm
(Collection of Clare Cooper, UK).

37. *Drift Of Days*, 1999.
Acrylic on paper, 138 x 143 cm
(Simon Lewty/Art First).

38. *Season Of Sun and Rain*, 1999.
Ink, acrylic on paper, 59 x 81 cm
(The British Museum, London).

39. *Day Of Heat, Day Of Storms*, 1999.
Ink, acrylic on paper, 140 x 140 cm
(Collection of James and Polly Moon, UK).

40. *Whispers From A Mysterious Revolt*, 1998.
Acrylic on paper, 138 x 148 cm
(Collection of Lucy and David Forster, UK).

41. *Perpetual Silence Amid Intrusive Noise*, 1999.
Ink, acrylic on paper, 57 x 202 cm
(Collection of Tom and Alison Baigrie, UK).

42. *Repetition and Dream I*, 2003.
Acrylic, graphite on paper, 29.5 x 42.5 cm
(Simon Lewty/Art First).

43. *Inscriptions Without Blame*, 2002.
Acrylic, photocopy on paper, 50 x 50 cm
(Simon Lewty/Art First).

44. *Diagram From A Dream*, 2002.
Photocopy, acrylic on paper, 50 x 50 cm
(Simon Lewty/Art First).

45. *Variant From A Book Of Rain*, 2002.
Acrylic on paper, 66 x 145 cm
(Collection of John and Tawna Farmer, USA)

46. *Strange Eyes*, 2007.
Typescript, various media, 59 x 42 cm
(Simon Lewty/Art First).

47. *Far From The Town And Yet Not Far*, 2001.
Acrylic on paper, 168 x 89 cm
(Collection of Ross and Vicky Cattell, UK).

48. *Character Situation, Outcome*, 2007.
Typescript, various media, 59 x 42 cm
(Collection of Ross Leckie, UK).

49. *Mythe*, 2006.
Acrylic on tissue paper, 98.5 x 99 cm
(Simon Lewty/Art First).

50. *Echo*, 2006.
Acrylic on tissue paper, 50 x 62 cm
(Collection of Clare Cooper, UK).

51. *First Spiral*, 2005.
Crayon on paper, 51 x 51 cm
(Simon Lewty/Art First).

52. *Emerging Spiral*, 2005.
Pigment, PVA on paper, 22.5 x 27 cm
(Simon Lewty/Art First).

53. *Second Spiral*, 2005.
Crayon on paper, 51 x 50 cm
(Simon Lewty/Art First).

54. *I took the frost for a writing, and the ice for its seal*, 2004. Crayon on tissue paper, 27 x 175 cm
(Collection of Carlo and Angela Zucchini, Italy).

55. *Legend*, 1974.
Pen, ink on paper, 25 x 100 cm (Simon Lewty).

56. *Sequence From Childhood*, 2002.
Acrylic, photocopy on paper, 41.5 x 214 cm
(Collection of Jonathan and Christine de Ferrars Green, UK).

57. *The Work of a Dismissed Servant*, 1990.
Ink, crayon, acrylic on paper backed on muslin, 186 x 154 cm (Wolverhampton Art Gallery, UK).

58. *Beach 1, 6.11.05*, 2005.
Pencil, pigment on tissue paper, 41 x 39 cm
(Simon Lewty/Art First).

59. *Beach 2, 7.11.05*, 2005.
Pencil, charcoal, pigment on tissue paper, 62 x 64 cm
(Simon Lewty/Art First).

60. *First Snow of Winter*, 1981.
Ink, crayon, acrylic on paper, 75 x 94 cm overall
(Simon Lewty).

61. *A Voice, a Recognition*, 2007.
Pencil on paper, 207 x 120 cm
(Simon Lewty/Art First).

62. *Figure 1*, 2007.
Photocopy, edition of 4, 41 x 29 cm
(Simon Lewty/Art First).

63. *Figure with Tyremarks*, 2007.
Photocopy, edition of 4, 41 x 29 cm
(Simon Lewty/Art First).

64. *Gift*, 2007.
Crayon, gesso on tissue paper, 51 x 70 cm
(Simon Lewty/Art First).

65. *A Cry Within a Mind*, 2007.
Crayon on conservation tissue, 160 x 170 cm
(Simon Lewty/Art First).

66. *Places, Voices*, 2007.
Typescript, various media, 68 x 79 cm + recording
(+ detail of 1 of 6 typed sheets)
(Collection of Benjamin Rhodes, UK).

67. *Passing Days and Nights of Oblivion Will Drain Reason Before the Strength of the Flower*, 2008.
Pen, ink on paper, 112 x 121 cm
(Simon Lewty/Art First).

68. *To Unexplained Day*, 2002.
Ink on paper, 100 x 143 cm (Simon Lewty/Art First).

69. *Secretary Exercise Card*, 2009.
Ink on paper, 17 x 24 cm (Simon Lewty/Art First).

70. *Proximity of Dream 3*, 2009.
Pen, ink, 21.5 x 21.5 cm (Simon Lewty/Art First).

71. *List: Train-Face*, 2010.
Typescript on tissue paper, 85 x 50.3 cm
(Simon Lewty/Art First).

BIOGRAPHY/LIST OF EXHIBITIONS

1941 Born, Sutton Coldfield.

1957–1960 Studied at Mid-Warwickshire School of Art.

1961–1963 Studied at Hornsey College of Art.

1964–1981 Lecturer at Mid-Warwickshire College of Further Education.

Lives and works in Leamington Spa, Warwickshire, and in Swanage, Dorset.

SOLO EXHIBITIONS

1968 Woodstock Gallery, London.

1984 Ikon Gallery, Birmingham.

1985 Anne Berthoud Gallery, London.
Serpentine Gallery, London.

1987 Anne Berthoud Gallery, London.

1988 Anne Berthoud Gallery, London.

1989 Chosen Objects, Birmingham Museum and Art Gallery.

1992 Austin/Desmond and Phipps, London, in association with Anne Berthoud.
Messages from the Past, Midlands Contemporary Art Ltd., Birmingham.
Terra Incognita, Castle Museum, Nottingham and Mead Gallery, University of Warwick.

1994 Drawings: Front Room Focus, Art First, London.

1995 Voices From Lost Fields, Art First, London.

1999 Towards Drawing, touring exhibition to Leicester, Wolverhampton, Stoke-on Trent, Preston, Bristol, Worcester, Leamington Spa.

2000 Episodes, Art First, London.

2004 Eclipses, Art First, London.
Eclipses, DKFA Projects, New York, with Art First.

2007 Imprimis, Atrium Gallery, Bournemouth University.

2008 The Self as a Stranger, Art First, London.

SELECTED GROUP EXHIBITIONS

1982 Midland View 2, Midland Group Gallery, Nottingham.

1983 6th Cleveland International Drawing Biennale, Cleveland City Museum & Art Gallery, Middlesbrough.

1984 TSWA National Open Art Exhibition, Newlyn Art Gallery, Penzance (and tour).
Midland View 3, (prizewinner) Midland Group Gallery, Nottingham.

1985 John Moores 14, Walker Art Gallery, Liverpool (prizewinner).
Figure 1, Young Figurative Painters & Sculptors, Aberystwyth Arts Centre (and tour).

1986 Walking and Falling, Interim Art, London, & Plymouth Arts Centre collaboration (toured to Kettles Yard, Cambridge).
Unheard Music—Contemporary Art on the Theme of Gardens, Stoke-on-Trent City Museum & Art Gallery.
Contrariwise—Surrealism and Britain 1930–1986, Glyn Vivian Art Gallery, Swansea (and tour).

1987 John Moores 15, Walker Art Gallery, Liverpool.
Athena Art Awards, Barbican Art Centre, London.
Knowing Your Place: Artists' Parish Maps, Common Ground, London.
8th Cleveland International Drawing Biennale, (prizewinner).

1988 Artists in National Parks, Victoria & Albert Museum, London (and tour).
Fragments of False Houses, Pomeroy Purdy Gallery, London (curated by Sharon Kivland).

1989 The Tree of Life, South Bank Centre, London (and tour).
Texts, Inscriptions & Calligraphy in Contemporary Art, Harris Museum & Art Gallery, Preston.

1990 Upturned Ark, Pitt-Rivers Museum, Oxford (curated by Chris Dorsett).

1991 The Discerning Eye, Mall Galleries, London (selected by John Russell Taylor).

1992 The Poetry Show, Rebecca Hossack Gallery, London.
The Beauty in Breathing, Ruth and Marvin Sackner Archive of Concrete & Visual Poetry, Miami Beach, Florida, USA

1994 Flowers, Coram Gallery, London.
Drawing Pairs, Adam Baumgold Fine Art, New York.

1995 National Trust Centenary Exhibition, Christies, London.

1996 Back to Nature, Art First, London.

2000 Blake's Heaven: A Tribute Exhibition to William Blake, Scolar Fine Art, in association with James Huntington-Whitely.

2003 Visual Poetics: Art and the Word, Miami Art Museum, Miami, Florida, USA.

2004 On Paper, Art First, London.

2005 A Full Emptiness, Art First, London (with Mary Riley).

2006 Charting a Decade, Art First, London (with Will Maclean).
Translations from the National Gallery, Art First, London.

2007 The Discerning Eye, Mall Galleries, London (selected by Charles Saumarez Smith).
Mapping the Imagination, V& A Museum, London.

2009 Beyond the Written Word, The Art Stable, Child Okeford (with Susan Michie).

2010 Summer Exhibition, Royal Academy of Arts, London.

ARTIST'S PUBLICATIONS

Chosen Objects, Birmingham Museum & Art Gallery, 1989.

Chosen Subjects, Mead Gallery, University of Warwick, 1992.

Cradles of the New, Prest Roots Press, 1994.

Towards Drawing, Art First, 1999.

RADIO, TELEVISION, FILM, SOUND RECORDINGS

Holding Your Ground, Central Television, Birmingham 1987

Maps for an Inner Landscape—The Work of Simon Lewty, film directed by Terry Bryan, 'Contrasts', Central Television, 1988.

Third Ear, Interview with Timothy Hyman, BBC Radio 3, 20th March 1992.

Sound recordings of the artist reading texts from his own work, Art First, 2008.

Artist's Lives, National Life Stories, The British Library (interviewed by Cathy Courtney), 2006–2009.

Through the Surface—The Work of Simon Lewty, film directed by Tom Hudson, Art First, 2010.

COLLECTIONS

Arts Council of Great Britain.

Birmingham Museum & Art Gallery.

The Bank of England.

The British Museum.

Cleveland Museum and Art Gallery, Middlesbrough.

Harris Museum & Art Gallery, Preston.

Leamington Spa Art Gallery.

Leeds City Art Gallery.

Mead Gallery, University of Warwick.

Sackner Archive of Concrete and Visual Poetry, Miami Beach, Florida.

Potteries Museum & Art Gallery, Stoke-on-Trent.

Wolverhampton City Art Gallery.

Worcester City Art Gallery.

Victoria & Albert Museum.

CREDITS

TEXTS

pp. 45–47 Stuart Morgan, *The Sadness of Dreams*, © Estate of Stuart Morgan.

pp. 49–71 Paul Hills, *Simon Lewty*, Anne Berthoud Gallery, London, 1991.

pp. 79–82 Peter Larkin, *Simon Lewty: Voices from Lost Fields*, Art First, London, 1995.

pp. 84–91 Paul Hills, *Simon Lewty: Episodes*, Art First, London, 2000.

pp. 96–97 Jessica Dubow, *Simon Lewty: Eclipses*, Art First, London, 2004.

pp. 107–125 Cathy Courtney's oral history recording with Simon Lewty is part of *Artists' Lives*, National Life Stories, The British Library (reference number: C466/235).

pp. 133–146 Simon Lewty, *Simon Lewty: The Self as a Stranger*, Art First, London, 2000.

pp. 150–169 Susan Michie/Simon Lewty, *Reveries and Transformations: a Dialogue*, Lacerta, UK, 2009.

PHOTOGRAPHS

Birmingham Museums & Art Gallery (plate 18)
David Clarke (plates 36, 37, 38, 39, 40, 41)
© DACS 2010 (page 160)
Harris Museum and Art Gallery (plate 30)
Stefan Kirkeby (plate 45)
George Meyrick (plates 48, 61,62, 63, 64, 65)
Justin Piperger (plates 15,16, 46, 64 (detail), 66, 70, 71, 72 / The Self as a Stranger 2008 installation shot)
Miki Slingsby (plates 4, 5, 25, 26 27,28, 57)
Storm Studios, Leamington Spa (plates 8, 11, 12, 13, 17, 55, 60)
The Potteries Museum and Art Gallery (plate 23)
Rutherford Photographic (1981 archive portrait)
Todd-White & Son (plates 14, 42, 43, 44, 47, 49, 50, 54, 56, 58, 59, 67, 69 / Episodes 2000 archive installation shot)
Luke Unsworth (plates 1, 10)
V&A Images (plate 19)
Edward Woodman (plates 3, 32, 34, 35 / 1995 archive portrait)

BIOGRAPHIES

Cathy Courtney. Writer and Project Director, *Artists' Lives*, National Life Stories, The British Library.

Jessica Dubow. Cultural geographer, University of Sheffield working at the intersections of geography, philosophy and aesthetic and critical theory.

Paul Hills. Author of *David Jones*, *Venetian Colour*, *The Light of Early Italian Painting*. Currently Professor, Courtauld Institute of Fine Arts.

Ian Hunt. Art critic and author of *Green Light*, a book of poems, currently teaching at Goldsmiths, London.

Peter Larkin. Poet and Philosophy and Literature Librarian, University of Warwick.

Susan Michie. Artist and film editor.

Stuart Morgan. Art critic for *Artscribe*, *Artforum*, *frieze*, whose writings are collected in two books, *What the Butler Saw* and *Inclinations*. He died in 2002.

ACKNOWLEDGMENTS

I would like to thank all those who have helped to make this book possible. Especially Clare Cooper, for her friendship and commitment to my work over the years. Thanks also to Benjamin Rhodes, Matt Incledon, Duncan McCorquodale and Rachel Pfleger.

My grateful thanks to the contributors, Cathy Courtney, Jessica Dubow, Ian Hunt, Paul Hills, Peter Larkin and Susan Michie.

I would like to thank Anne Berthoud; and to remember with affection and gratitude Stuart Morgan, for his encouragement of my early work.

Simon Lewty, 2010

Ross and Vicky Cattell

Clare Cooper

Jonathan and Christine de Ferrars Green

Lucy and David Forster

John and Tawna Farmer

Joe and Moira Gallagher

Ross Leckie

James and Polly Moon

Benjamin Rhodes

The Sackner Archive of Visual and Concrete Poetry

Carlo and Angela Zucchini

Simon Lewty and Art First would like to express their heart-felt thanks to everyone named above, both for being patrons of the artist's work and for their support for this publication.

Black Dog Publishing Limited
10A Acton Street
London
WC1X 9NG

t. +44 (0)207 713 5097
f. +44 (0)207 713 8682
e. info@blackdogonline.com

Edited by Clare Cooper at Art First
Designed by Rachel Pfleger at Black Dog Publishing

British Library Cataloguing-in-Publication Data.
A CIP record for this book is available from the British Library.

ISBN 978 1 907317 07 1

Black Dog Publishing is an environmentally responsible company.
The Self as a Stranger: Simon Lewty is printed on FSC accredited paper.

ART FIRST

reuse recycle reduce

architecture art design
fashion history photography
theory and things

www.blackdogonline.com

black dog publishing
london uk